Embedding Perl in HTML
with Mason

Embedding Perl in HTML with Mason

Dave Rolsky and Ken Williams

O'REILLY®

Beijing · Cambridge · Farnham · Köln · Paris · Sebastopol · Taipei · Tokyo

Embedding Perl in HTML with Mason
by Dave Rolsky and Ken Williams

Editor:	Linda Mui
Production Editor:	Philip Dangler
Cover Designer:	Ellie Volckhausen
Interior Designer:	David Futato
Production Services:	TIPS Technical Publishing, Inc.

Printing History:

October 2002:   First Edition.

0-596-00225-4

[M]

Table of Contents

Foreword ix

Preface xi

1. **Introduction** **1**
   A First Example   2
   The Main Features of Mason   2
   Alternatives to Mason   6
   Philosophy   14
   Getting Started with Mason   14

2. **Components** **18**
   Mason from 10,000 Feet   18
   Core Concepts   19
   Basic Component Syntax   20
   Component Arguments   32
   Component Return Values   36
   Special Globals   37
   Sample Component   37

3. **Special Components: Dhandlers and Autohandlers** **39**
   Dhandlers   39
   Autohandlers   42
   Using Autohandlers and Dhandlers Together   49

4. **APIs** **50**
   Request Class and Object API   50
   Component Object API   64
   Buffers   68

5. Advanced Features **69**

Subcomponents   69

Creating Components on the Fly   70

Sharing Data Among Component Sections   71

Methods and Attributes   73

Calling Components with Content Blocks   80

Advanced Inheritance   84

Subrequests   88

6. The Lexer, Compiler, Resolver, and Interpreter Objects **90**

Passing Parameters to Mason Classes   91

The Lexer   92

The Compiler   92

The Resolver   97

The Interpreter   98

7. Using Mason with mod_perl **101**

Configuring Mason   102

Document Root Versus the Component Root   107

Not OK   108

$r   109

ApacheHandler Parameters   110

To Autoflush or Not to Autoflush   111

Generating Something Besides HTML   111

Apache::Status and Mason   112

8. Building a Mason Site **113**

Functionality   114

Directory Layout   116

File Extensions   116

Apache Configuration   116

The Components   117

Components with Access Controls   152

All Done   165

Further Directions   165

9. Mason and CGI **167**

CGI-Appropriate Situations   167

CGI-Inappropriate Situations   169

Creating a CGI-Based Site in Mason 170
Using Mason Templates Inside Regular CGI Scripts 171
Differences Between Mason Under CGI and mod_perl 174

10. Scalable Design **176**
Modules Versus Components 176
Components as Independent Units 182
Component Layout 183
File Naming and Directory Layout 184
Random Advice 184

11. Recipes **185**
Sessions 185
Making Use of Autoflush 193
User Authentication and Authorization 194
Co-Branding Color Schemes 200
Developer Environments 202
Using Mason Outside of Dynamic Web Sites 205

12. Custom Mason Subclasses **214**
Class::Container as a Superclass 214
Syntax: Your Very Own Lexer 216
Output: Compiling to a Different Output 224
Storage: Replacing the Resolver 228
Request: A Request Object with a Built-in Session 232
Argument Munging: ApacheHandler 235
More Reader Exercises 236

A. The Mason API **237**

B. Object Constructor Parameters **253**

C. Text Editors That Understand Mason **257**

D. Content Management with Bricolage **260**

Glossary **281**

Index **285**

Foreword

When Dave asked last year if I wanted to cowrite a book about Mason, I mused over the idea for a few hours but ultimately declined. I've already written a good deal about Mason in documentation and articles and wouldn't want the book to become a rehash of my particular point of view. On a more personal level, the thought of creating any text longer than a few pages fills me with trepidation. Given the choice of eight hours of backbreaking Perl coding or an hour of writing, I'd take the code any day.

This book was authored, instead, by two Mason developers who have a fresh perspective and who, apparently, like writing as well as coding. Dave and Ken have been involved with Mason for years; they've contributed to the project immeasurably, first in discussions and later to the Mason core itself. I cannot imagine two people better suited for this book.

When authors have unfettered access to the CVS repository, as Dave and Ken do, the writing process ends up shaping the product itself (e.g., "I just wrote about this feature but it turns out it doesn't exist—I'm going to implement it" or "I just wrote about this feature and it's horrible, can we kill it?"). As a result, Mason has grown over the past year in ways I never would have predicted.

Read Chapter 12, for example, to see the new parsing/compiling infrastructure so insanely flexible that one can compile Mason into Embperl or replace Mason's syntax with an XML variant. (Consider the original parser, a single 371-line subroutine, and you get an idea of how far we've come.)

Or Chapter 5 to see how "Calling Components with Content Blocks" turns content filtering from a limited hack into a first-class language feature and opens the door to the creation of custom language tags.

Or Chapter 9 to see how support for CGI (and its high-powered cousins FastCGI and SpeedyCGI) has gone from a few paragraphs in the FAQ to a full-fledged handler, inside a new modular architecture just begging for additional platforms.

Such changes expand Mason's reach to an ever larger set of problems. At the same time, the reference sections and copious recipes in this book help to fulfill Mason's original mission: to provide a fun, simple, and powerful environment for mod_perl development. Should we stray too far from this path, we will certainly hear of it from the users.

Reading this book has taught me a surprising number of techniques about a product I used to know everything about and has reignited my enthusiasm for building cool web applications. I hope it does the same for you.

—Jonathan Swartz
swartz@pobox.com

Preface

Mason is a tool for embedding the Perl programming language into text, in order to create text dynamically, most often in HTML. But Mason does not simply stop at HTML. It can just as easily create XML, WML, POD, configuration files, or the complete works of Shakespeare.

Mason was originally written by Jonathan Swartz, with the help of the rest of the CMP development team at CMP Media in 1996, and in its earliest incarnations it was known as Scribe.

Mason was first made publicly available as Version 0.1 in August of 1998. Since that time, Jonathan Swartz has invited your humble authors to participate in the further development of Mason. Mason has been expanded, and rewritten and is much changed from those early days. This book covers Version 1.12 of Mason.

Intended Audience

This book assumes that the reader is familiar with Perl at an intermediate level and that common Perl idioms don't stop you in your tracks. While you need not have written your own modules previously, familiarity with Perl's object-oriented syntax will be helpful.

Since Mason is most often used in the generation of web sites, this book frequently presents its example in terms of generating HTML pages. You definitely do not need to be an HTML expert to read this book, but a passing familiarity with HTML will be helpful in understanding what the output is intended to look like.

As previously mentioned, Mason is well-suited for the generation of any sort of dynamic text, including markup languages such as XML, as well as configuration files, email bodies (think mail merge, perhaps), or even code.

Finally, experience with mod_perl and Apache will be helpful for Chapters 7 and 9, which discuss integrating Mason with mod_perl and CGI, respectively, though the rest of the book should be easily comprehensible regardless of your familiarity with those particular topics.

Requirements

As of Version 1.12, Mason requires Perl Version 5.00503 or later, as well as the following modules available from CPAN: Class::Container 0.07+, File::Spec 0.8+, Params::Validate 0.24+, Exception::Class 1.01+, and Cache::Cache 1.00+.

If you want to run Mason under mod_perl, you will need to have at least Version 1.22 of mod_perl installed (although installing the very latest version in the 1.*x* series is highly recommended). You'll also probably want Apache::Request 0.31+, though this is not strictly required.

Some of the examples are designed to work in a web server context and may require either CGI or mod_perl capabilities. For the CGI examples, any CGI-capable web server is sufficient, though our configuration examples always assume Apache.

Mason itself is designed to be platform-agnostic. Any behavior to the contrary should be considered a bug in Mason, and bug reports are always welcome.

In writing this book, we did our testing with Perl 5.6.1 and mod_perl 1.25, with Apache 1.3.22, so it is possible that something shown here may not work as expected with other versions of these pieces of software. If you find this to be the case, please let us know and we'll either fix the example or make a note of the dependencies.

How to Read This Book

This book is not a reference manual. While certain chapters, notably Chapter 4, are reference-like in nature, the book as a whole builds chapter upon chapter and often refers to material covered earlier. Nonetheless, some readers may prefer to look at Chapter 8 early, so an alternate path through the book might be to read that chapter right after Chapter 1.

Once you become more familiar with Mason, we expect that much of the book will still be useful as a reference, particularly chapters 4, 5, 6, and 7.

Appendixes A and B present much of the same material as those chapters in a more streamlined reference style, and should also be useful long after you have become a Mason guru. Appendix C is a short discussion of editors you can use with Mason, and Appendix D covers Bricolage, a content management system based on Mason.

Finally, the book includes a short glossary for those of you who are new to Mason and its terminology.

Overview

Chapter 1, *Introduction*

    This chapter goes into more detail on what Mason is, highlights a few of its most notable features, and also discusses some alternatives to Mason.

Chapter 2, *Components*

    Components are the basic building block in Mason. This chapter covers component syntax and how components can call one another, much like Perl subroutines.

Chapter 3, *Special Components: Dhandlers and Autohandlers*

    The topic of this chapter is dhandlers and autohandlers, two features unique to Mason that really can help you maximize code reuse.

Chapter 4, *APIs*

    This chapter is a bit more of a reference than those before it, as it has a lot of ground to cover. We cover the APIs of various objects that you might want to access from your components, primarily the Mason request object.

Chapter 5, *Advanced Features*

    Now that you know about component syntax, dhandlers, autohandlers, and a good chunk of the Mason API, it's time to learn about some of Mason's more complex features, like component methods and attributes, components that filter content, and Mason subrequests.

Chapter 6, *The Lexer, Compiler, Resolver, and Interpreter Objects*

    These objects form the core of Mason itself, and their constructor parameters and object APIs let you customize the way Mason handles requests.

Chapter 7, *Using Mason with mod_perl*

    Mason and mod_perl are designed to play nice together, and this chapter shows you how to make this happen.

Chapter 8, *Building a Mason Site*

    The obligatory sample site. See Mason at work on a real, live, on-the-Internet, usable-by-you web site.

Chapter 9, *Mason and CGI*

    If you can't use mod_perl, you may still want to use Mason to generate web pages via CGI scripts.

Chapter 10, *Scalable Design*

    Mason is cool, but it's not magic. You still need to think about architecture and design when designing a Mason-based application. We try to give you a few things to think about here.

Chapter 11, *Recipes*

    This chapter demonstrates a number of different uses of Mason in order to stimulate your thinking, as well as provide some easily customized example code.

Chapter 12, *Custom Mason Subclasses*
    A how-to on creating your own customized Mason subclasses.

Appendix A, *The Mason API*
    All the APIs we covered earlier, in a more concise form.

Appendix B, *Object Constructor Parameters*
    A spiffy table of constructor parameters.

Appendix C, *Text Editors That Understand Mason*
    Information on using Emacs and Vim to edit Mason components.

Appendix D, *Content Management with Bricolage*
    David Wheeler explains how to use Bricolage, a content management system
    built with Mason that can use Mason to generate web pages.

Other Resources

The most important online resource for Mason is the Mason HQ site located at
http://www.masonhq.com/. This site includes an online copy of the documentation, a Frequently Asked Questions database, news, user-contributed code and
documentation, and much more. The bug tracker on Mason HQ is kept up-to-
date, and it is a good source of information about limitations in certain versions of
Mason. There is also a to-do list that can give you insights on future directions
planned by the Mason developers.

Mason HQ also provides information on subscribing to the various Mason mailing lists,
of which the most important is the *mason-users* list. See *http://www.masonhq.com/
resources/mailing_lists.html* for more details.

This book's web site, at *http://www.masonbook.com/*, will always contain the latest
digital version of the book, freely available. In addition, we will make sure to report
any errata found in the published edition(s), as well as providing downloadable versions of all of the source code found in the book.

Typographic Conventions

Constant width
    is used for literal text, module names, function names, method names, and key-
    words

Italics
    is used for filenames, components, commands, URLs, emphasis, and terms
    when they are first introduced

We'd Like to Hear from You

Please send comments and questions concerning this book to the publisher at the following address:

O'Reilly & Associates, Inc.
1005 Gravenstein Highway North
Sebastopol, CA 95472
(800) 998-9938 (in the United States or Canada)
(707) 829-0515 (international or local)
(707) 829-0104 (fax)

We have a web page for this book, where we list errata, examples, or any additional information. You can access this page at:

http://www.oreilly.com/catalog/perlhtmlmason

To comment or ask technical questions about this book, send email to:

bookquestions@oreilly.com

For more information about our books, conferences, Resource Centers, and the O'Reilly Network, see our web site at:

http://www.oreilly.com

Open Publication License

This book is published under the Open Publication License (OPL), as follows:

Open Publication License Draft v1.0, 8 June 1999

I. REQUIREMENTS ON BOTH UNMODIFIED AND MODIFIED VERSIONS

The Open Publication works may be reproduced and distributed in whole or in part, in any medium physical or electronic, provided that the terms of this license are adhered to, and that this license or an incorporation of it by reference (with any options elected by the author(s) and/or publisher) is displayed in the reproduction.

Proper form for an incorporation by reference is as follows: Copyright (c) 2003 by David Rolsky and Ken Williams. This material may be distributed only subject to the terms and conditions set forth in the Open Publication License, v1.0 or later (the latest version is presently available at *http://www.opencontent.org/openpub/*). Commercial redistribution of Open Publication-licensed material is permitted.

Any publication in standard (paper) book form shall require the citation of the original publisher and author. The publisher and author's names shall appear on all outer surfaces of the book. On all outer surfaces of the book the original publisher's name shall be as large as the title of the work and cited as possessive with respect to the title.

OPTION B: Distribution of the work or derivative of the work in any standard (paper) book form for commercial purposes is prohibited unless prior permission is obtained from the copyright holder.

II. COPYRIGHT

The copyright to each Open Publication is owned by its author(s) or designee.

III. SCOPE OF LICENSE

The following license terms apply to all Open Publication works, unless otherwise explicitly stated in the document. Mere aggregation of Open Publication works or a portion of an Open Publication work with other works or programs on the same media shall not cause this license to apply to those other works. The aggregate work shall contain a notice specifying the inclusion of the Open Publication material and appropriate copyright notice.

SEVERABILITY. If any part of this license is found to be unenforceable in any jurisdiction, the remaining portions of the license remain in force.

NO WARRANTY. Open Publication works are licensed and provided "as is" without warranty of any kind, express or implied, including, but not limited to, the implied warranties of merchantability and fitness for a particular purpose or a warranty of non-infringement.

IV. REQUIREMENTS ON MODIFIED WORKS

All modified versions of documents covered by this license, including translations, anthologies, compilations and partial documents, must meet the following requirements:

1. The modified version must be labeled as such.
2. The person making the modifications must be identified and the modifications dated.
3. Acknowledgement of the original author and publisher if applicable must be retained according to normal academic citation practices.
4. The location of the original unmodified document must be identified.
5. The original author's (or authors') name(s) may not be used to assert or imply endorsement of the resulting document without the original author's (or authors') permission.

V. GOOD-PRACTICE RECOMMENDATIONS

In addition to the requirements of this license, it is requested from and strongly recommended of redistributors that:

1. If you are distributing Open Publication works on hardcopy or CD-ROM, you provide email notification to the authors of your intent to redistribute at least thirty days before your manuscript or media freeze, to give the authors time to provide updated documents. This notification should describe modifications, if any, made to the document.

2. All substantive modifications (including deletions) be either clearly marked up in the document or else described in an attachment to the document.

3. Finally, while it is not mandatory under this license, it is considered good form to offer a free copy of any hardcopy and CD-ROM expression of an Open Publication-licensed work to its author(s).

For more information about the Open Publication License, visit the Open Content web site at *http://www.opencontent.org/openpub*.

Acknowledgments

Ken would like to thank Dunn Brothers Coffee in St. Paul, Minnesota, where huge chunks of this book were written over steamy mochas in between crossword puzzle sessions. He would like to thank Apple Computer for creating the iBook, Cyclic Software for creating the CVS revision control system, and Larry Wall for creating the much-overstressed POD markup language, all of which were essential tools in the creation of this book. He'd like to thank Helen Plotkin and the rest of the Math Forum for turning a naive young mathematician into a salty programmer of the world. He'd like to thank his friends and family for not asking too many questions about what he does all day. Most importantly, he would like to thank Sheri Schechinger for being proud of a lowly open source programmer, for asking questions about what he does all day, and for giving him something so wonderful to come home to.

Dave would first and foremost like to thank his wife, Huey-Ling Chen, for her support and humor, particularly the "juice guy" incident (he'd explain, but then he'd have to juice you). He also wants to thank DoTheGood, Inc., in particular Gabriel Cheifetz, for providing such a great place to work while at the same time giving him enough free time to actually write this thing. Jonathan Swartz deserves thanks and sympathy for letting Dave muck up his code in such a cruel and twisted manner. Jon will no doubt get over the shock one day. Finally, Dave wants to thank any friend or family member who had the good grace not to cruelly mock him when they asked "when will the book be out?" and he responded with something like "oh, it's almost done, it should be out in a few months." How wrong he was!

Both authors would like to thank our unshockable editor, Linda Mui, and our crack team of technical reviewers: Alex Edelman, Jules Cook Graybill, Joe Johnston, Mike Stok, Jonathan Swartz, David Wheeler, and John Williams. David Wheeler in particular needs to be singled out for praise, not only for his excellent appendix on Bricolage (Appendix D), but also for his careful, detailed review. If his review comments were printed in the same typeface as this book, they would be about 100 pages long! Without his comments, and those of our other reviewers, this book would pretty much suck.

Joshua Chamas, Mark-Jason Dominus, Gerald Richter, and Sam Tregar provided invaluable feedback on the comparisons to other templating systems, in many cases defending their own systems from the ham-handed errors we made in describing them.

The entire group of overseers is responsible for transforming a disorganized and error-ridden draft into what we hope is a useful resource for billions and billions of Mason users. Or at least a few dozen.

## CHAPTER 1

Introduction

At its heart, Mason is simply a mechanism for embedding Perl code into plain text. It is only one of many such mechanisms that all do more or less the same thing. However, Mason represents a particular set of choices about how this embedding should be done, and many people have found that the way Mason does things is very straightforward and extremely conducive to getting jobs done.

In this chapter we'll introduce you to some of Mason's key features and strengths, show you a couple of examples of how to use Mason, and talk about some alternatives to Mason. After reading this chapter, you should have a fairly good idea of how Mason relates to its peers and what kinds of tasks you can accomplish with Mason.

The most common application of Mason is in building large dynamic web sites, and this book focuses mostly on web site building. Mason is broadly applicable to any situation in which fine control over document content is required, however, such as generating mail-merged form letters, creating custom configuration file sets, and even building dynamic GIF images based on varying input parameters. We intend to give you enough facility with Mason that after reading this book, you can imagine Mason-based solutions to problems we haven't ever thought of.

Before we get into the details of Mason and comparisons with its alternatives, we'll just briefly mention some of its guiding design principles. Mason was designed to help you build, organize, and maintain large web sites or other groups of dynamically generated documents. It cooperates fully with Perl, leveraging all the solutions and techniques that Perl developers have come to depend on and that have made Perl such a powerful and widespread tool. It encourages thinking about your site in structural terms rather than as a collection of procedural scripts or modules. All of these things are conducive to getting your job done effectively, letting you concentrate on your goals while Mason takes care of the details.

A First Example

To help make this discussion a little more concrete (this thing is called Mason, after all), let's look at an example. We'll give more in-depth treatment to the details of Mason's syntax later in the book; these examples are just to put some Mason code in front of your eyes and show you what it looks like.

The following code is a complete chunk of Mason code, called a *component*:

```
% my $planet = "World";
Hello, <% $planet %>!
```

When Mason runs this code, the output is:

```
Hello, World!
```

We'll talk more about the details of component syntax in Chapter 2, but two basic elements in the preceding example deserve mention here. The first is that any line that begins with a % character tells Mason that the line contains Perl code. The Perl code can be any syntactically correct Perl—Mason doesn't care what it is or what it does. In this case, it simply sets the value of a variable that will be used later in the component.

The other element in the previous Mason component is the substitution tag, denoted by the sequence <% %>. Mason will evaluate the contents of any such tag and insert the result into the surrounding text. In this case, the variable $planet evaluates to World, and the output of the entire component is Hello, World!

Note that any text that isn't a special Mason construct simply becomes part of the output of the component.

These two lines are relatively simple and not particularly exciting, but they should give you a taste for how Mason code looks in its simplest form.

The Main Features of Mason

There are more templating systems written in Perl than you could possibly keep in your head all at once. To help you make sense of Mason's place in the world, this section presents Mason's most important and distinctive features. By the end of this section, you should see that Mason pushes the boundaries of the term "templating system," with lots of features aimed at helping you manage the larger tasks of site design and maintenance.

Components: Modular Design Elements

As we mentioned before, the basic unit of Mason code is called a component. It is a chunk of Mason code that can accept input parameters and generate output text. An important feature of Mason is that any component may call any other component at any point during its execution, much like a Perl subroutine calling another Perl sub-routine. Because of this feature, a component may represent a single web page, a part of a web page (like a side navigation bar), or even a shared utility function that gener-ates no output of its own. This separation of design elements allows you to use Mason as a sort of glorified server-side include (SSI) mechanism, as in Examples 1-1, 1-2, and 1-3. Executing *mainpage.mas* will produce a full page of HTML with the header and footer inserted in place.

Example 1-1. header.mas

```
<html>
<head><title>Welcome to Wally World!</title></head>
<body bgcolor="#CCFFCC">
```

Example 1-2. footer.mas

```
<center><a href="/">Home</a></center>
</body></html>
```

Example 1-3 introduces the component call tag syntax, `<& &>`, which is used to call another component and insert its output into the surrounding text. The component tag can also accept arguments, which in this case can help unify site design by mov-ing the page header text into the *header.mas* component.

Example 1-3. mainpage.mas

```
<& header.mas &>
<center><h1>Wally World Home</h1></center>
Here at Wally World you'll find all the finest accoutrements.
<& footer.mas &>
```

The *header.mas* component in Example 1-4 now accepts an argument called $head that contains the text that should get inserted into the <h1> tags. A component's arguments are declared by using an <%args> block, which you'll see in more detail later in the book. The $head argument becomes an honest-to-goodness Perl variable that can be used throughout the rest of the component. It's lexically scoped in the *header.mas* component using Perl's my( ) function.

Example 1-4. header.mas

```
<%args>
 $head
</%args>
<html>
<head><title>Welcome to Wally World!</title></head>
<body bgcolor="#CCFFCC">
<center><h1><% $head %></h1></center>
```

The *footer.mas* component in Example 1-5 is fairly straightforward. It just provides a link to the document root.

Example 1-5. footer.mas

```
<center><a href="/">Home</a></center>
</body></html>
```

In the *mainpage.mas* component in Example 1-6, the arguments are passed to the *header.mas* component by using standard Perl syntax (i.e., commas, quotes, and the => operator). In fact, any Perl syntax for passing a list can be used, because the argument list is specified in real Perl syntax.

Example 1-6. mainpage.mas

```
<& header.mas, head => "Wally World Home" &>
Here at Wally World you'll find all the latest accoutrements.
<& footer.mas &>
```

Mason will take the list of arguments passed to the *header.mas* component and assign the proper values to the variables specified in the <%args> block.

Object-Style Component Inheritance

Aside from the fact that there's a little bit of Perl thrown into the mix for passing parameters, the examples we've seen don't really show anything that you couldn't do using standard server-side include (SSI) techniques. In fact, the usage demonstrated in these examples is relatively uncommon in building Mason sites, because there are better ways to get the job done. One of the greatest features of Mason is that components can inherit behavior from other components, much like classes and objects in an object-oriented hierarchy.* Typically, each component will inherit from a single component called the *autohandler*. The autohandler implements general behavior for all components, such as the content of headers and footers. Individual components implement specific behavior, such as the body text of the individual pages.

Using component inheritance, we can rewrite Examples 1-4 through 1-6 in a more common Mason idiom, as shown in Examples 1-7 and 1-8.

Example 1-7. autohandler

```
<html>
<head><title>Welcome to Wally World!</title></head>
<body bgcolor="#CCFFCC">
<center><h1><% $m->base_comp->attr('head') %></h1></center>
% $m->call_next;
<center><a href="/">Home</a></center>
</body></html>
```

---

* A caveat is necessary when using the term "object-oriented" to describe Mason's content-wrapping and inheritance schemes, because Mason merely borrows some ideas from the object-oriented world rather than employing Perl's (or any other language's) built-in object-oriented inheritance.

Example 1-8. mainpage.mas

```
<%attr>
 head => "Wally World Home"
</%attr>
Here at Wally World you'll find all the finest accoutrements.
```

Notice that the header and footer are now both all in one file, the autohandler. Visually, this helps unify the page content, because tags like `<html>` and `<body>` that are opened in the header are closed in the same file. The other important difference here is that *mainpage.mas* no longer has to call the header and footer components explicitly, but rather Mason calls the parent component automatically and it wraps its header and footer around the main content. The page header is now specified by an attributes block, one of Mason's object-oriented mechanisms. An attribute is a component property that inherits via Mason's component inheritance chain.

There are zillions of other uses for Mason's inheritance mechanism, which will be further explored in Chapter 5.

Intelligent Caching Mechanisms

Anyone who has built any dynamically generated web sites knows that sometimes certain portions of a site can take longer to generate and serve than you want to make your users wait. Furthermore, portions of a site might be only "semidynamic," meaning that their content changes periodically but stays static for a long time between changes. Alternatively, as might happen on a news site or for an online poll, content may change continually, but a lag time of a few minutes in updating the content would be acceptable if it improves site performance. For cases like these, Mason provides a very sophisticated caching mechanism that you can use to control how often the output of a component is rebuilt. You can base the expiration decision on time, on certain key parameters like username or content ID, or on an explicit agent that decides when specific data has expired.

The caching mechanism can be used for the output of a component, for an arbitrary block of text, or for any Perl data structure you might want to cache. The first-class support for caching is one of Mason's most endearing qualities, and you'll learn to appreciate it the first time it saves you from spending hours optimizing sluggish code.

To aid overall performance, Mason also has an intelligent internal caching mechanism. During execution, Mason turns each component into Perl source code on disk, then compiles the Perl code into bytecode, then executes the bytecode to produce the component's output. It would be a waste of computing resources to repeat this cycle every time a component needs to be executed, so Mason caches at each stage. As an aid to rapid development, Mason will check your components' modification times and invalidate its cache when you make changes to your components, ensuring that any changes you make to your site take effect immediately. When your site moves from development to production, you probably won't be making frequent changes to your site, so you can disable the freshness checks in order to improve your site's responsiveness.

Integration with Apache and mod_perl

As mentioned before, the most common use of Mason is in building large, dynamic, data-driven web sites. The most popular web server around is Apache, and one of Apache's most powerful features is mod_perl, which lets you use the full power of Perl within the Apache server process. Therefore, it should come as no surprise that Mason is designed to cooperate fully with mod_perl. Mason comes with drop-in mod_ perl handlers that let Apache serve your Mason components directly. It lets you take advantage of the sophisticated decision-making mechanisms that Apache has evolved to support, such as custom authentication methods, content negotiation, and dynamic URL rewriting. Mason's caching mechanism and other performance considerations are designed specifically for the task of serving dynamic content efficiently and with enough flexibility to let you design creative solutions to your specific problems. Although Mason lets you build a site without relying very much on assumptions about the server environment, learning about mod_perl and Apache's request cycle can help you use Mason to create slick and powerful features.

Alternatives to Mason

Much of this chapter so far may have sounded like a sales pitch, because we wanted you to know about Mason's biggest strengths so you could have some solid reasons for reading the rest of this book. However, you should also be aware that there are many alternatives to using Mason, and an awareness of these alternatives will help you form an accurate picture of the context for which each system was created. It will also help you decide which system to use for each individual project, because no single system was designed to be a solution to all the problems you might encounter. Just as importantly, different people find that different systems suit the way they think better than others do.

There are generally two kinds of systems that people consider to be alternatives to Mason: lightweight solutions and heavyweight solutions. Lightweight solutions generally have the goal of being small and fast and leave much of the major work up to you. They are often simple templating modules like Text::Template or HTML::Template or even homegrown templating schemes. Using templates is certainly a good idea, and it is one of the core ideas in Mason itself. However, when designing an entire site, you're usually going to need some more sophisticated system that helps you manage your site-building resources; if you choose a templating-only solution, you'll probably end up writing this management code yourself. You may have a good idea of what such a system would entail only after writing and maintaining dozens of complicated web sites, so you'd likely spend more time working on your management code than on building your sites. This is the main trade-off with lightweight solutions: you gain flexibility because you can manage your site however you want, but since the burden rests entirely on you, you might end up preferring to use a tool that handles many of these management issues for you.

By contrast, heavyweight solutions implement several layers on top of their templating capabilities. Despite some disagreement on proper use of the term, "application server" is often used to describe such heavyweight systems. Each anticipates the typical needs of a large, sophisticated web site and provides methods for dealing with these situations cleanly. A heavyweight system will typically have support for integrating a site with a database, working with HTML and URLs, preserving state from one request to the next, caching often-used resources, and dealing with error conditions. Each heavyweight solution is tailored to different site requirements and makes different assumptions about the best ways to deal with them.

Good solutions, such as Mason, Embperl, and `Apache::ASP`, also help you organize your site code in a way that lets you think about your site's structure in an organized way, both on the small scale and the large scale. They help you design a site that is easy to build and easy to maintain.

Mason itself is sort of a unique offering. It sits somewhere in the middle between lightweight and heavyweight solutions, though it leans a bit toward the heavy. It doesn't directly provide support for database connections, HTML munging, or sessions, but it makes it so easy for you to use regular Perl tools for these purposes that you'll never miss the functionality. If you do decide that Mason is missing a feature you really need, it's easy to add functionalities to Mason and use them just as if they were built in. In a sense, Mason's main strengths lie in the ways it lets you interface various parts of your site with one another and with outside resources.

Consider these design goals as you read the following descriptions. When possible, we have worked with the authors of these systems to make sure the descriptions highlight each system's best features. Keep in mind, though, that our list of alternatives is by no means exhaustive. There are countless other solutions. We have tried to pick the most popular solutions, but for more information on any product you might want to use, read its documentation, find an appropriate mailing list in which to ask questions, and make your own decision.

Embperl

Of the systems presented in this chapter, Embperl may be the most similar one to Mason. Embperl is one of the oldest heavyweight systems that is still in widespread use. It has been used for several years under the name `HTML::Embperl`, but recent beta releases have switched the module name to just `Embperl`. Its author, Gerald Richter, is generally very responsive to bug reports and feature requests.

Embperl is targeted specifically toward generating HTML and has several "magical" HTML-manipulation features. For instance, HTML tables can be autogenerated by using the special Embperl variables $row, $col, and $cnt:

```
[- @k = qw(zero one two) -]
<table>
 <tr>
  <td>[+ $row    +]</td>
  <td>[+ $k[$row] +]</td>
 </tr>
</table>
```

This would output:

```
<table>
 <tr>
  <td>0</td>
  <td>zero</td>
 </tr>
 <tr>
  <td>1</td>
  <td>one</td>
 </tr>
 <tr>
  <td>2</td>
  <td>two</td>
 </tr>
</table>
```

This means that Embperl does some scanning of your HTML and your Perl code to decide when you mean to use its magical generation. Some people find this assistance useful, and others would prefer to manage the generation themselves (the approach that Mason takes). The equivalent Mason code would require an explicit loop:

```
% my @k = qw(zero one two);
<table>
% foreach my $row (0..$#k) {
 <tr>
  <td><% $row    %></td>
  <td><% $k[$row] %></td>
 </tr>
% }
</table>
```

Notice that the Embperl delimiters for embedded Perl code are based on square brackets like [+ +]. This is so that Embperl code can be written by using a WYSI-WYG HTML editor that might get confused by angle brackets and treat them as HTML code. Embperl takes this even further and lets you write Perl code that is HTML-escaped by the editor, like so:

```
[- $i = 0; -]
[$ while ($i &lt; 5) $]
  Row: [+ $i++ +]<br>
[$ endwhile $]
```

The text < will be converted to < by Embperl before execution.

Notice also that Embperl uses its own custom loop control syntax rather than Perl's built-in loop control. There is experimental support in Version 1.2b2 and higher for using native Perl loops, and it will be part of the stable feature set in Embperl Version 2.

Embperl has a feature called EmbperlObjects, which is an inheritance system similar to Mason's autohandler functionality. It also offers integrated support for preserving state between requests with Apache::Session via another special variable, %udat. This can be very handy; see Chapter 12 for how you can accomplish a similar effect with Mason.

Variables you create in Embperl are usually dynamically scoped as either local or global variables (not lexical my() variables), which can sometimes be a bit unnerving in a persistent environment like mod_perl. Fortunately, after each request, Embperl will clean up any variables you created during the request. Variables declared with local() or my() in Embperl are usually scoped to the substitution tag enclosing them. Contrast this to Mason, in which the default scope of localized variables is the entire component. Because of this, it is more common to see my() in Mason code and global variables in Embperl code.

Embperl Version 1.x also provides some support for using the Safe.pm module, which can provide some protection against executing malicious Perl code. This strategy is somewhat dubious, however, because the Safe module is fairly easily defeated and because we hope your page designers aren't going to be trying to sabotage your servers in the first place. Moreover, when using Safe mode, you won't be able to access outside resources like databases, so it might not even be an option in the first place. Because of these problems, support for Safe mode has been removed in Embperl Version 2.

Embperl 2 will add several new features, including support for XML/XSLT processing, custom template syntax, and a highly customizable data caching and output filtering system.

Apache::ASP

Apache::ASP, by Joshua Chamas, is a package for writing Active Server Pages under mod_perl. It is fairly mature (its initial release was in 1998), and several years of development and active use by the Perl community have created a feature set that includes several useful extensions to the Microsoft standard.

With Apache::ASP, instead of using VBScript or JScript for the dynamic portions of the pages, you use Perl.[*] The ASP feature set has been neatly translated to Perl, so you have

---

[*] A third-party PerlScript option is also available, but it is not as widely used as VBScript or JScript.

access to all of ASP's built-in features such as session management (using a custom session manager, not `Apache::Session`), email integration, and the ASP object model.

The Perl embedding syntax is very simple: `<% %>` tags get wrapped around Perl control structures or miscellaneous Perl instructions, and `<%= %>` tags are wrapped around Perl expressions whose values you wish to insert into the surrounding HTML. For example:

```
<h2>Font sizes:</h2>
<% foreach my $i (1..5) { %>
  <font size="<%= $i %>">Size = <%= $i %></font><br>
<% } %>
```

The Mason equivalent is very similar:

```
<h2>Font sizes:</h2>
% foreach my $i (1..5) {
  <font size="<% $i %>">Size = <% $i %></font><br>
% }
```

The output of both examples is:

```
<h2>Font sizes:</h2>
  <font size="1">Size = 1</font><br>
  <font size="2">Size = 2</font><br>
  <font size="3">Size = 3</font><br>
  <font size="4">Size = 4</font><br>
  <font size="5">Size = 5</font><br>
```

Because it is built on the ASP model, `Apache::ASP` is a natural choice when porting an ASP/IIS application to the Apache platform. You will need to translate the scripting language from VBScript or JScript into Perl, but the overall structure of the site should remain unchanged.

Besides the standard ASP feature set, `Apache::ASP` supports several additional features, including extra event handlers, XML/XSLT processing, and component output caching. It also supports a cookieless mode for maintaining session data, which can be very handy for end users unwilling or unable to store session cookies. The XSLT support is particularly interesting, since combining it with the output caching features means that you can use dynamic XSLT transformations in web publishing, a technique that might be computationally prohibitive without caching.

For more information on `Apache::ASP`, please visit *http://www.apache-asp.org/*.

HTML::Template

Sam Tregar's `HTML::Template` module falls into the lightweight category. Its chief goal is to allow site builders to separate a site's HTML from its Perl controlling code, and it enforces this division quite strictly. No Perl code is ever embedded within templates, and control structures like `if`, `include`, and various loops are all implemented by custom `HTML::Template` tags. Any variables to be interpolated into the HTML template are explicitly fed to the template by the controlling Perl code.

Philosophically, the reason for this strict division of HTML and Perl is so that a division of labor can be enforced in an organization, with HTML designers and Perl coders working independently, not worrying about whether they're editing the same files. It is also possible to apply the same controlling code to several different templates, so that designers can create different look-and-feel templates without involving programmers.

`HTML::Template` is generally very fast at filling in HTML templates, especially if you use its just-in-time compiler `HTML::Template::JIT`. It also provides a caching mechanism, somewhat similar to Mason's, that allows for caching templates in private memory, on disk, in memory shared between processes, or in combinations thereof. Unlike Mason, `HTML::Template`'s caching handles the caching only of templates themselves, not of their output or arbitrary data.

Example syntax:

```
<h1>Employee listing:</h1>
<TMPL_LOOP NAME=EMPLOYEE_INFO>
  Name: <TMPL_VAR NAME=NAME> <br>
   Job: <TMPL_VAR NAME=JOB> <br>
</TMPL_LOOP>
```

To make this actually do something, you need to write Perl code to call the template. For this template, we might write something like this:

```
my $template = HTML::Template->new( filename => 'emp_list.tmpl' );
$template->param( EMPLOYEE_INFO =>
                    [ { NAME => 'Dave', JOB => 'Grouper of Bumpers' },
                      { NAME => 'Ken',  JOB =>  'Bumper of Groupers'} ] );
print "Content-Type: text/html\n\n";
print $template->output;
```

Note that the top layer for the system is a Perl script. Some people love this, some people hate it. You may know by now which category you fall into.

Text::Template

`Text::Template`, written by Mark-Jason Dominus, is a lightweight solution similar to `HTML::Template`, but has some philosophical differences. First, it does not assume that the template contains HTML but is designed to work with any kind of text in the template (in truth, `HTML::Template` can work with arbitrary text, too, but it was designed specifically to work with HTML). Second, it uses native Perl control structures instead of its own custom macros, so Perl programmers have less to keep in their heads. This has the effect of breaking down the barrier that `HTML::Template` maintains between code and HTML, so in an environment in which designers and programmers need exclusive control over their own work products, HTML::Template may be the better choice.

Like Embperl, Text::Template also supports code sequestering via the Safe.pm module, with the same caveats as mentioned earlier. Template variables can be passed explicitly to the template for substitution or drawn from Perl variables in a specified Perl package. Text::Template also allows the user to customize what delimiters are used to indicate the special Perl code or variable substitution sections. The default delimiters are curly braces:

```
my $string = q[
  Dear {$recipient},
    Congratulations!  You have won {$amount} dollar{$plural}!
];
my $template = Text::Template->new(TYPE => 'STRING', SOURCE => $string );
$T::recipient = int(rand 2) ? 'Mary' : 'John';
$T::amount    = int(rand 10) - 5;
$T::plural    = $T::amount == 1 ? '' : 's';

print $template->fill_in(PACKAGE => 'T');
```

Text::Template was first released in 1995 and has undergone many revisions in its life cycle. It is considered a mature product, and its author is very responsive to comments and questions about it. There is also a low-volume mailing list for users of Text::Template, the details of which can be found in the module documentation.

Template Toolkit

In order to combat the proliferation of zillions of templating modules that all look and act similar but contain maddening and meaningless differences, the Template Toolkit package by Andy Wardley aims to be the only templating package you'll ever need and offers an extremely full-featured templating system. Like HTML::Template, it uses a large set of custom control macro tags like IF, SWITCH, FOREACH, FILTER, and so on, as well as more advanced tags like FILTER, TRY and CATCH, and MACRO. It can either allow embedded Perl as Text::Template does or disallow it as HTML::Template does. Like Mason, it lets you build a site in terms of modular components. There is also an Apache::Template module that facilitates building a mod_perl-based site out of Template Toolkit components.

An example of Template Toolkit usage follows:

```
my $string = q(
  Dear [% recipient %],
    Congratulations!  You have won [% amount %] dollar[% plural %]!
);

my $template = new Template;
my %vars = (recipient => (int(rand 2) ? 'Mary' : 'John'),
            amount    => int(rand 10) - 5);
```

```
$vars{plural} = $vars{amount} == 1 ? '' : 's';

$template->process(\$string, \%vars);
```

Because of its many features and its well-supported development, the Template Toolkit is becoming the modern standard for standalone templates. It is quite different in philosophy from Mason, though, so we do not consider it to be in direct competition as a tool for the same situations we'd use Mason for.

PHP

PHP (*http://www.php.net/*) is pretty far removed from Mason, but we mention it here because of its popularity. PHP is another mechanism for embedding functionality into web pages, but PHP does *not* use Perl as its scripting language. The name PHP can refer variously to the embedding system itself, the scripting language, or the interpreter that renders the HTML pages.

It is important to understand some of the properties of PHP before deciding to use it. One of the design goals of PHP is to be as simple as possible to install and start using, and in some cases this means that features that experienced Perl programmers rely on are not present. For instance, PHP lacks support for private namespaces, there is no way to create three-tiered applications that separate business logic and presentation code, and there is no mechanism for creating reusable code modules. The Apache mod_php module is only a content generation module, so it cannot cooperate with other request phases in the same way Mason can cooperate with mod_perl's authentication or filename translation phases.*

Importantly, although there is a lot of user-contributed code in the PHP world, it cannot match the breadth and depth of Perl's CPAN. It has often been said that the CPAN is Perl's "killer app," and programmers most appreciate the CPAN when they least expect it.

Finally, although you can theoretically use PHP for general-purpose programming, it wasn't designed for that. PHP is typically used only for embedding PHP code into templates, whereas Perl is a full-featured programming language used for more purposes than any single programmer could imagine. While this does make PHP well-suited for the common tasks of web scripting, it may be limiting. For instance, a certain Perl programming friend was recently contracted to write a "simple shopping cart system" that had one small addition: it had to do some horribly complex optics calculations. For situations like these, a general-purpose programming language like Perl can be quite handy.

---

* Although Mason is also just a content generation module, it cooperates with the other request phases by virtue of mod_perl's support for sharing information among the request phases.

Philosophy

The final criterion in evaluating an application platform is peace of mind: your peace of mind as a developer, your company's peace of mind as a provider of services and maintainer of site resources, and your users' peace of mind to enjoy (or suffer through) your final product.* If you are continually frustrated by your development tools and environment, you will almost certainly not be able to create a satisfactory product.

Mason was created to help you with tasks when you need help and get out of your way when you don't. It was designed to cooperate with Perl to the fullest extent possible. The Mason templating language is extremely simple but full featured and leverages Perl to do all the things that a programming language is good at. Mason is not explicitly tied to the HTML markup language, but it was designed to function well in an HTML environment. Mason's design choices were made to encourage a structural approach to site building rather than a procedural approach, and this often makes building large sites with a consistent feel very simple.

If you're interested in learning more about alternatives to Mason, you might be interested in another book from O'Reilly and Associates, Inc., *CGI Programming with Perl*, written by Scott Guelich, Shishir Gundavaram, and Gunther Birznieks. It contains more extensive discussions of many of the modules mentioned here.

Getting Started with Mason

To help you try out the various examples you'll see throughout the book, we'll walk you through the typical installation and configuration steps. First we'll describe a fairly bare-bones standalone installation that can be used without a web server, and then we'll describe the more common situation, which is to install Mason for use in conjunction with the Apache web server and its mod_perl-embedded Perl interpreter.

A Standalone Installation

Mason can be installed just like any other typical Perl module and used as a toolset for templating. You'll need these ingredients:

Perl 5.005 or later
> Available from *http://www.cpan.org/src/*. Perl may already be installed on your system, especially if it's a variety of Unix. Mason requires at least Version 5.005 of Perl, though Version 5.6.1 is recommended. Instructions for installing Perl are contained in the *INSTALL* file, included with the distributions. If you're on some

---

* An excellent exposition on the importance of peace of mind when designing and maintaining systems is *Zen and the Art of Motorcycle Maintenance* by Robert M. Pirsig.

variety of Windows, you may find it much easier to install a version of Perl supplied by ActiveState, available at *http://www.activestate.com/Products/ActivePerl/*.

Mason 1.10 or later

To install Mason, download it from *http://www.cpan.org/modules/by-module/HTML/*, *http://www.masonhq.com/code/download/*, or your favorite CPAN mirror, and issue the standard commands for installing Perl modules: `perl Makefile.PL`, then `make`, then `make test`. If no errors are encountered, issue the command `make install`. This last step may need to be done as the administrative user, so that Mason is made available to all the users of the computer.

During some of these steps, you'll notice Mason looking around for Apache and `mod_perl`. You can skip these parts of the installation process when asked, since you won't be using them in this scenario.

You'll also need several other Perl modules that Mason depends on, such as `Exception::Class`, `Class::Container`, and `Params::Validate`. Since it can get fairly tedious to follow all these dependencies yourself, you may want to use the `CPAN.pm` module to help automate the process. In this case, you can start the `CPAN` shell with the command `perl -MCPAN -e shell`, and then type `install HTML::Mason` at the prompt.

A mod_perl Installation

Most of the examples in this book will assume that Mason is being used in a web context. Most people using Mason also use it in conjunction with Apache and `mod_perl`. The main ingredients involved in setting up this paradigm are:

Perl 5.005 or later

You can follow the same procedure as in the standalone scenario. Perl itself doesn't care how you're going to use Mason.

Apache

You can get Apache from *http://httpd.apache.org/dist/httpd/*. Mason has no direct dependencies on any specific version of Apache, but you'll probably want the latest version in the 1.3.x sequence, which is 1.3.26 at the time of this writing. Mason has not yet been tested extensively with Apache 2.x, though it probably will be by the time this book hits the shelves. Instructions for installing Apache are included in its *INSTALL* file—or, if you're building `mod_perl` too, you can just let `mod_perl` build and install Apache for you.

`mod_perl`

You can get `mod_perl` from *http://perl.apache.org/dist/*. `mod_perl` follows the standard installation procedure for a perl module (even though it is actually much more than that), so you can issue the same `perl Makefile.PL`, `make`, `make test`, and `make install` commands mentioned previously. Several configuration options are available in the first step—for full Mason compatibility, build mod_ perl with the command perl Makefile.PL EVERYTHING=1. We do *not* recommend building mod_perl as a Dynamic Shared Object (DSO), because that configuration has been associated with instability on several platforms.

Mason

After you've installed mod_perl, you can install Mason. The process is exactly the same as we described previously in the standalone configuration, but if mod_perl is installed, the make test step will test Mason with a live mod_perl-enabled Apache server. Make sure all the tests succeed before issuing the make install command.

Apache configuration files

In order to enable Mason for certain sections of your web site, you'll need to configure Apache so that it hands off requests for Mason components to Mason. A simple configuration that will suffice for many users is the following, put in the *httpd.conf* for the site:

```
PerlModule HTML::Mason::ApacheHandler
<FilesMatch "\.html$">
 SetHandler perl-script
 PerlHandler HTML::Mason::ApacheHandler
</FilesMatch>
```

This tells Apache that all files ending in *.html* are Mason components and should be handled by the HTML::Mason module via mod_perl. Of course, you can use standard Apache configuration directives to specify different criteria for passing requests to Mason. For instance, if you'd rather restrict Mason's influence to a certain directory, you can use something like this:

```
PerlModule HTML::Mason::ApacheHandler
<Directory /path/to/subdirectory>
 <FilesMatch "\.html$">
  SetHandler perl-script
  PerlHandler HTML::Mason::ApacheHandler
 </FilesMatch>
</Directory>
```

Lots of configurations are possible. If you have more complex needs for your site, you'll need to be familiar with Apache's configuration directives. The relevant documentation on general Apache configuration are available at *http://httpd.apache.org/docs/*, and more advanced Mason configuration is discussed in Chapter 7.

Trying It Out

Once Mason is installed, you can write a simple test program like the one in Example 1-9 to show that it's actually working.

Example 1-9. handshake.pl

```
#!/usr/bin/perl

use strict;
use HTML::Mason;
my $interp = HTML::Mason::Interp->new();
my $comp = $interp->make_component(comp_source => <<'END');
 Greetings, <% ("Earthlings", "Martians")[rand 2] %>
END
$interp->exec($comp);
```

When you run this program, you should see either Greetings, Earthlings or Greetings, Martians. The code between the <% %> tags is just regular Perl code, not anything to do specifically with Mason. It randomly selects an element from the two-element list ("Earthlings", "Martians"). Of course, we'll explain the details of how the rest of the program works later in this book.

If you've installed mod_perl and configured Apache as we described earlier, then you should test out your setup now. Assuming the first configuration option we showed you, you can place the same component at the top level of your web server's documents directory, as shown in Example 1-10.

Example 1-10. handshake.html

```
Greetings, <% ("Earthlings", "Martians")[rand 2] %>
```

When you request the URL *http://www.example.com/handshake.html* from your server, you should again see a random selection of either Greetings, Earthlings or Greetings, Martians.*

Assuming you've gotten Mason installed properly and everything's working right, congratulations. If you've run into a problem that you can't figure out, several sources of help are available. First check out the Frequently Asked Questions file at *http://www.masonhq.com/docs/faq/*, as it contains answers to the most commonly encountered problems. If you don't get any satisfaction there, try searching the archives of the Mason mailing list, available at *http://www.masonhq.com/resources/mailing_lists.html*, or post a message to *mason-users@lists.sourceforge.net*. Try to be as specific as possible about your problems if you go this route.

Finally, a word of advice as you read this book—try out all the examples! You'll have a lot more fun and you'll retain the techniques better if you take a hands-on approach. And of course, if you find any errors in the examples, be sure to let us know.

---

* Throughout this book, we'll use the fictional domain *example.com* for many of our examples. Unless you own this domain (and you don't, since it's reserved for examples in books like this one), you should replace it with the real name of your web server.

## CHAPTER 2

Components

As mentioned in Chapter 1, the basic building block of Mason is called a component. A component consists of text of any sort as well as Mason-specific markup syntax. This chapter briefly introduces some core Mason concepts and then goes into the nitty-gritty of component syntax.

In this chapter we'll introduce you to the *syntax* of Mason components, but we won't spend much time on semantics. In most of the sections, we refer to other parts of the book where you can find out more about each concept.

Mason from 10,000 Feet

In order to put Mason into perspective, a basic understanding of how Mason processes a request is helpful. Each request is defined by an initial component path and a set of arguments to be passed to that component.

Requests are handled by the Interpreter object. You can use it directly or its API can be called by the ApacheHandler or CGIHandler modules provided with Mason.

The Interpreter asks the Resolver to fetch the requested component from the filesystem. Then the Interpreter asks the Compiler to create a "compiled" representation of the component. Mason's compilation process consists of turning Mason source code into Perl code, which is then executed in order to create an object representing the component. Mason stores this generated Perl code on disk, so that it doesn't need to go through the parsing and compilation process for every request, and stores the compiled code in an LRU (least recently used) cache in memory.

Once Mason has an object representing the initial component, it creates a request object and tells it to execute that component. The initial component might call several other components during the request. Any output a component generates is sent to STDOUT, which is a reasonable default for most environments in which Mason might be used. Of course, it is possible to change this default and send output elsewhere.

Several parameters can change how elements of this process happen, and you can replace the core Mason classes with your own customized subclasses for specialized behavior. When using the ApacheHandler module, all of these parameters can be specified in the web server's configuration file.

If a fatal error occurs during any part of this process, Mason throws an exception via Perl's built-in die( ) function. In a mod_perl or CGI environment, Mason will make sure that this exception is handled in a reasonable way, by showing the error in the browser and/or recording the error in the server's error log. You can also catch exceptions in your own code and handle them as you please.

Core Concepts

Before diving into component syntax, it is important to understand a few basic Mason concepts, with the key concepts highlighted *in italics*.

First there is the *component*. A component is a combination of text and Mason-specific markup. The markup sections may contain Perl code or special Mason directives. A component can correspond to a single web page, but more often a page is built up from several components. However, a component always corresponds to a single file.

A component is usually expected to generate output of some sort, whether HTML, an email message, or an image file. Components are closely analogous to Perl subroutines.

The *component root* is a directory or list of directories on the filesystem under which Mason expects to find all of your components. This is important in determining how component calls are resolved. If you ask Mason to execute the component */view/ books.comp*, Mason needs to know where to find such a thing. If your component root is */var/www/mason*, Mason will look for a file called */var/www/mason/view/ books.comp*.

The process of resolving a *component path* to a component can actually be a bit more complex than that, because you may actually specify multiple directories in which to search for components or use another storage mechanism altogether. We'll leave those complexities aside for now.[*]

When running under Apache, either via mod_perl or CGI, Mason will default to using the web server's document root as the component root. Mason may also be used in ways that don't require a component root at all, such as from a standalone perl

---

[*] For the curious, these issues are covered in Chapter 3, Chapter 5, and Chapter 12.

script. Since the focus of this book is on building sites, we will generally assume that there is a component root unless we mention otherwise.

It is very important to understand that component paths, like URL paths, always use the forward slash (/) as their directory separator, no matter what operating system Mason is running on. In other words, a component path can be thought of as a unique identifier for a particular component, in much the same way that a URL is a unique identifier for a particular resource. Also much like a URL, a component path usually corresponds to a file on disk with a related path, but it needn't necessarily.

Basic Component Syntax

Mason parses components by taking the text of a component and translating it into actual Perl code. This Perl code, when executed, creates a new HTML::Mason:: Component object. This object, in turn, can be used to generate the text originally found in the component. In a sense, this inverts the component, turning it from text with embedded Perl into Perl with embedded text.

The markup language Mason uses can give certain parts of the component special semantics, just like any other markup language such as XML or HTML. In this case, the syntax is used to tell Mason that certain parts of the component's text represent either Perl code, special instructions for Mason, or in some cases both.

The markup language used for Mason components contains a simple tag to do in-place substitution of Perl expressions, a way to mark a single line as being a line of Perl, and a set of block tags, most of which contain Perl code that is given a special meaning based on the particular tag being used (see Table 2-1).

Table 2-1. A portion of Mason's markup language

Tag	Name	Contains
<% ... %>	Substitution	Perl that is evaluated and sent as output
% ...	Perl line	A single line of Perl code [a]
<%perl> ... </%perl>	Perl block	Perl code
<& ... &>	Component call	A call to another component, possibly with arguments
<%init> ... </%init>	init block	Perl code that executes before the main body of the component
<%args> ... </%args>	args block	A component's input argument declarations

[a] The percent sign (%) must occur at the beginning of the line.

Substitution Tags: <% %>

The simplest kind of Mason tag is the substitution tag, used to insert the results of a Perl expression into your text. This tag is quite similar to those found in other templating systems. A simple example might look like this:

```
% $cd_count = 207; # this is embedded Perl
You have <% $cd_count %> CDs.
```

The output of this example would be:

```
You have 207 CDs.
```

The contents of the tag are evaluated in a list context and joined together just as if they had been passed as arguments to Perl's built-in `print()` function.

It is possible, and often desirable, to put more complicated Perl expressions into your substitution tags. For example, to handle plurals properly, the second line in the previous example could be rewritten as:

```
You have <% $cd_count %> CD<% $cd_count != 1 ? 's': '' %>
```

This could output any of the following, depending on the value of the `$cd_count` variable:

```
You have 207 CDs.
You have 1 CD.
You have 0 CDs.
```

The contents of the substitution tag are evaluated as Perl code, so whitespace is ignored, meaning `<%$cd_count%>` would be perfectly valid, though perhaps a bit difficult to read. Our style is to always include whitespace in a substitution tag.

Escaping substitutions

One very useful feature provided by Mason is the ability to escape the contents of a tag before it is sent as output. Escaping is the process of making unsafe characters safe. In a web context, safe means that we do not generate output that could be mistaken for HTML. In addition, we may need to do URL-style escaping as well.

Substitution escaping is indicated with a pipe (|) followed by one or more escape flags placed before the close of the tag. Currently, there are three valid escape flags, h for HTML entity escaping (i.e., > into >), u for URI escaping (i.e., > into %3E), and n for no escaping. The HTML and URI escape flags can be combined (i.e., hu) or used separately. An example might look like:

```
Name: <% $name | h %>
Homepage: <a href="redirect?url=<% $homepage | u %>">
```

The HTML escaping mode escapes the string using the `HTML::Entities` module, which means that all control and high-bit characters are escaped, as well as the greater-than and less-than signs (< and >), the ampersand (&), and the double quote character (").

HTML escaping is particularly useful when you're populating a page with data from an external data source like a database. For instance, consider the following code:

```
<textarea name="foo"><% $foo_data %></textarea>
```

If $foo_data contains the string </textarea>, your HTML will be broken. Guard against this possibility by escaping the output:

```
<textarea name="foo"><% $foo_data | h %></textarea>
```

However, the current implementation of HTML escaping in Mason comes with one giant caveat. Mason uses HTML::Entities internally but does not provide a way to tell HTML::Entities not to escape certain characters. By default, HTML::Entities assumes that you are using the ISO-8859-1 character set and escapes characters accordingly. If you are generating text for another character set, such as Big5, this will simply not work. As of this very moment, Mason does not provide a workaround for this problem, but it will in a near-future release and perhaps already has by the time you are reading this.

The URI escaping mode escapes any character besides alphanumerics, the underscore (_), dash (-), and period (.).

The "no escape" escaping mode is used when you have set a default escaping mode via the default_escape_flags parameter (see Chapter 6 for details). The n flag turns off the default escaping for the substitution tag in which it is used.

If you want to escape using a different mode than the default, you can combine the n escape with another flag, for example:

```
# default is 'u'
<% $contains_html | nh %>
```

The use of spaces around the pipe is optional.

The purist will note that $variable | h is perfectly valid Perl syntax for obtaining the value of $variable bitwise OR'ed against the output of the h subroutine (or perhaps the bareword string h), and therefore this valid Perl construct has a different meaning in <% %> tags than it has in other Perl environments. If you *really* mean to do the bitwise OR (in which case we strongly suspect you really *shouldn't* mean to), a workaround looks like this:

```
<% ($variable | h) %>
```

No doubt this will cause much consternation among those who write code that involves OR-ing together variables and the output of subroutines with single character names, who are being made second-class citizens in the Mason world. Sorry, but we're standing firm here.

In a near-future release of Mason we plan to make this escaping behavior customizable, so that you will be able to create your own escaping flags.

Embedded Perl: % Lines and <%perl> Blocks

There are two ways to embed Perl code into text with Mason. The first, the Perl line, is a line that starts with a percent sign (%). The rest of that line (up to the newline character) is interpreted as Perl code. This percent sign cannot be preceded by any horizontal whitespace such as spaces or tabs. A typical use of these lines is to implement Perl control structures. For example:

```
% foreach my $person (@people) {
  Name: <% $person->{name} %>
  Age: <% $person->{age} %>
  Height: <% $person->{height} %>
  Weight: <% $person->{weight} %>
% }
```

You can put any valid piece of Perl code on these lines. It is possible to use a Perl line for a larger chunk of code too—the previous code could have been equivalently written like the following:

```
% foreach my $person (@people) {
%    print "Name: ", $person->{name}, "\n";
%    print "Age: ", $person->{age}, "\n";
%    print "Height: ", $person->{height}, "\n";
%    print "Weight: ", $person->{weight}, "\n";
% }
```

If you have more than a few lines of Perl code in a row, however, it is probably best to use a Perl block instead. A Perl block is equivalent to a bunch of Perl lines in a row. It begins with the start tag <%perl> and ends with the end tag </%perl>. The contents of these blocks may be any valid Perl code.

You may want to use this tag if you need to do some data processing in the midst of your text. For example:

```
<%perl>
 my @words = sentence =~ /\b(\S+)\b/g;
 my @small_words = grep { length <= 3 } @words;
 my @big_words = grep { length > 3 } @words;
</%perl>
There were <% scalar @words %> in the sentence.
The big words were:
% foreach my $word (@big_words) {
  <% $word %>
% }
The small words were:
% foreach my $word (@small_words) {
  <% $word %>
% }
```

Calling Other Components: <& &> Tags

One of the most powerful features in Mason is the ability of one component to execute another, causing the called component's output to appear inside the calling component's output. The called component can, in turn, call other components, and so on. There are several ways to call components, but the simplest way is via the ampersand tag, like this:

```
<html>
<head>
<title>The Goober Guide</title>
</head>
<body>
<h1>Welcome to The Goober Guide!</h1>
<& menu &>
...
</body>
</html>
```

The menu component might contain a navigation bar used on all the pages for a site. Other example calls might look like this:

```
<& /path/to/menu &>
<& $component &>
<& menu, width => 640, admin => 1 &>
```

These calls illustrate several facets of Mason's component call tag. First, the component can be specified either directly using its name in plain text or indirectly as the result of Perl expression like $component in the example. In addition, component calls can take arguments (like width and admin in the third example) just like a Perl subroutine—internally, they actually *are* subroutines.

How does Mason figure out which component calls are specified directly and which indirectly? It applies some simple parsing rules. In a component call tag, if the first nonwhitespace character is a letter, number, underscore (_), slash (/), or period (.), Mason assumes that this text is a plain text component path rather than a Perl expression. In that case, everything up to the first comma or end of the tag (&>), whichever comes first, is assumed to be a string specifying the component path. Anything after a comma, if present, will be considered a list of arguments to pass to the called component.

If the first nonwhitespace character is something else, it is assumed that the component call contains a Perl expression (perhaps a variable or function call) whose value indicates the desired component.

These rules may seem a little arcane, but they manage to capture most people's expectations pretty well. Most of the time you can just specify the component in the most natural way, and it will just work. If you want to use a Perl expression (the "indirect" syntax) starting with one of the special characters mentioned in the previous paragraph, however, it is necessary to do something to force Mason to see it as Perl. An easy way to do this is to wrap the Perl expression in parentheses or to prefix it with Perl's no-op unary plus operator (+). For example:

```
<& ( component_path_returner() ) &>
<& +component_path_returner() &>
```

An alternative to the `<& &>` syntax for calling other components is the `$m->comp()` method. The `$m` variable contains the `HTML::Mason::Request` object for the current request, and you may use the `$m->comp()` method in Perl code just as you would use a `<& &>` tag in the component body.[*] In fact, in the current version of Mason, the `<& &>` tag is implemented internally with the `$m->comp()` method. So the following two lines are equivalent to each other:

```
<& menu, width => 640, admin => 1 &>
% $m->comp('menu', width => 640, admin => 1);
```

Notice how we used a Perl line, starting with a %, to embed the `$m->comp()` call in the component.

In this section we have been intentionally vague about how a Perl expression "specifies" a component. There are two ways it may do so: it may either evaluate to a string that gives the path to the component or evaluate to a component *object*,[†] rather than a path, and that object will then be executed. There are a few idioms in which this is useful, but they're used fairly rarely, and you'll mostly call components by their paths.

Components called with content

With Version 1.10, Mason introduced support for a powerful new construct, which we call "components called with content." Using this construct, it is possible to pass a Mason content block as part of a component call. Here is an example:

```
<%args>
 $name
</%args>
<&| /i18n/itext, lang => $lang &>
%# The bits in here will be available from $m->content in the /i18/text
  <en>Hello, <% $name %>.  These words are in English.</en>
  <fr>Bonjour, <% $name %>, ces mots sont français.</fr>
  <pig>Ellohay <% substr($name,2) . substr($name,0,1) . 'ay' %>,
       esethat ordsway areyay inyay Igpay Atinlay.</pig>
</&>
```

---

[*] The `HTML::Mason::Request` object provides access to several properties and methods concerning the currently executing chain of components. It is treated in detail in Chapter 4.

[†] Component objects are returned by several of the `HTML::Mason::Request` and `HTML::Mason::Interp` methods, covered in detail in Chapter 4 and Chapter 6.

Presumably, we expect the /i18n/itext component to filter this text so that only the correct language, as specified in $lang, is used. The /i18n/itext component would probably look something like this, using the $m->content() method to retrieve the content block:

```
<% $text %>
<%args>
 $lang
</%args>
<%init>
 my ($text) = $m->content =~ m{<$lang>(.+?)</$lang>}s;
</%init>
```

The content block gets executed when $m->content() is called, but it still has access to the variables as declared in the original component, such as $name. Components called with content will be covered in more depth in Chapter 5.

Other Named Blocks

Mason has a variety of other named blocks. These all have the same start and end tag syntax as <%perl> blocks, and most of them contain plan Perl. However, these other blocks are interpreted as having special meanings by Mason.

If any of these blocks, or a <%perl> block, is immediately followed by a newline, then that newline is discarded from the text output. This is a convenience to prevent you from having to do this all over the place:

```
<%args>
 ...
</%args><%init>
 ...
</%init><%perl>
 ...
</%perl>This is the start of the component ...
```

<%init> blocks

This is one of the most commonly used Mason blocks. The Perl code it contains is run before any other code except for code in <%once> or <%shared> blocks. It is run every time the component is called.

Using this block achieves the same effect as putting a <%perl> block at the top of a component but may be aesthetically more pleasing, because it allows you to isolate code at the bottom of a component, out of the way of the component's main body.

The <%init> block is typically used for doing things like checking arguments, creating objects, or retrieving data from a database. The variables created here are used in substitutions and perl lines throughout the rest of the component.

```
It is currently <% $temperature %> degrees.
<%init>
 my $temp = $dbh->selectrow_array("SELECT temperature FROM current_weather");
</%init>
```

<%args> blocks

As we have mentioned, components can take a variety of arguments, from either an external source (an HTTP request, for example) or an internal one (one component calling another).

It is usually desirable to declare the names and datatypes of the arguments that a component expects, as well as default values for these arguments, if they have any. This is done via the <%args> block. A typical block might look like this:

```
<%args>
 $color
 $size  => 20  # A default value
 @items => ( 1, 2, 'something else' )
 %pairs => ( key1 => 1, key2 => 'value' )
</%args>
```

This example demonstrates all the syntax possibilities for this block. First of all, we have argument types and names. The valid types are scalar, array, and hash, represented by their corresponding Perl sigil ($, @, or %), exactly as would be expected.

It is possible to give an argument a default value to be used if none is provided when the component is called. Any argument without a default is considered a *required* argument. Calling a component without specifying all its required arguments will cause a fatal exception to be thrown.

An argument's default can refer to an earlier argument, so this is completely legal:

```
<%args>
 $x
 $y => $x * 2 > 20 ? 50 : 100
</%args>
```

While this block looks as if it contains Perl, it is important to realize that its syntax is actually something unique to Mason. Importantly, lines should not end with a semicolon or comma, and each variable definition must be on a single line.

It is possible to have comments both after an argument declaration and on their own line. Comments start with the # character and continue to the end of the line, just as in Perl. Blank lines are also allowed.

<%filter> blocks

A <%filter> block is called after a component has finished running. It is given the entire output of the component in the $_ variable, and any changes to this variable are reflected in the output of the component. For example, this filter uppercases all of the component's output:

```
<%filter>
 s/(\w+)/\U$1/g
</%filter>
```

<%once> blocks

This block is executed whenever the component is loaded into memory. It is executed before any other block (including an <%init> block). Any variables declared here remain in existence (and in scope) until the component is flushed from memory or the Perl interpreter running Mason shuts down, whichever comes first. The <%once> section is useful for things like creating database handles or instantiating large, resource-intensive objects.

```
The universe is this big: <% $size %>
<%once>
 my $size = calculate_size_of_universe();
</%once>
```

<%cleanup> blocks

The cleanup block is executed right before the component exits and is the counterpart to the <%init> block. It is useful if you have created resources—such as circular references—that need to be freed. Technically, it is the same as placing a <%perl> block at the end of a component.

```
<%init>
 my $resource = get_a_resource();
</%init>

... do something interesting with that resource

<%cleanup>
 $resource->dispose;
</%cleanup>
```

Since cleanup code tends to be put at the end of the component anyway, <%cleanup> blocks aren't very common. Their chief advantage is that their name is cleanup.

Cleanup blocks are *not* executed if the component dies or aborts.

<%text> blocks

The contents of this block are output exactly as they are, without any parsing. This if useful if you need to write a component containing text about Mason. For example:

```
<%text>
 Substitution tags look like this: <% $var %>.
</%text>
```

<%doc> blocks

This block is intended for use by component authors for documentation purposes. Its contents are completely ignored. In the future Mason may do something more useful with them.

```
<%doc>
=head1 My Story

This is the part where I tell you what the component does.  But I'd
rather tell you a story about my childhood.  When I was but a
child, my mother said to me ...
</%doc>
```

As you can see, there's no reason not to use POD (Perl's Plain Old Documentation markup language) in these blocks, and you can even run perldoc on a component file.

<%flags> and <%attr> blocks

These two blocks share the same syntax and are used to declare one or more key/value pairs. The key can contain only letters, numbers, and the underscore character (_). The value can be any Perl expression whose results can fit into a scalar (such as a number, string, reference, or undef).

As in the <%args> block, the syntax in these blocks *looks* like Perl, but it is not. First, you cannot end a line with a comma or semicolon. Second, the whole key/value pair must be on a single line.

The difference between these two is that the <%flags> block may contain only official Mason flags, which are used to affect the component's behavior. Currently, there is only one flag defined, inherit. This is used to specify the component's parent component. Component inheritance is discussed in Chapter 3.

The <%attr> block may contain any keys that you want, as the variables defined in this block are not used by Mason but may be used in your code. Its contents are available by calling the object's attr() method and giving the desired key as the argument. See Chapter 5 for the details.

```
<%flags>
 inherit => '/some/other/component'
</%flags>

<%attr>
 color => "I'm so blue"
 size => 'mucho grande'
</%attr>

My color: <% $m->base_comp->attr('color') %>
```

There is one other important difference between flags and attributes: flags refer to only the current component, whereas attributes are part of Mason's inheritance scheme, discussed in Chapter 5.

<%def> and <%method> blocks

These two blocks use a syntax slightly different from any other Mason block because their contents are, in turn, components. The <%def> block contains a *subcomponent*, an embedded component that can be called via the normal Mason component calling syntax. A <%method> block also contains an embedded component, but one that may be inherited by a component's children. <%def> and <%method> blocks require a name in the initial tag. In the following example, a subcomponent named .make_a_link is defined:

```
<%def .make_a_link>
 <a href="<% $url %>"><% $text %></a>
 <%args>
  $path
  %query => ()
  $text
 </%args>
 <%init>
  my $url = ...
 </%init>
</%def>
```

The name of a subcomponent or method may contain alphanumerics, underscores (_), dashes (-), or periods (.). Customarily, a period is the first character of subcomponent names, in order to distinguish them from nonembedded components. Methods generally do not follow this convention; they have names without leading periods.

The main difference between subcomponents and methods is simply that subcomponents are visible only within the component in which they are defined, whereas methods are visible outside of the component and can be inherited via Mason's component inheritance mechanism. Subcomponents and methods are covered in Chapter 5.

<%shared> blocks

This block also contains Perl code. Code in this block is executed once per request, before the <%init> block, but unlike in an <%init> block, the variables declared in this block are in scope both in the component's main body and in any subcomponents or methods it may contain. This is useful for sharing a common chunk of code between all the parts of a single component. The uses of this block are discussed in Chapter 5.

Escaping a Newline

When using Mason, you may find that you want to suppress a newline in your text. A typical example is this:

```
<pre>
I am
% if ($height < 5) {
 not
% } elsif ( $height < 5.75 ) {
 not very
% } elsif ( $height > 6.25 ) {
 very
% }
tall
</pre>
```

This will generate the following output if $height is less than 5:

```
<pre>
I am
 not
tall
</pre>
```

The newlines in the output are not desirable but are unavoidable because of the need for the Perl code to exist on separate lines. Mason therefore provides the ability to get rid of a newline simply by preceding it with a backslash (\).

If we rewrote the preceding example with escaped newlines, it would look like this:

```
<pre>
I am\
% if ($height < 5) {
 not\
% } elsif ( $height < 5.75 ) {
 not very\
% } elsif ( $height > 6.25 ) {
 very\
% }
tall
</pre>
```

Given this, the output for a $height less than 5 would then be:

```
<pre>
I am not tall
</pre>
```

This example could be redone on a single line using multiple <%perl> blocks, but it would be pretty hideous looking.

Component Arguments

Most components will expect to receive named arguments, and these can be passed in one of two ways. Components can receive arguments as the result of external requests, such as those via HTTP, or they can receive arguments when they are called from another component. These arguments are available in the called component via several mechanisms. But from a component's perspective, how it is called is largely irrelevant.

<%args> Block Revisited

Since we are talking about arguments, it is worth revisiting the <%args> block discussed previously. This block is used to declare the arguments that a component expects. In addition, it can also be used to specify a default value if none is given when the component is called.

The block we used earlier was:

```
<%args>
$color
$size => 20
@items => ( 1, 2, 'something else' )
%pairs => ( key1 => 1, key2 => 'value' )
</%args>
```

This says, in English, that this component expects two scalars, one named color, which is mandatory, and one named size, which is not mandatory and defaults to 20. It also expects an array named items, which defaults to (1, 2, 'something else') and a hash named pairs, which defaults to (key1 => 1, key2 => 'value'). Neither of these latter two arguments is mandatory.

These arguments are all available in your component as lexically scoped variables. For example, your component will have a lexically scoped $color variable available. You do not need to declare it anywhere but in the <%args> block.

If a mandatory argument (one with no default) is not provided in the call to the component, an exception is thrown. If an argument with a default is not given a value, the default is transparently assigned to the variable. Just to be clear, we will explicitly note that undef is a valid value for an argument. It is the absence of an argument that causes the exception.

%ARGS

In addition to any lexically scoped variables created via their declaration in an <%args> block, each component body also has a lexically scoped hash called %ARGS. This hash contains all of the arguments with which the component was called.

One point of confusion for those new to Mason is the difference between %ARGS and the <%args> block. The %ARGS hash contains the arguments exactly as they were *passed* to a component, whether or not they are declared in the <%args> block. The keys of the %ARGS hash do not contain the Perl sigils ($, @, or %). An argument declared as $color in the <%args> block would therefore be available via $ARGS{color}. Any assignment of defaults by the <%args> block is not visible in %ARGS; the values are given exactly as they were passed.

In addition, the %ARGS hash is always present,* but the <%args> block is optional.

If you are expecting input with a large number of similarly named items, such as input1, input2, and so on through input20, declaring all of them in an <%args> block may be a bit unwieldy. In this case, the %ARGS hash can be quite handy.

%ARGS is also useful if you expect arguments with names that cannot be used for Perl variables. For example, when submitting a web form by clicking on an image named submit, the browser will generate two additional form values, called submit.x and submit.y. You cannot have a Perl variable named $submit.x, so the only way to get at this argument is to check $ARGS{'submit.x'}.

There are other ways to retrieve the arguments passed to a component, which are discussed in Chapter 4.

%ARGS Versus @_

The Mason tradition has always been to use named arguments. However, for simple components, you may prefer to use @_ to access the arguments, just as in Perl subroutines. There are several caveats here. If your component contains an <%args> section, Mason expects it to receive an even number of arguments in @_ so that it can assign @_ to %ARGS. If it receives an odd number of arguments, a fatal error will occur. But regardless of how arguments are passed, @_ is always available in components.

So the following pieces of code are near-identical when a component receives an even number of arguments:

```
% foreach (sort %ARGS) {
  <% $_ %>
% }

% foreach (sort @_) {
  <% $_ %>
% }
```

---

* Unless the component is called with an odd number of arguments. See the next section for details on this exception.

Argument Examples

Let's take a look at a number of scenarios involving argument passing, first via an HTTP URL query string and then via an internal component call. Then we will see how this interacts with the component's <%args> block and the %ARGS hash.

Arguments submitted via POST and GET requests are treated in exactly the same way, and if both are present they are merged together before the component is called.

Let's assume that the component being called contains this <%args> block:

```
<%args>
$colors
@colors
%colors
</%args>
```

For each example, we show you two ways to call that component. The first is via an HTTP query string, which is how a component is called to generate a web page. The second is via a component call tag, as a component would be called from another Mason component.

/some/component?colors=blue
<& /some/component, colors => 'blue' &>

> In both cases, $colors is the string "blue" and @colors is a single-element array containing ('blue'). In addition, $ARGS{colors} would be the string "blue" as well.
>
> This component will die when it is called, however, because Mason does not allow you to assign an odd number of elements to a hash, so the assignment to %colors is fatal.

/some/component?colors=blue&colors=red&colors=green
<& /some/component, colors => ['blue', 'red', 'green'] &>

> Again the URL and internal example give the same result. The $colors variables contains a reference to a three-element array, ['blue', 'red', 'green']. This time, $ARGS{colors} contains the same three-element array reference as $colors and the @colors array contains a three-element array with those same elements.
>
> Again, assigning an odd number of elements to the %colors hash causes a fatal error.

/some/component?colors=blue&colors=cyan&colors=green&colors=mint
<& /some/component, colors => ['blue', 'cyan', 'green', 'mint'] &>

> Now, $colors contains a reference to a four-element array, and the @colors array has four elements as well. Finally, the assignment to %colors works without an error and will result in a hash containing ('blue' => 'cyan', 'green' => 'mint'). $ARGS{colors} contains the same *array* reference as $colors.

```
<& /some/component, colors => { blue => 'cyan', green => 'mint' } &>
```

This set of arguments isn't representable with a query string, because there's no way to indicate that the arguments are structured in a hash via a web request.

In this call, $colors contains a reference to a hash, not an array, though the @colors array contains four elements, just as in the previous example. The %colors hash is likewise the same as the previous example. Now, the $ARGS{colors} hash entry contains a *hash* reference.

This discrepancy in how hash assignments are treated, depending on the way a call is made, is probably not too important because Mason simply does the right thing based on the contents of %args. You declare %colors as an argument, and as long as an even number of colors elements are passed in, you get a hash.

Arguments via Component Calls

When calling another component that expects named arguments, it is important to remember that arrays and hashes need to be passed as references. For example, a component named /display with an <%args> block like this:

```
<%args>
@elements
%labels
</%args>
```

Should be called like this:

```
<& /display, elements => \@some_data, labels => \%data_labels &>
```

Mason will do the right thing and translate the references back into an array and a hash in the /display component.

Arguments via HTTP Requests

When using Mason to make a web application, you must understand the details of how external HTTP requests are converted into component calls. Specifically, we are interested in how query string and POST parameters are converted into arguments.

These requests are expected to be in the standard name/value pair scheme used by most web interfaces. If a parameter is given only once (i.e., component?foo=1&bar=2), it will be present in the %ARGS hash as a simple scalar, regardless of how it is declared in the <%args> section.

If a parameter is declared as a scalar ($foo) but given multiple values (i.e., component?foo=1&foo=2), the $foo parameter will end up containing a reference to an array, as will $ARGS{foo}. Future versions of Mason may provide the ability to coerce these arguments into specific data structures.

If a parameter is declared as an array (@foo), it will contain zero or more values depending on what is in the query string and/or POST data. A hash is treated more or less like an array, except that giving a parameter declared as a hash an odd number of values will cause a fatal error.

One caution: the key/value associations in a declared hash are determined by the order of the input. Let's assume we have a component with this <%args> block:

```
<%args>
 %foo
</%args>
```

A request for `component?foo=1&foo=2` will result in a different hash from `component?foo=2&foo=1`. This isn't generally a problem because you can usually control the order of the arguments by their position in an HTML form. However, neither the HTTP or HTML specifications specify that a client needs to respect this ordering when submitting the form, and, even if it were, some browsers would probably screw it up eventually.* It's not a great idea, therefore, to use hashes as arguments in a top-level component that may be called via an HTTP request generated by a form. When you can control the query string yourself, this is not a problem.

Component Return Values

So far, we know three ways to call components: by using the inline component call tag (<& &>), by using the $m->comp() method, or via a URL. When using a component call tag, the called component's output is placed exactly where the tag was. When a component is called via a URL, its output is sent to the client. The $m->comp() tag offers an additional channel of component output: the return value. By default, Mason components return undef. If you want to return something else, you can add an explicit return() statement inside that component, such as this:

```
<%init>
 my $size = 20;
 return $size;
</%init>
```

Perl's return() function will end processing of the component, and any values specified will be the return value of $m->comp(). Since Perl's normal rules of scalar/list context apply, a component may return either a scalar or a list.

---

* We know of no browsers that actually screw it up, but surely there must be some out there. Browsers have a history of simply making up their own unique behaviors, even when there *is* a specification.

Special Globals

All Mason components are given access to certain special variables. We have already discussed %ARGS, which is lexically scoped for each component. Mason also has a few special global variables available.

$m

This variable is an HTML::Mason::Request object, which has a number of methods that allow you to do things such as retrieve information on the current request, call other components, or affect the flow of execution. This object is discussed in detail in Chapter 4.

$r

If Mason is running under mod_perl (as is the case in most Mason setups), all components also have access to the Apache request object via the global variable $r. Mason's special hooks into mod_perl are covered in Chapter 7.

Sample Component

The component shown in Example 2-1 is part of our sample site and the focus of Chapter 8. The component here is responsible for displaying news about the site. It is called *news.mas* and is not intended to standalone by itself, but rather to form one part of a complete page.

It demonstrates a typical small Mason component. Its <%init> block does some very simple work to figure out the time that the file was last altered, and then it turns that time into a human-readable string.

Example 2-1. news.mas

```
<table width="100%" cellspacing="0" cellpadding="5">
 <tr>
  <td class="heading"><h2 class="headline">What's New?</h2></td>
 </tr>
 <tr>
  <td>
   <p>
   The whole site, at this point.
   </p>

   <p>
   <em>Last modified: <% $last_mod %></em>
   </p>
```

Example 2-1. news.mas (continued)

```
  </td>
 </tr>
</table>
<%init>
 my $comp_time = (stat $m->current_comp->source_file)[9];
 my $last_mod =
     Time::Piece->strptime( $comp_time, '%s' )->strftime( '%B %e, %Y %H:%M' );
</%init>
```

No single component can demonstrate all of Mason's features, so if you're curious to see more, browse some of the components shown in Chapter 8.

## CHAPTER 3

Special Components: Dhandlers and Autohandlers

In previous chapters you've seen an overview of the basic structure and syntax of Mason components, and you've seen how components can cooperate by invoking one another and passing arguments.

In this chapter you'll learn about *dhandlers* and *autohandlers*, two powerful mechanisms that help lend reusable structure to your site and help you design creative solutions to unique problems. Mason's dhandlers provide a flexible way to create "virtual" URLs that don't correspond directly to components on disk, and autohandlers let you easily control many structural aspects of your site with a powerful object-oriented metaphor.

Dhandlers

The term "dhandler" stands for "default handler." The concept is simple: if Mason is asked to process a certain component but that component does not exist in the component tree, Mason will look for a component called dhandler and serve that instead of the requested component. Mason looks for dhandlers in the apparent requested directory and all parent directories. For instance, if your web server receives a request for */archives/2001/March/21* and passes that request to Mason, but no such Mason component exists, Mason will sequentially look for */archives/ 2001/March/dhandler*, */archives/2001/dhandler*, */archives/dhandler*, and */dhandler*. If any of these components exist, the search will terminate and Mason will serve the first dhandler it finds, making the remainder of the requested component path available to the dhandler via $m->dhandler_arg. For instance, if the first dhandler found is */archives/dhandler*, then inside this component (and any components it calls), $m-> dhandler_arg will return *2001/March/21*. The dhandler can use this information to decide how to process the request.

Dhandlers can be useful in many situations. Suppose you have a large number of documents that you want to serve to your users through your web site. These documents might be PDF files stored on a central document server, JPEG files stored in a database, text messages from an electronic mailing list archive (as in the example from the previous paragraph), or even PNG files that you create dynamically in response to user input. You may want to use Mason's features to create or process these documents, but it wouldn't be feasible to create a separate Mason component for each document on your server.

In many situations, the dhandler feature is simply a way to make URLs more attractive to the end user of the site. Most people probably prefer URLs like *http://www.yoursite.com/docs/corporate/decisions.pdf* over URLs like *http://www.yoursite.com/doc.cgi?domain=corporate&format=pdf&content=decisions*. It also lets you design an intuitive browsing interface, so that people who chop off the tail end of the URL and request *http://www.yoursite.com/docs/corporate/* can see a listing of available corporate documents if your dhandler chooses to show one.

The alert reader may have noticed that using dhandlers is remarkably similar to capturing the PATH_INFO environment variable in a CGI application. In fact, this is not exactly true: Apache's PATH_INFO mechanism is actually available to you if you're running Mason under mod_perl, but it gets triggered under different conditions than does Mason's dhandler mechanism.

If Apache receives a request with a certain path, say, */path/to/missing/component*, then its actions depend on what the final existing part of that path is. If the */path/to/missing/* directory exists but doesn't contain a *component* file, then Mason will be invoked, a dhandler will be searched for, and the remainder of the URL will be placed in $m->dhandler_arg. On the other hand, if */path/to/missing* exists as a regular Mason component instead of as a directory, this component will be invoked by Mason and the remainder of the path will be placed (by Apache) into $r->path_info. Note that the majority of this handling is done by Apache; Mason steps into the picture after Apache has already decided whether the given URL points to a file, what that file is, and what the leftover bits are.

What are the implications of this? The behavioral differences previously described may help you determine what strategy to use in different situations. For example, if you've got a bunch of content sitting in a database but you want to route requests through a single Mason component, you may want to construct "file-terminating" URLs and use $r->path_info to get at the remaining bits. However, if you've got a directory tree under Mason's control and you want to provide intelligent behavior for requests that don't exist (perhaps involving customized 404 document generation, massaging of content output, and so on) you may want to construct "directory-terminating" URLs and use $m->dhandler_arg to get at the rest.

Finer Control over Dhandlers

Occasionally you will want more control over how Mason delegates execution to dhandlers. Several customization mechanisms are available.

First, any component (including a dhandler) may decline to handle a request, so that Mason continues its search for dhandlers up the component tree. For instance, given components located at */docs/component.mas*, */docs/dhandler*, and */dhandler*, */docs/ component.mas* may decline the request by calling $m->decline, which passes control to */docs/dhandler*. If */docs/dhandler* calls $m->decline, it will pass control to */dhandler*. Each component may do some processing before declining, so that it may base its decision to decline on specific user input, the state of the database, or the phase of the moon. If any output has been generated, $m->decline will clear the output buffer before starting to process the next component.

Second, you may change the filename used for dhandlers, so that instead of searching for files called *dhandler*, Mason will search for files called *default.mas* or any other name you might wish. To do this, set the dhandler_name Interpreter parameter (see Chapter 6 for details on setting parameters). This may be useful if you use a text editor that recognizes Mason component syntax (we mention some such editors in Appendix C) by file extension, if you want to configure your web server to handle (or deny) requests based on file extension, or if you simply don't like the name *dhandler*.

Dhandlers and Apache Configuration

You may very well have something in your Apache configuration file that looks something like this:

```
DocumentRoot /home/httpd/html

<FilesMatch "\.html$">
  SetHandler perl-script
  PerlHandler HTML::Mason::ApacheHandler
</FilesMatch>
```

This directive has a rather strange interaction with Mason's dhandler mechanism. If you have a dhandler at */home/httpd/html/dhandler* on the filesystem, which corresponds to the URL */dhandler* and a request arrives for the URL */nonexistent.html*, Mason will be asked to handle the request. Since the file doesn't exist, Mason will call your dhandler, just as you would expect.

However, if you request the URL */subdir/nonexistent.html*, Apache will never call Mason at all and will instead simply return a NOT FOUND (404) error. Why, you ask? A good question indeed. It turns out that in the process of answering the request, Apache notices that there is no */home/httpd/html/subdir* directory on the filesystem before it even gets to the content generation phase, therefore it doesn't invoke Mason. In fact, if you were to create an empty */home/httpd/html/subdir* directory, Mason *would* be called.

One possible solution is simply to create empty directories for each path you would like to be handled by a dhandler, but this is not a very practical solution in most cases. Fortunately, you can add another configuration directive like this:

```
<Location /subdir>
    SetHandler perl-script
    PerlHandler HTML::Mason::ApacheHandler
</Location>
```

This tells Apache that it should pass control to Mason for all URL paths beginning with */subdir*, regardless of what directories exist on disk. Of course, using this Location directive means that *all* URLs under this location, including images, will be served by Mason, so use it with care.

Autohandlers

Mason's autohandler feature is one of its most powerful tools for managing complex web sites.

Managing duplication is a problem in any application, and web applications are no exception. For instance, if all pages on a given site should use the same (or similar) header and footer content, you immediately face a choice: should you simply duplicate all the common content in each individual page, or should you abstract it out into a central location that each page can reference? Anyone who's worked on web sites knows that the first approach is foolhardy: as soon as you need to make even a minor change to the common content, you have to do some kind of find-and-replace across your entire site, a tedious and error-prone process.

For this reason, all decent web serving environments provide a way to include external chunks of data into the web pages they serve. A simple example of this is the Server Side Include mechanism in Apache and other web servers. A more sophisticated example is Mason's own ability to call one component from inside another.

Although an include mechanism like this is absolutely necessary for a manageable web site, it doesn't solve all the duplication problems you might encounter.

First, the onus of calling the correct shared elements still rests within each individual page. There is no simple way for a site manager to wave a wand over her web site and say, "Take all the pages in this directory and apply this header and this footer." Instead, she must edit each individual page to add a reference to the proper header and footer, which sounds remarkably like the hassle we were trying to avoid in the first place. Anyone who has had to change the header and footer for one portion of a site without changing other portions of the site knows that include mechanisms aren't the cat pajamas they're cracked up to be.

Second, include mechanisms address only *content* duplication, not any other kind of shared functionality. They don't let you share access control, content filtering, page initialization, or session management, to name just a few mechanisms that are typically shared across a site or a portion of a site.

To address these problems, Mason borrows a page from object-oriented programming. One of the central goals of object-oriented programming is to allow efficient and flexible sharing of functionality, so that a Rhododendron object can inherit from a Plant object, avoiding the need to reimplement the photosynthesize() method. Similarly, each component in Mason may have a parent component, so that several components may have the same parent, thereby sharing their common functionality.

To specify a component's parent, use the inherit flag:

```
<%flags>
  inherit => 'mommy.mas'
</%flags>
```

If a component doesn't specify a parent explicitly, Mason may assign a default parent. This is (finally) how autohandlers come into the picture:

- The default parent for any "regular" component (one that isn't an autohandler—but might be a dhandler) is a component named "autohandler" in the same directory. If no autohandler exists in the same directory, Mason will look for an autohandler one directory up, then one more directory up, and so on, until reaching the top of the component root. If this search doesn't find an autohandler, then no parent is assigned at all.

- The default parent for an autohandler is an autohandler in a higher directory. In other words, an autohandler inherits just like any other component, except that it won't inherit from itself.

Note that these are only the defaults; any component, including an autohandler, may explicitly specify a parent by setting the inherit flag. Be careful when assigning a parent to an autohandler, though: you may end up with a circular inheritance chain if the autohandler's parent inherits (perhaps by default) from the autohandler.

Just like dhandlers, you can change the component name used for the autohandler mechanism from *autohandler* to something else, by setting the Mason interpreter's autohandler_name parameter.

We'll use the standard object-oriented terminology when talking about the inheritance hierarchy: a component that has a parent is said to be a "child" that "inherits from" its parent (and its parent's parent, and so on). At runtime, the hierarchy of parent and child components is often referred to in Mason as the "wrapping chain," for reasons you are about to witness.

Examples 3-1 and 3-2 show how to use autohandlers for our simple content-sharing scheme, adding common headers and footers to all the pages in a directory.

Example 3-1. /autohandler

```
<html>
<head><title>Example.com</title></head>
<body>
% $m->call_next;
<br><a href="/">Home</a>
</body>
</html>
```

Example 3-2. /welcome.html

```
<p>Welcome to a very wonderful site.  We hope you enjoy your stay.</p>
```

This demonstrates the first property of inheritance, which we call "content wrapping"—any component that inherits from the autohandler in Example 3-1, like */welcome.html* in Example 3-2, will automatically be wrapped in the simple header and footer shown. Note that */welcome.html* doesn't need to explicitly insert a header and footer; that happens automatically via the autohandler mechanism.

Let's trace through the details of the component processing. A request comes to the web server for *http://example.com/welcome.html*, which Mason translates into a request for the */welcome.html* component. The component is found in the component path, so the dhandler mechanism is not invoked. */welcome.html* doesn't explicitly specify a parent, so Mason looks for a component named */autohandler*, and it finds one. It then tries to determine a parent for */autohandler*—because there are no directories above */autohandler* and */autohandler* doesn't explicitly specify a parent, */autohandler* remains parentless, and the construction of the inheritance hierarchy is complete.

Mason then begins processing */autohandler,* the top component in the parent hierarchy. The first part of the component doesn't contain any special Mason sections, so it simply gets output as text. Mason then sees the call to $m->call_next, which means that it should go one step down the inheritance hierarchy and start processing its child component, in this case */welcome.html*. The */welcome.html* component generates some output, which gets inserted into the middle of */autohandler* and then finishes. Control passes back to */autohandler*, which generates a little more output and then finishes, ending the server response.

Using Autohandlers for Initialization

As we mentioned earlier, the autohandler mechanism can be applied to more than just header and footer generation. For the sake of dividing this material into reasonably sized chunks for learning, we're leaving the more advanced object-oriented stuff like methods and attributes for Chapter 5. However, several extremely common autohandler techniques are presented here.

First, most interesting sites are going to interact with a database. Generally you'll want to open the database connection at the beginning of the response and simply make the database handle available globally for the life of the request.* The autohandler provides a convenient way to do this (see Examples 3-3 and 3-4).

Example 3-3. /autohandler

```
<html>
<head><title>Example.com</title></head>
<body>
% $m->call_next;
<br><a href="/">Home</a>
</body>
</html>

<%init>
 $dbh = DBI->connect('DBI:mysql:mydb;mysql_read_default_file=/home/ken/my.cnf')
   or die "Can't connect to database: $DBI::errstr";
</%init>
```

Example 3-4. /view_user.mas

```
<%args>
 $user
</%args>

% if (defined $name) {
 <p>Info for user '<% $user %>':</p>
 <b>Name:</b> <% $name %><br>
 <b>Age:</b>  <% $age  %><br>
% } else {
 <p>Sorry, no such user '<% $user %>'.</p>
% }

<%init>
 my ($name, $age) = $dbh->selectrow_array
   ("SELECT name, age FROM users WHERE user=?", undef, $user);
</%init>
```

Note that the $dbh variable was not declared with my( ) in either component, so it should be declared using the Mason allow_globals parameter (or, equivalently, the MasonAllowGlobals directive in an Apache config file). The allow_globals parameter tells the compiler to add use vars statements when compiling components, allowing you to use the global variables you specify. This is the easiest way to share variables among several components in a request, but it should be used sparingly, since having too many global variables can be difficult to manage.

---

* This strategy can be used in conjunction with the Apache::DBI module, which allows for database connections that persist over many requests.

We'll give a brief trace-through of this example. First, Mason receives a request for *http://example.com/view_user.max?user=ken*, which it translates to a request for the */view_user.mas* component. As before, the autohandler executes first, generating headers and footers, but now also connecting to the database. When the autohandler passes control to */view_user.mas*, its <%init> section runs and uses the same $dbh global variable created in the autohandler. A couple of database values get fetched and used in the output, and when control passes back to the autohandler the request is finished.

Since this process is starting to get a little complicated under scrutiny, you may wonder how the user parameter is propagated through the inheritance hierarchy. The answer is that it's supplied to the autohandler, then passed automatically to */view_user.mas* through $m->call_next. In fact, $m->call_next is really just some sugar around the $m->comp method, automatically selecting the correct component (the child) and passing the autohandler's arguments through to the child. If you like, you can supply additional arguments to the child by passing them as arguments to $m->call_next.

Using Autohandlers as Filters

Example 3-5 is another common use of autohandlers. Often the content of each page will need to be modified in some systematic way, for example, transforming relative URLs in <img src> tags into absolute URLs.

Example 3-5. /autohandler

```
% $m->call_next;

<%init>
 # Images are on images.mysite.com
 (my $host = $r->hostname) =~ s/^.*?(\w+\.\w+)$/images.$1/;
 # Remove final filename from path to get directory
 (my $path = $r->uri)      =~ s,/[^/]+$,,;
</%init>

<%filter>
 # Matches site-relative paths
 s{(<img[^>]+src=\")/}        {$1http://$host/}ig;

 # Matches directory-relative paths
 s{(<img[^>]+src=\")(?!\w+:)} {$1http://$host$path/}ig;
</%filter>
```

This particular autohandler doesn't add a header and footer to the page, but there's no reason it couldn't. Any additional content in the autohandler would function just as in our previous example and also get filtered just like the content from call_next( ).

We make two substitution passes through the page. The first pass transforms URLs like `<img src="/img/picture.gif">` into `<img src="http://images.mysite.com/img/picture.gif">`. The second pass transforms URLs like `<img src="picture.gif">` into `<img src="http://images.mysite.com/current_dir/picture.gif">`.

Filter sections like this can be very handy for changing image paths, altering navigation bars to match the state of the current page, or making other simple transformations. It's not a great idea to use filters for very sophisticated processing, though, because parsing HTML can give you a stomach ache very quickly. In Chapter 5 you'll see how to use inheritance to gain finer control over the production of the HTML in the first place, so that often no filtering is necessary.

Inspecting the Wrapping Chain

When Mason processes a request, it builds the wrapping chain and then executes each component in the chain, starting with the topmost parent component and working its way toward the bottommost child. Inside one of these components you may find it necessary to access individual components from the chain, and several Mason methods exist for this purpose.

For orientation purposes, let's define a little more terminology. The term "requested component" refers to the component originally requested by a URL or to a dhandler if that component doesn't exist. The term "current component" refers to the component currently executing at any given time. The term "base component" refers to the bottommost child of the current component. The base component starts out as the requested component, but as components call one another during a request, the base component will take on several different values. Note that the requested component is determined only once per request, but the current component and the base component will typically change several times as the request is handled

An example scenario is illustrated in Figure 3-1. If */subdir/first.html* is called as the requested component, its parent will be */subdir/autohandler* and its grandparent will be */autohandler*. These three components make up the initial inheritance chain, and while */subdir/first.html* is executing, it will be designated as the base component. Its content gets wrapped by its parents' content, so the component execution starts with */autohandler*, which calls */subdir/autohandler* via $m->call_next, which in turn calls */subdir/first.html* by the same mechanism. While any of these components is executing, it temporarily becomes the current component, though the base component stays fixed as */subdir/first.html*.

If */subdir/first.html* calls `<& called.mas &>` during the request, */subdir/called.mas* temporarily becomes both the current component and the base component. Note that its parents do *not* go through the content wrapping phase again; this happens only for the requested component. When */subdir/called.mas* finishes, control passes back to */subdir/first.html*, which becomes the base component and current

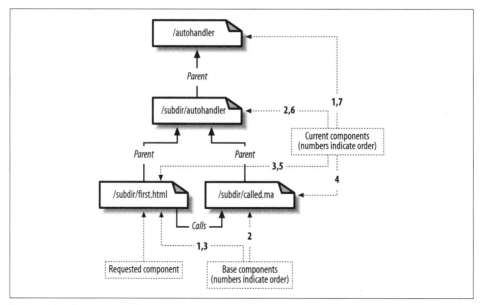

Figure 3-1. The wrapping chain

component again. It remains the base component for the duration of the request as its parents become the current components so they can finish their content wrapping.

To access the base component, current component, or requested component in your code, you can use the $m->base_comp, $m->current_comp, or $m->request_comp request methods. Each of these methods returns an object representing the component itself. These objects inherit from the HTML::Mason::Component class, and they can be used in several ways.

First, a component object can be used as the first argument of $m->comp( ) or <& &> in place of the component name. Second, you can access a component's parent by calling its parent( ) method, which returns another component object. Third, you can access methods or attributes that a component or its parents define in <%method> or <%attr> blocks. Finally, the HTML::Mason::Component class and its subclasses define several methods that let you query properties of the component itself, such as its creation time, what arguments it declares in its <%args> section, where its compiled form is cached on disk, and so on. See Chapter 4 for more information on the HTML::Mason::Component family of classes.

Using Autohandlers and Dhandlers Together

Despite their similar names, the autohandler and dhandler mechanisms are actually totally distinct and can be used independently or in tandem. In this section we look at some ways to use autohandlers and dhandlers together.

Most important about the way dhandlers and autohandlers interact is that Mason *first* figures out how to resolve a path to a component name, *then* figures out the inheritance of that component. In other words, Mason determines dhandlers before it determines autohandlers. This has several consequences.

First, it means that a dhandler may use the inheritance mechanism just like any other component can. A component called */trains/dhandler* may specify its parent using the inherit flag, or it may inherit from */trains/autohandler* or */autohandler* by default.

Second, if Mason receives a request for */one/two/three.mas*, and the component root contains components called */one/two/autohandler* and */one/dhandler* but no */one/two/three.mas*, Mason will first determine that the proper requested component for this request is */one/dhandler*, then it will search the component root for any appropriate parents. Since the autohandler is located in the */one/two/* directory, it won't be invoked when serving */one/*.

An example from John Williams (a frequent and important contributor to the Mason core) helps illustrate one powerful way of using dhandlers and autohandlers together. Suppose you're running a web site that serves news articles, with articles identified by the date they were written. Normally articles get published once a day, but once in a while there's a day without an article published.

Say you get a request for */archive/2001/march/21*. A dhandler at */archive/dhandler* could provide the content for any missing files, for example by finding the latest article whose date is before the requested date. An autohandler at */archive/autohandler* or */autohandler* could provide the sitewide header and footer in a uniform fashion, not caring whether the article had its own component file or whether it was generated by the dhandler.

Remember, autohandlers and dhandlers are distinct features in Mason, and by combining them creatively you can achieve very powerful results.

CHAPTER 4

APIs

Mason is more than just a templating system. It provides a framework for translating requests into output.* This framework has a number of class/object APIs worth knowing about. You certainly won't need to use *most* of these methods very often, but you will probably want to use at least *some* of them in many of your Mason-based projects. This chapter documents those APIs. For a more concise reference to these methods, see Appendix B.

Request Class and Object API

The request object in Mason represents the context of the current request process. For example, it knows where in the component wrapping chain it is, what arguments have been passed to various component calls, if you've been bad or good, and so on. It also allows you to change that context in various ways, such as by calling another component or aborting the request.

The request API provides access to some of the most frequently used Mason features, particularly those relating to component calls, autohandlers, and aborting in the middle of a request.

Recall, as first mentioned in Chapter 2, that the Mason request object is available in all components as $m.

The request class has only two *class* methods. The first, HTML::Mason::Request->new( ), is intended for use by other Mason objects and is not documented for external use. If you want to make a new request object, use the make_subrequest( ) method provided by the request object, which is covered as part of the discussion of Mason's subrequest mechanism in Chapter 5.

---

* You may or may not choose to call this an application server.

The second class method, `HTML::Mason::Request->instance()`, returns the current Mason request object. This is useful if you have code outside of a Mason component that needs to access the request object. Inside components, you can just use `$m`.

The request object's methods can be grouped together into several functional areas.

Constructor Parameters

A number of parameters can be set when creating a new request object. You will most often set these by passing them to the ApacheHandler's constructor or by setting them in your *httpd.conf* file. You may occasionally want to set one of these parameters on the fly for the current request. Finally, you will create a new request object when you want to make a subrequest, and you may want to set these parameters then.

All of the following parameters are also available as get/set methods of the same name:

autoflush

> This attribute is discussed in "Buffer-Related Methods," later in this chapter.

data_cache_defaults

> This returns a hash reference containing default options for the Request object's cache() method.

dhandler_name

> This is the name used for dhandlers. This defaults to "dhandler."

error_format

> This may be `brief`, `text`, `line`, or `html`. These produce an error message with no trace, a multiline error with trace information, a single-line error with tab-separated fields (suitable for writing to a log), and a fancy HTML format.

> Each of these methods corresponds to a method in the `HTML::Mason::Exception` class, such as `as_text()` or `as_line()`. You can create your own method in the `HTML::Mason::Exception` namespace, such as `as_you_wish()`, in which case you could set this parameter to "you_wish." This method will receive a single argument, the exception object, and is expected to return a string containing the formatted error message.

> In a `mod_perl` or CGI environment, this defaults to `html` format. Otherwise, the default is `text`.

error_mode

> This may be either `fatal` or `output`. In fatal mode, errors are thrown as exceptions. In output mode, the exception is converted to a text representation and sent to the same output stream as normal content.

> In a `mod_perl` or CGI environment, the default is `output`, which means that errors go the client. In any other environment, the default is `fatal`. If you set this to

fatal in a web environment, errors will end up in your web server's logs. If you wish to implement your own exception-handling mechanism around Mason, set this to fatal and catch the exceptions yourself.

max_recurse

This can be used to set the maximum stack size for component calls and subrequests. It defaults to 32, which is likely to be more than enough for any application. But if for some reason you need more, you can set this to a higher number.

out_method

This parameter indicates where output should be sent and must be a reference to either a scalar or a subroutine. If it is a scalar reference, output will be appended to this scalar. If it is a subroutine reference (often called a code reference in Perl parlance), this subroutine will be called with a list of arguments whenever output needs to be sent, which occurs after the output has passed through all of Mason's buffers.

The default out_method will print its arguments to STDOUT. In a mod_perl or CGI environment, this means that output gets sent to the client.

Calling Other Components

Besides the component call tag (<& &>) discussed in Chapter 2, there are several other ways for one component to call another:

comp(component, arguments)

This method is exactly like the <&...&> tag discussed in Chapter 2. It allows you to call another component, specified either by path or by supplying a component object as the first argument. Arguments are passed exactly as with the component call tag.

The return value of this method is the return value of the component being called. Most components will not have an explicit return value and will return undef. Any output generated by the called component becomes part of the output of that particular request.

As of Mason 1.10, a hash reference can be provided as an additional first argument to this method. The contents of this hash reference are used to modify the way the component call is processed. Right now, only one parameter—store—is accepted for this hash reference.

The value of the store key should be a reference to a scalar, into which Mason will place the output for the component. For example:

```
$m->comp( { store => \$content }, 'Hello.comp', to => 'World' );
```

The output of *Hello.comp* would be available in the $content variable. This functionality is fundamentally the same as that provided by the scomp() method except that it allows you to capture the component's return value in addition to its output.

scomp(component, arguments)

> This is exactly like the comp( ) method except that the called component's output is returned as a string instead of being sent to the output stream. This is analogous to the use of sprintf( ) instead of printf( ) in C. Components called via this method go through all of the normal steps of component execution.
>
> If you have a component that generates output and has a return value and you want to capture that output in a scalar, you should use the store component call modifier.

content

> This method is relevant only inside a component called with content, a feature we saw briefly in Chapter 2 but will cover more completely in Chapter 5.
>
> This method returns the block of content wrapped by the component call. This will make more sense once you've read the section on "Calling Components with Content Blocks" in Chapter 5.

Aborting the Flow of Execution

Mason provides a way to abort the flow of execution during a request. Several request object methods relate to doing so and examining what happened afterward.

abort(optional argument)

> Calling this method will immediately abort the execution of the current request.
>
> If an argument is given to this method, this value will be available via the aborted_value( ) method after calling abort( ).
>
> Since this method is implemented internally via Perl's die( ) function, it may be caught by an eval block (eval {...}). In this case, you may call the aborted( ) method to distinguish this exception from one generated by something else in your code. The value of $@ will be an exception object of the class HTML::Mason:: Exception::Abort.
>
> In a web context, if you don't catch the abort call via an eval block, the return value will be used as the server status code. The following example takes advantage of that fact to deny access unless a user has authenticated himself to Apache:

```
<%init>
use Apache::Constants;
$m->abort(FORBIDDEN) unless $r->connection->user;
</%init>
```

aborted

> This method returns a boolean value indicating whether or not abort( ) has been called previously during the current request.

aborted_value

When aborted() is true, this method returns whatever value was passed to the abort() call.

If you are using eval blocks for exception handling in your components, it is important to propagate exceptions generated from a call to abort(). Here is one way do this:

```
eval { $m->call_next(%ARGS) };
if ($@) {
  if ($m->aborted) {
    # pass this up to a higher level
    die $@;
  } else {
    # something else that's bad happened
    $m->comp( 'exception_handler', exception => $@ );
  }
}
```

The Wrapping Chain

These are methods related to the wrapping chain, which was discussed in Chapter 3.

call_next(arguments)

When the currently executing component is part of a wrapping chain, this method will call the next component in the chain, passing it the current component's arguments and any arguments specified in the call to call_next().

If there is no next component to call, it will throw an exception.

fetch_next

This method returns the next component object in the wrapping chain. This is the same component that would be run upon calling call_next(). This object may then be passed to a component call via the <& &> tag or the comp() method.

fetch_next_all

This method returns an array of all of the components in the wrapping chain that have yet to be executed. They are returned in order based on their position in the wrapping chain.

Dhandler-Related Methods

Certain request object methods are specifically related to dhandlers:

decline

This method was discussed in detail in Chapter 3. Calling this method indicates that the current component does not wish to handle the request, in which case Mason will look for the next available dhandler to handle it.

dhandler_arg

> This method was also discussed in Chapter 3. This method returns the remainder of the component path after stripping off the dhandler's directory. Given a call to */archives/2002/02/30/all* and a dhandler component at */archives/dhandler*, dhandler_arg( ) returns *2002/02/30/all*.

Miscellaneous Methods

The request object also has some general-use methods:

file(filename)

> Given a file path, Mason will look for this file and return its contents as a string.
>
> If a relative path is given, Mason will prepend the path with the current component's directory if the component is file-based or the system's root directory otherwise.

comp_exists(component path)

> Given a component path, this method returns true if this path would successfully resolve to a component when passed to comp( ).

print(output)

> This method takes a list of scalars, which will be sent as output. For example, the following two lines are identical:
>
> ```
> % $m->print($output);
> <% $output %>
> ```
>
> If you feel a need to call Perl's print( ) function from your Mason code, don't. Your code will be faster if you use $m->print( ) instead, though the result will be the same in the end.

interp

> This returns the Interp object associated with the current request. Chapter 6 documents this object's API.

count

> This method returns this request's number, which is unique for a given request and interpreter.

Introspection

The Mason request object provides numerous methods allowing introspection of the details of the current request. Some of these methods return one or more component objects, while others return information about the arguments passed to components.

These methods are useful if you are using autohandlers (particularly more than one) and you want to get some information about the components in a request.

Using some of these methods requires an understanding of autohandlers and the wrapping chain, a topic that was covered in Chapter 3.

base_comp

> This method returns the base component for a request. Initially, the base component is the component that was called for a request. This may differ from the current component when you are in an autohandler.
>
> The base component is the first component looked at when a component method is called in the form:
>
> ```
> <& SELF:method &>
> ```
>
> Methods are discussed in Chapter 5.
>
> The base component is changed when you call another component during the context of that component's execution:
>
> ```
> $m->comp( '/some/other/comp' );
> ```
>
> In this case, the base component will now be the component */some/other/comp*. This will be reset to the original base component after the call is finished.
>
> If you pass a component object to a component call, Mason assumes that you know what you are doing and doesn't change the base component.
>
> If your brain now feels like oatmeal after reading this, simply rest assured that the goal of all this is to make Mason just do the right thing and surprise you as little as possible.
>
> But why would you use the base_comp() method, you ask? The primary reason for doing this is to get access to a component's attributes and methods.
>
> Let's say that I call a component called */people/faye_wong/bio.html* and it is wrapped by both */people/faye_wong/autohandler* and */people/autohandler*. While in one of the autohandlers, I may wish to access the attributes of the component that was called.
>
> The easiest way to do this is via the base_comp() method, like so:
>
> ```
> my $name = $m->base_comp->attr('name');
> ```
>
> The attr() method starts looking for an attribute in the component on which it is called, then ascends the inheritance hierarchy from there. We want to start at the last component in the hierarchy—the "child component"—in order to give it a chance to override any attributes defined in its parents.

request_args

> This method returns the arguments passed to the originally requested component. In scalar context, it returns a hash reference. In list context, it returns a list.

callers(stack level)

> This method is analogous to the Perl caller() function. It returns one or more component objects in the current component stack. When called without an argument, it simply returns the entire array of components in the stack up to, and including, the current component. The first element of the array will be the current component and the last will be the first component in the stack.

If this method is called with an integer argument, then that number is used as an index number into the stack. Just as with Perl arrays, negative integers start at the end of the stack and count backward.

```
my @comps = $m->callers    # all components
$m->callers(0)             # current component
$m->callers(1)             # component that called us
$m->callers(-1)            # first component executed
```

caller

This method is equivalent to $m->callers(1).

caller_args(stack level)

This method returns the arguments passed to the component on a given part of the stack. Unlike the callers() method, this method requires an integer argument to specify a stack index. When called in a list context, this method returns a list. In a scalar context, it returns a hash reference.

If the arguments to the given component were not specified as key/value pairs (see "%ARGS Versus @_" in Chapter 2), you will need to assign the returned value to an array in order to avoid an error.

```
# arguments passed to current component
my %args = $m->caller_args(0)

# arguments passed to component that called us
my $args_ref = $m->caller_args(1)

# arguments passed to first component executed
my @args = $m->caller_args(-1)
```

Using an index of -1 is equivalent to calling the request_args() method.

request_comp

This method returns a component object representing the requested component. For example, if your wrapper chain looks like this:

```
/autohandler
/tasks/autohandler
/tasks/show_task.html
```

this method would return the component object representing */tasks/show_task.html*.

Note that this is very similar to base_comp(). The difference between them is that request_comp() will always refer to */tasks/show_task.html* for the entire duration of the request, whereas base_comp() may change when other components are called.

current_comp

This method returns the component object that is currently being executed.

request_depth

This method tells you the depth of the current component, which is defined as the number of components in the component stack before the current component plus one. For the first component executed, this value is 1.

Buffer-Related Methods

The following methods all deal with Mason's buffer objects. A typical request starts off with a single base buffer. For each component that is called in the component stack, another buffer will be added to the stack. In addition, filtering and other special Mason features will add and remove additional buffers.

The buffer objects have their own API, detailed later in this chapter, but you will rarely need to use this unless you have a need to implement a subclass of Mason's default buffer class, HTML::Mason::Buffer.

The request API offers several methods for dealing with the buffer stack as a whole:

autoflush(boolean)

> This method can be used to turn autoflushing on and off. When autoflushing is on, output is sent as soon as it is generated. Otherwise, it is buffered until all components have run.
>
> By default, autoflushing is off.
>
> Remember that if you turn autoflush on, the first piece of output generated by a component will end up being sent immediately. In a web context, this will prevent you from aborting execution later (to issue a redirect, for example).
>
> Also, while autoflushing may give the impression of a snappier response because the first output arrives quicker, it is usually a bit slower overall than buffering all the output and sending it at once.

flush_buffer

> This method flushes any output that the top buffer on the stack contains, sending it to the next buffer below it in the stack. Depending on what other buffers are below it, the flushing may continue through the entire stack, meaning output will be sent, or it may stop part of the way through because some buffers are set to ignore flushes.
>
> If autoflush is on, this method is meaningless as no output is ever buffered.
>
> Attempts to flush the buffers are ignored within the context of a call to scomp() or when output is being stored in a scalar reference, as with the { store = \$out } component call modifier for the comp() method.
>
> Additionally, if a component has a <%filter> block, that component is buffered until its entire output is generated. This means that inside that component and any components that it calls, the buffer cannot be flushed.
>
> This method can be used to send output to the client more quickly in a web context:
>
> ```
> Processing your request...
> % $m->flush_buffer;
> <% very_slow_function() %>
> ```

If you are running Mason under mod_perl, this method will also call rflush() on the Apache object.

clear_buffer

This method clears all buffered output in the buffer stack. This is useful if you generate some output and then need to discard it without outputting it. For obvious reasons, this method does nothing when autoflush is on.

Caching

One of the easiest ways to gain a quick performance boost for an application is to cache the results of operations that are slow, such as a complicated database query that cannot be optimized. Even when you *can* optimize some code, it might be simpler to just cache its result rather than optimize your code at the expense of increasing its complexity, thus making it less maintainable.

Caching can also be a big win in providing scalability when you have a bottleneck like an RDBMS. For example, if your web site traffic quadruples in one day, caching the results of some database queries can be the difference between serving pages and watching your database box grind to a bloody, overloaded death.

Because caching is so useful, Mason has a simple caching system that you can use from within your components. Mason's caching system is merely a thin wrapper over DeWitt Clinton's excellent Cache::Cache modules. These modules provide a number of caching backends such as file or shared memory caches with a simple, feature-rich API. All caches can be limited to a certain size using an LRU algorithm. In addition, it is possible to specify expiration times for stored data using a very flexible syntax.

For more information on Cache::Cache, simply install it from CPAN and type perldoc Cache::Cache on the command line. Also check out *http://perl-cache.sourceforge.net/* for more information online.

cache(...)

This method returns the Cache::Cache object associated with this component, taking several options that allow you to control the parameters used to access the cache.

Each component has its own cache, and it is not possible for a component to access another component's cache.

The most important parameter is cache_class. This can be either the full name of a Cache::Cache subclass, such as Cache::FileCache or Cache::MemoryCache, or you can simply leave off the initial Cache:: part and use something like FileCache or MemoryCache. The default is Cache::FileCache.

All other parameters given to this option will simply be passed on to the new() method of the designated Cache::Cache subclass. For example, if you are using the Cache::FileCache subclass, valid parameters would include namespace, default_expires_in, auto_purge_interval, and cache_root. The Cache::Cache and Cache::FileCache documentation contains more details on these and other parameters.

Since Mason provides intelligent defaults for all of the needed parameters, it is possible to simply call the cache() method without any parameters at all. In this case, the return value will be a new Cache::FileCache object, which stores data under the data_dir specified by the Interp object. Each component will have an entirely unique cache object and storage, so two components can store data using the same keys without worrying about conflicts.

Here is a typical cache example:

```
<%init>
 my $cache = $m->cache;

 my $data;

 unless ($data = $cache->get('complex_data')) {
     $data = complex_calculation();
     $cache->set('complex_data' => $data);
 }
</%init>
```

If your data calculation depends on an incoming parameter, you can simply use that as your key (or part of the key):

```
<%args>
 $name
</%args>
<%init>
 my $cache = $m->cache;

 my $data;

 unless ($data = $cache->get("complex_data_$name")) {
     $data = complex_calculation($name);
     $cache->set("complex_data_$name" => $data);
 }
</%init>
```

To set an expiration time for a piece of cached data, simply pass that as the third argument to set():

```
$m->cache->set("complex_data_$name" => $data, '3h'); # expires in 3 hours
```

To iterate through all the keys currently in your cache object, you can use the cache's get_keys() method.

```
% foreach my $key ($m->cache->get_keys) {
  <% $key %> = <% $m->cache->get($key) %>
% }
```

Mason reserves all keys beginning with __mason for its own internal use.

The Cache::Cache API also includes methods that allow you to remove cached data, examine cache metadata such as when a piece of data was added or last accessed, and much more. See the Cache::Cache documentation for more details.

cache_self(...)

This method is used when a component wants to cache its entire output and/or its return value. This is one of Mason's greatest features—it allows you to design a site in a way that makes sense for you as a developer, then go back and sprinkle in a few cache_self() calls if performance is too slow.

The cache_self() method takes all of the optional arguments that can be passed to cache(), as well as two others, both of which are also optional:

key

An optional key used to identify the cached data, as would be given to the cache object's get() and set() methods. This identifies a unique set of cached data and allows you to store multiple versions of the component's output.

expire_in

An expiration time as would be given to the $cache->set() method, such as 5m, meaning five minutes. The default is for cached data to last until the cache is intentionally wiped out.

The idiom for using this method looks like this:

```
<%init>
 return if $m->cache_self;

 ... # rest of init and output generation
</%init>
```

The first time this component is called, its output will be generated normally and then stored in the cache. In the future, all calls to this component will use this cached output.

Of course, we may need to generate different output depending on what parameters are given as input. In this case, we do something like this:

```
<%args>
 $name
</%args>
<%init>
 return if $m->cache_self( key => $name );

 ... # rest of init and output generation
</%init>
```

For every different value of $name, the component will be rerun and its output will be cached.

If your component has a return value that you would like to cache, the cache_self() idiom looks like this:

```
<%init>
 my @retval = $m->cache_self;

 return @retval if pop @retval;
</%init>
```

We need to pop @retval because Mason must append a true value to the end of the returned list, in order to ensure that the return value of cache_self() is always true when it is returning cached output. This is important because the cached return value could simply be an empty list, (), which evaluates to false, in which case the caching would be useless because the return value of cache_self() would always be false, even when it was returning a cached value! Yes, it's a hack, but we think it's better than simply having this method not work for a return value that is an empty list.

Subrequests

Subrequests are request objects that inherit all their settable properties from their parent. The main difference between calling a component with a subrequest versus using a regular component call is that subrequests will invoke the autohandler and dhandler mechanisms, whereas a regular component call will execute only the called component. Subrequests are covered in a more detail in Chapter 5.

make_subrequest(comp => component, args => [...], ...)

This method creates a new subrequest object, which you can then execute via its exec() method. This gives you a chance to override the parent object's properties by passing in arguments to this method.

subexec(comp, args)

This combines the make_subrequest() method and the subrequest's exec() method in one step. Any argument list given to subexec() will become the argument list for the called component. This doesn't give you a chance to set properties of the request, however. For that, you'll need to use the full two-step approach of calling make_subrequest() and then exec() on the returned object.

is_subrequest

This method returns a boolean value indicating whether the given object is a subrequest.

parent_request

Calling this method returns the parent request object for a subrequest. If called on the top-level request object, it just returns undef.

Methods Available Only When Using ApacheHandler

When you are using Mason under mod_perl with the HTML::Mason::ApacheHandler class, which is covered in Chapter 7, the Request object will contain several additional methods.

ah
> This method returns the current HTML::Mason::ApacheHandler object for this request.

apache_req
> This method returns the current Apache object for the request. This object is also available in all components as the variable $r.
>
> If you chose to use Apache::Request to handle incoming parameters by setting args_method to mod_perl, this object will be an Apache::Request object; otherwise, it will be an Apache object.
>
> Incoming parameter handling is covered in Chapter 7.

Methods Available When Using ApacheHandler or CGIHandler

Two additional methods are available in the HTML::Mason::ApacheHandler or HTML::Mason::CGIHandler classes. The latter class is covered in Chapter 9.

cgi_object
> This method is always available when using HTML::Mason::CGIHandler.
>
> If you are using HTML::Mason::ApacheHandler, this is available only if you chose to use the CGI.pm module to handle incoming request parameters.
>
> This method will return the CGI.pm object that was used to handle incoming parameters.

redirect(url)
> Given a URL, this generates a proper HTTP redirect, which is then sent immediately to the client. This will not work if any output has been previously sent, which may be the case if flush_buffer() has been called or if the request is in autoflush mode.

Getting in Close with Buffers

Underneath the hood of the request object, output is handled via buffer objects, which by default are of the HTML::Mason::Buffer class.

The request object maintains a buffer stack. Output goes to the top buffer on the stack, which can then manipulate it and pass it on to the next buffer in the stack, which can in turn do the same, and so on.

Buffers are also used to implement features like the request's scomp() method.

So why would *you* want to play with buffers? Chances are you won't want to simply add more plain old HTML::Mason::Buffer objects to the stack. That wouldn't achieve much.

But if you were to create a custom buffer subclass, you might want to selectively stick one onto the stack. For example, if you made a buffer that traced the source of all output it received, you might want to put it on the stack only for certain parts of your site during debugging. Just be sure to remove any buffers you add, or Mason may get confused and your output may never get sent.

The other buffer-related methods are potentially useful for introspection and debugging:

top_buffer
> Returns the current top-level buffer object for the request. This is the buffer to which output is currently being sent.

buffer_stack
> Returns all the buffers on the stack, starting from the top buffer and ending with the bottom buffer, which is the one at the bottom of the stack.

push_buffer_stack(Buffer object)
> Pushes a new buffer onto the top of the stack. Mason pushes new buffers onto the stack when calling new components.

pop_buffer_stack
> Pops the top buffer off the stack and returns it. Mason pops a buffer each time a component finishes executing.

Component Object API

Objects that you will deal with in this class actually fall into three categories. The majority will be objects of the HTML::Mason::Component::FileBased class, which is used for components generated from component source files. The next most common will be HTML::Mason::Component::Subcomponent objects, which represent subcomponents and methods. Finally, anonymous components created via the HTML::Mason::Interp->make_component() method (covered in Chapter 5 and Chapter 6) will simply be of the HTML::Mason::Component class.

For the most part, these objects all share the same interface.

Component objects are returned from a number of Request object methods as well as the interpreter object's make_component() method.

These first methods are the ones you most likely want to use:

attr(name)
> Looks for the specified attribute in the component and its parents, returning the first value found. If the attribute is not found, this method throws an exception.

Attributes are declared in <%attr> blocks, as covered in "<%flags> and <%attr> blocks" in Chapter 2.

attr_if_exists(name)

Works just like the attr() method except that it simply returns undef if the specified attribute does not exist.

Of course, this makes it impossible to distinguish between an attribute with undef as its value and an attribute that is not found. To make that distinction, use the attr() method and wrap it in an eval {} block, or use this method in conjunction with the attr_exists() method.

attr_exists(name)

Returns true if the specified attribute exists in the component or its parents.

call_method(name, arguments)

Calls the specified method with the given arguments. If the method is not present in the component or any of its parents, an exception is thrown.

scall_method(name, arguments)

This is analogous to the scomp() method for the Request object. This method calls the named method with the given arguments and returns the output as a string. If the method is not present in the component or any of its parents, an exception is thrown.

method_exists(name)

Returns true if the specified method exists in the component or its parents.

Much of the component API is interesting only for introspection, though we're sure creative developers can think of ways to work strange magic with this API.

comp_id

Returns a unique ID for this component. This ID may be in the form of a component path, though this is not guaranteed.

load_time

Returns the Unix epoch time when this object was created.

declared_args

Returns a hash reference containing an entry for each argument declared in the component's <%args> section. These keys include the variable prefix, so they are strings like $foo or %bar. Each key's value is itself a hash reference, which contains a single key, default, the value of which is the string given as the argument's default value, or undef if no default was given.

For example, the following <%args> section:

```
<%args>
$foo
@bar => (1, 2, 3)
%baz => () # an empty hash
$undefined => undef
</%args>
```

would cause the following to be returned from the declared_args() method:

```
{
  '$foo' => { default => undef },
  '@bar' => { default => ' (1, 2, 3)' },
  '%baz' => { default => ' () # an empty hash' },
  '$undefined' => { default => ' undef' }
}
```

Note the difference between an argument with no default value and an argument with a default value of undef. Also, as you can see, the default value for each argument is returned as a string, not a data structure. This is because Mason does not actually parse these values as Perl does, but rather simply drops them into the code it generates in one piece.

dir_path

Returns the component's notion of the current directory, relative to the component root. For file-based components, this is the full component path minus the filename. For subcomponents and methods, this will be the same as its parent component. For anonymous components, this will be undef.

This path is like a URL path and always uses forward slashes (/) as separators.

To get the filesystem path and filename for file-based components, see the source_dir() and source_file() methods.

flag(name)

Returns the value of the specified flag. Flags are declared in <%flags> blocks, as covered in "<%flags> and <%attr> blocks" in Chapter 2.

is_subcomp

Returns true if the specified component is a subcomponent or a method.

is_file_based

Returns true if the given component is file-based.

name

Returns the name of the component. For file-based components, this is the component filename without any path information. For subcomponents and methods, it is the name given in the <%def> or <%method> tag. For anonymous components, this method returns the same value as comp_id().

owner

For subcomponents and methods, returns the component in which the component was defined.

parent

Returns the parent component object, if one exists. The way a parent component is determined was discussed in Chapter 3.

path

Returns the component path for file-based components. This path starts from the component root, not the filesystem root. In other words, this is an absolute path that could be used to call this component from another component. For a subcomponent object, this returns a string containing its parent object's path and its own name, separated by a colon (:).

As with dir_path(), the path returned here is a URL-style path and uses the forward slash (/) as its separator.

subcomps

With no arguments, returns a hash reference containing all the subcomponents defined in the component. The keys of this hash reference are component names, while the values are the component objects themselves.

If an argument is given, it returns the subcomponent of that particular name, or undef if there is no such subcomponent.

methods

Operates exactly like the subcomps() method but for methods instead of subcomponents.

title

Returns a printable string identifying this component. It is intended to uniquely identify a component within a given interpreter although this is not 100% guaranteed.

For file-based components, this is the component's path. If you have multiple component roots, this path will also be supplemented by a string indicating which component root the component was found in.

For subcomponents, this is its owner's title plus its own name, as returned by the name() method.

For anonymous components, this is the same as comp_id().

Methods for File-based Components

A few additional methods are available only for file-based components.

source_file

Returns the full absolute path to the file that contains the original component source. This is given in the native dialect of the filesystem, so its directory separators will be / on Unix, : on Mac OS, and who knows what on VMS.

source_dir

Returns the full path to the source component's directory on the filesystem. As with source_file(), the path is given in the native dialect of the filesystem.

object_file

Returns the object filename for the component if the component is file-based, otherwise undef.

The object file is the file that contains the code Mason generates from the component's source file.

Buffers

Playing with buffers is not for the everyday user but may be useful to you during debugging. Buffer objects have only a few methods:

output

> For buffers that store output in a scalar, this method returns the output they have stored so far. If the buffer is a filtering buffer, the output will be filtered before it is returned.

flush

> This forces the buffer to pass its output on to its parents, if it has any. Buffers can be set to ignore flushes, in which case this method does nothing.

receive(output, ...)

> This method is used to pass output to the buffer. It takes an array of scalars, each of which is considered a piece of output.

clear

> This method clears any stored output that the buffer may contain.

## CHAPTER 5

Advanced Features

In the previous chapters you have been introduced to the basic features of Mason, and you should have a fairly good idea by now of how you might actually go about constructing a dynamic web site from Mason components. You have seen a few of Mason's unique features, such as the autohandler mechanism, the dhandler mechanism, and the ability to pass arbitrary data between components.

In this chapter we'll go beyond the basics and learn more about advanced ways to use Mason components to design large dynamic sites. You'll learn how to define multiple components in the same text file, how to create components on the fly from Perl strings, how to manage multiple component root directories, and (finally!) how to use all of Mason's object-oriented features.

Subcomponents

Although we often imagine a one-to-one correspondence between text files and Mason components, it is actually possible to define multiple components in a single text file. This is achieved by using a <%def></%def> block, a special Mason directive that defines one component from within another. The component embedded within the <%def> block is called a *subcomponent*, and it is visible only to the component within which it resides: component A may not access component B's subcomponents directly.

The subcomponent may use any of the standard Mason component directives, such as <%args>, <%init>, %-lines, and so on. The only exceptions are that you may not use <%def> or <%method> blocks within subcomponents nor may you use "global" blocks like <%once> or <%shared>.

Subcomponents are most useful when you have some piece of processing to repeat several times that is used only in a certain specific situation and doesn't merit its own separate component file.

Here is an example of defining and calling a subcomponent. Note that the component is assigned a name inside the <%def> tag (the name often starts with a period, purely by convention) and that you use the regular component-calling mechanisms ($m->comp() or a <& &> tag) to invoke it.

```
<h2>Information about certain Minnesota cities:</h2>

% my @cities = ("Young America", "Sleepy Eye", "Nisswa", "Embarrass",
%               "Saint Cloud", "Little Canada", "Burnsville", "Luverne");
% foreach my $name (@cities) {
 <hr>
 <& .city_info, city => $name, state => 'MN' &>
% }

<%def .city_info>
<%args>
 $city
 $state
</%args>
 <table border="2">
  <tr> <th colspan="2"><% $city %></th> </tr>
  <tr> <td>Population:</td>  <td><% $population %></td>                </tr>
  <tr> <td>Coordinates:</td> <td><% "$latitude, $longitude" %></td> </tr>
  <tr> <td>Mayor:</td>       <td><% $mayor %></td>                   </tr>
 </table>
<%init>
 my ($population, $latitude, $longitude, $mayor) =
   $dbh->selectrow_array("SELECT population, latitude, longitude, mayor
                          FROM cities
                          WHERE city=? and state=?",
                          undef, $city, $state);
</%init>
</%def>
```

Since a subcomponent is visible only to the component that defines, and because it has all the capabilities that regular components have, you may think of subcomponents as roughly analogous to privately scoped anonymous subroutine references in Perl.

Creating Components on the Fly

You may encounter situations in which you want to use Mason's templating features and data management tools, but you don't want to create a full-blown component root hierarchy on disk to house your components. Perhaps you want to create a component from an isolated file or directly from a string containing the component text.

For these situations, the Mason interpreter provides the make_component() method. It accepts a comp_file or comp_source parameter (letting you create a component from a file or a string, respectively) and returns a Component object.

```
# Creating a component from scratch
#!/usr/bin/perl -w

use strict;
use HTML::Mason;

my $source = <<'EOF';
<%args>
 $planet
</%args>
Hello, <% $planet %>!
EOF

my $interp = HTML::Mason::Interp->new();
my $comp = $interp->make_component(comp_source => $source);
$interp->exec($comp, planet => 'Neptune');
```

And here is a component that creates another component at runtime:

```
<& $comp &>

<%init>
 my $comp = $m->interp->make_component(
   comp_file => '/home/slappy/my_comps/foo',
 );
</%init>
```

Of course, creating components at runtime is slower than creating them ahead of time, so if you need to squeeze out all the performance you possibly can, you might need to think of a speedier method to achieve your goals. And as always, benchmark everything so you really know what the effects are.

If the compiler encounters syntax errors when attempting to compile the component, a fatal exception will be thrown inside the make_component() method. If you want to trap these errors, you may wrap the make_component() method in Perl's eval {} block, and check $@ after the method call.

Sharing Data Among Component Sections

By default, the scope of variables created within an <%init> block, a Perl line, or any other Mason markup sections is the entire component. This is tremendously convenient, because it lets you initialize variables in the <%init> block, then use their values across the rest of the component. So most of the time, the techniques discussed in this section won't be needed.

There is one limitation to variables created within the <%init> section, however: their values won't be seen by any subcomponents you might define. This is true for two reasons. First, the subcomponents may themselves contain an <%init> section, so the relevance of the main component's <%init> section isn't necessarily clear. Second, a subcomponent may actually be a *method* (more on this later), in which case it is accessible to the outside world without first calling the main component, so the <%init> section never has a chance to run.

Sometimes you need to share data between a component and its subcomponents, however, and for these situations Mason provides the <%shared> and <%once> blocks. A <%shared> block runs before the main component or any of its methods or subcomponents and may run initialization code. Any variables created here will be visible to the entire main component and any of its subcomponents, including the main component's <%init> section, if any. The <%once> block is similar—the only difference is that code in the <%once> block won't run every time the component is called. It will run only when the component itself is loaded. The initialized values will remain intact for the lifetime of the component object, which may be until you make changes to the component source file and Mason reloads it or until the web server child expires and gets replaced by a new one.

A <%shared> section is great when a component and its subcomponents have a tight relationship and may make complicated use of shared data. In contrast, <%once> sections are useful for caching values that change infrequently but may take a long time to compute. See Example 5-1.

Example 5-1. sharing_example.mas

```
<%def .subcomponent>
 visible $color in .subcomponent is <% $color %>
</%def>

visible $color in main component is <% $color %>
<& .subcomponent &>

<%shared>
 my $color = 'bone';
</%shared>
```

A similar example, but using a <%once> section, is shown in Example 5-2.

Example 5-2. once_example.mas

```
<%def .subcomponent>
 visible $flavor in .subcomponent is <% $flavor %>
</%def>

visible $flavor in main component is <% $flavor %>
<& .subcomponent &>

<%once>
 my $flavor = 'gamey';
</%once>
```

A cautionary note about the <%shared> and <%once> sections: they do *not* let you transparently share data among Apache children (this would require actual shared memory segments and can be done with modules like IPC::Shareable), or among multiple components (this can easily be done with global variables). It is also unwise to use variables created in a <%once> section for saving state information that you intend to change, since the next time the component is loaded your changes will be lost.

You should also remember that variables defined via an <%args> block are not visible in a <%shared> block, meaning that the only access to arguments inside a shared block is via the %ARGS hash or one of the request object methods such as request_args.

Methods and Attributes

The ability to use Mason's component-level object-oriented methods and attributes can give you powerful techniques for managing your site.

As explained in Chapter 3, one of the major benefits of object-oriented techniques is that they help you reduce redundancy in your site. Site redundancy is a much bigger problem than most people realize. How many times have you forgone a site revision because performing the revision would be "too intrusive," and you can't afford the downtime? How many Internet web sites have you seen that look promising at first, but fail to fix problems and don't adapt to usage patterns over the long run? Nobody likes to be stuck with an unmaintainable site, and the only way to avoid it is to design the site to be adaptable and extensible in the first place. Eliminating redundancy goes a long way toward this goal.

Methods

Methods in Mason are actually quite simple. A method is just like a subcomponent, but instead of defining it with a <%def> section, you use a <%method> section:

```
<%method .my_method>
 Any regular component syntax here...
</%method>
```

The difference between subcomponents and methods is primarily in how they can be invoked from other components. A method can only be invoked using special method syntax. We present three ways of doing this here:

```
# Fetch the bottommost child of the current component
my $self = $m->base_comp;
$self->call_method('.my_method');

# Shortcut for the above two lines
$m->comp('SELF:.my_method');

# Same thing, using <& &> syntax
<& SELF:.my_method &>
```

Let's think about what happens when you invoke a method. Suppose there is a component called */staff/flintoff.mas*, whose parent is */staff/autohandler*, whose parent is in turn /autohandler. While *any* of these components are executing (which might be when a top-level request comes in for /staff/flintoff.mas or when /staff/flintoff.mas is called from another component), calling $m->base_comp from within any of these three components will return a component object representing /staff/flintoff.mas. In the example, that component object is stored in $self. Invoking call_method('.my_method') will search $self and its hierarchy of parents for a method called .my_method, starting the search at $self and proceeding upward. If such a method is found, it gets executed. If no such method is found, a fatal error occurs. You may want to call $self->method_exists('.my_method') first if you're not sure whether the method exists.

Remember that methods are full-blown subcomponents, so you may also pass them arguments when you invoke them. Examples 5-3 and 5-4 demonstrate a more sophisticated example of method invocation.

Example 5-3. /autohandler

```
<html>
<& $m->call_next &>
</html>
<%method .body_tag>
 <%args>
  $bgcolor => 'white'
  $textcolor => 'black'
 </%args>
 <body onLoad="prepare_images()" bgcolor="<% $bgcolor %>" text="<% $textcolor %>">
</%method>
```

Example 5-4. /important_advice.mas

```
<head><title>A Blue Page With Red Text</title></head>

<& SELF:.body_tag, bgcolor=>'blue', textcolor=>'red' &>
 Never put anything bigger than your elbow into your ear.
</body>
```

The central thing to note about this example is the way the main component and the autohandler cooperate to produce the <body> tag. The designer of this site has chosen to make the bgcolor and textcolor page attributes configurable by each page, and the autohandler will generate the rest, including the call to the JavaScript function prepare_images().

Incidentally, note that the autohandler took responsibility for the <html> and </html> tags, while the main component generated everything in the <head> and <body> sections. This is not necessarily good design—you must determine the right factorization for each site you create—but it made the example straightforward.

Now that you know what methods are and how they work, we can explore some ways that you can use them to design your site to be flexible and maintainable.

Using Methods for Titles and Headers

The most familiar example of commonality within a site's structure is probably the overall design of pages. Most web sites want to have a common design structure across multiple pages, including common colors and fonts, common navigational elements and headers, common keywords in <META> tags, and so on. In this section, we explore how you can use methods for the specific problem of generating commonly styled headers and titles for your pages.

Generating titles and headers was the major motivation behind developing Mason's method capabilities in the first place. Consider for a moment the "title and header problem": it is often desirable to control the top and bottom of an HTML page centrally, for all the reasons we've tried to drum into your skull throughout this chapter. However, while large portions of the top and bottom of the page may be the same for all pages on your site, certain small pieces may be different on every page—titles and headers often fall into this category. So, you would like a way to generate the large common portions of your pages centrally but insert the noncommon titles and headers where they belong.

Mason's methods provide a perfect answer. Each title and header can be specified using a method. Then an autohandler can generate the common headers and footers, calling the base component's title and header methods to insert the page-specific information in its proper place (Examples 5-5 and 5-6).

Example 5-5. autohandler

```
<html>
<head><title><& SELF:title &></title></head>
<body>
 <center><h3><& SELF:header &></h3></center>
% $m->call_next;
 <center><a href="/">-home-</a></center>
</body>
</html>
<%method title>
 www.Example.com
</%method>
<%method header>
 Welcome to Example.com
</%method>
```

Example 5-6. fancy_page.html

```
<p>This page isn't all <i>that</i> fancy, but it might be the
fanciest one we've seen yet.</p>
<%method title>
 Fancy Page
</%method>

<%method header>
```

Example 5-6. fancy_page.html (continued)

```
 A Very Fancy Page
</%method>
```

The autohandler provides a default title and header, so if the base component fancy_page.html didn't provide a title or header method, the autohandler would use its default values. If none of the components in the parent hierarchy (*autohandler* and *fancy_page.html* in this case) defines a certain method and that method is invoked, a fatal exception will be thrown. If you don't want to have a default title and header, ensuring that each page sets its own, you can simply omit the default methods in the autohandler. If a page fails to set its title or header, you will know it pretty quickly in the development cycle.

Remember that methods are Mason components, so they can contain more than just static text. You might compute a page's title or header based on information determined at runtime, for example.

Methods with Dynamic Content

As you know, methods and inheritance may be used to let a page and its autohandler share the responsibility for generating page elements like headers and titles. Since these elements may often depend on user input or other environmental conditions (e.g., "Welcome, Jon Swartz!" or "Information about your 9/13/2001 order"), you'll need a way to set these properties (like "Jon Swartz" or "9/13/2001") at runtime. Why is this an issue? Well, the following *won't* work:

```
<%method title>
 <!-- this method is invoked in the autohandler -->
 Information about your <% $order_date %> order
</%method>

Your order included the following items:
 ...generate item listing here...

<%init>
 my $order_date = $session{user}->last_order_date;
</%init>
```

The reason that won't work is that variables set in the <%init> block won't be visible inside the <%method title> block. Even if the scope of $order_date included the <%method title> block (it doesn't), the sequence of events at runtime wouldn't allow its value to be seen:

1. A request for */your_order.html* is received. Mason constructs the runtime inheritance hierarchy, assigning */autohandler* as */your_order.html*'s parent.

2. Mason executes the */autohandler* component, which invokes its SELF:title method. The title method invoked is the one contained in */your_order.html*.

3. The /your_order.html:title method runs, and the value of the $order_date is still unset—in fact, the variable is undeclared, so Perl will complain that the Global symbol "$order_date" requires explicit package name. Let's suppose you trapped this error with eval {}, so that we can continue tracing the sequence of events.

4. Control returns to /autohandler, which eventually calls $m->call_next and passes control to /your_order.html.

5. /your_order.html runs its <%init> section and then its main body. Note that it would set $order_date much too late to affect the title method back in step 3.

6. /your_order.html finishes and passes control back to /autohandler, and the request ends.

What's a Mason designer to do? The solution is simple: use a <%shared> block instead of an <%init> block to set the $order_date variable. This way, the variable can be shared among all the methods of the /your_order.html component, and it will be set at the proper time (right before step 2 in the previous listing) for it to be useful when the methods are invoked.

The proper code is remarkably similar to the improper code; the only difference is the name of the block in which the $order_date variable is set:

```
<%method title>
 <!-- this method is invoked in the autohandler -->
 Information about your <% $order_date %> order
</%method>

Your order included the following items:
 ...generate item listing here...

<%shared>
 my $order_date = $session{user}->last_order_date;
</%shared>
```

<%shared> blocks are executed only once per request, whenever the first component sharing the block needs it. Its scope lasts only to the end of the request. Because of this, <%shared> blocks are ideal for sharing scoped variables or performing component-specific initialization code that needs to happen only once per request.

Now imagine another scenario, one in which the method needs to examine the incoming arguments in order to generate its output. For instance, suppose you request /view_user.html?id=2982, and you want the title of the page to display some information about user 2982. You'll have to make sure that the user ID is available to the method, because under normal conditions it isn't. The two most common ways to get this information in the method are either for the method to call $m->request_args() or for the autohandler to pass its %ARGS to the method when calling it. The method could then either declare $id in an <%args> block or examine the incoming %ARGS hash directly. An example using request_args( ) follows:

```
<%method title>
 <!-- this method is invoked in the autohandler -->
 User page for <% $user->name %>
</%method>

... display information about $user ...

<%shared>
 my $user = MyApp::User->new(id => $m->request_args->{id});
</%shared>
```

Note that we cached the $user object with a shared variable so that we didn't have to create a new user object twice.

Attributes

Sometimes you want to take advantage of Mason's inheritance system, but you don't necessarily need to inherit the full components. For instance, in our first title and header example, the title and header methods contained just plain text and didn't use any of the dynamic capabilities of components. You might therefore consider it wasteful in this case to bring the full component-processing system to bear on the generation of headers and footers.

If you find yourself in this situation, Mason's component *attributes* may be of interest. An attribute is like a method in the way its inheritance works, but the value of an attribute is a Perl scalar variable, not a Mason component.

Examples 5-7 and 5-8 rewrite our previous autohandler example using attributes instead of methods.

Example 5-7. autohandler

```
<html>
<head><title><% $m->base_comp->attr('title') %></title></head>
<body>
 <center><h3><% $m->base_comp->attr('header') %></h3></center>
% $m->call_next;
 <center><a href="/">-home-</a></center>
</body>
</html>

<%attr>
 title  => "FancyMasonSite.Example.com"
 header => "Welcome to FancyMasonSite.Example.com"
</%attr>
```

Example 5-8. fancy_page.html

```
<p>This page isn't all <i>that</i> fancy, but it might be the
fanciest one we've seen yet.</p>

<%attr>
 title  => "Fancy Page"
 header => "A Very Fancy Page"
</%attr>
```

Attributes can be used like this, for small bits of text that become part of every page, but whose values vary from page to page. They can also be used to set properties of the component, such as whether to display a certain navigation bar or to omit it, whether the user must have certain characteristics in order to view this page,* and so on.

In the current version of Mason, each attribute in an <%attr> block must be on a single line. This means that you cannot use multiple lines for clarity or to specify multiline values. Future versions of Mason may provide additional syntax options for multiline attributes. If you run up against this limitation, you may want to use a method instead of an attribute anyway, since methods can more easily deal with more complex definitions.

Another limitation of attributes in the current version of Mason is that their values are completely static properties of the component and can't change from one request to the next. This may or may not be addressed by a future version of Mason. In any case, if you think you need dynamic attributes, you probably actually need to use methods instead.

Top-Down Versus Bottom-Up Inheritance

The attentive reader will have noticed that there are two distinct facets to Mason's inheritance—the first is the "content wrapping" behavior, by which a parent component can output some content, then call its child component, then output some more content. The typical example of this is an autohandler that generates headers and footers, wrapped around the output of its base component. The second facet of inheritance is the method and attribute system, by which designers can define general behavior and properties in the parent components and specific behavior in the children.

A major difference between these two facets is the direction of inheritance. Mason will begin the search for methods and attributes by starting with the bottommost

---

* In a mod_perl setting, authentication and authorization often happen before the content generation phase (i.e., before Mason even steps into the picture). However, you may wish to bypass the auth control phases and do your own authorization in the autohandler, just so that you can use Mason's attributes to control the behavior. For instance, you might give an unauthenticated user a different view of a certain page, rather than denying access outright.

child and working its way toward the parent, but it will begin the component's content generation by starting at the topmost parent and working its way toward the bottommost child (assuming each parent calls $m->call_next).

Although this behavior may seem odd if this is the first time you've encountered it, the inheritance system will seem like second nature after you've worked with it for a while. To help form an intuitive notion of what's happening, simply remember that autohandlers (or other parent components) specify general behavior, whereas top-level (i.e., child; i.e., "regular") components dictate specific behavior, overriding the parents.

Calling Components with Content Blocks

As you saw earlier, <%filter> blocks can be quite handy. The example we showed in Chapter 3 altered the src attribute of <img> tags in order to point them to a different server.

In Chapter 8 we will show an example that filters a link menu of <a href> tags to find the link for the current page and changes it to a <b> tag instead, in order to highlight the current page.

Both of these examples work just fine as long as we are willing to filter the output of an entire component, but sometimes we'd like to limit the filtering to just one section of the component. Consider the following autohandler:

```
<html>
<head>
<title><& SELF:title &></title>
</head>
<body>

<& SELF:top_menu, %ARGS &>

% $m->call_next;

</body>
</html>
```

This component calls the top_menu method, expecting it to produce some sort of menu of links. We'd like to use the menu-filtering trick just mentioned, but using a regular <%filter> block in this component would filter not only the menu of links but also the entire page. That's a waste of processing, not to mention a potential source of bugs—and we hate bugs.

Another option would be to insert a <%filter> block directly into the source of the top_menu method. However, the method may be defined in many different places; the whole point of using a method instead of a regular component call is that any component may redefine the method as it chooses. So we'd end up adding the *same* filter block to every definition of the top_menu method. That's a pretty poor solution.

What we really want is a solution that allows us to write the code once but apply it to only the portion of the output that we choose. Of course, there is such a thing called a "component call with content," introduced in Mason Version 1.10. It looks just like a regular <& &> component call, except that there's an extra pipe (|) character to distinguish it and a corresponding end tag, </&>. Using a component call with content, we can apply the desired filter to just the menu of links:

```
<html>
<head>
<title><& SELF:title &></title>
</head>
<body>

<&| .top_menu_filter &>
 <& SELF:top_menu, %ARGS &>
</&>

% $m->call_next;

</body>
</html>
```

So the .top_menu_filter component—presumably a subcomponent defined in the same file—is somehow being passed the output from the call to <& SELF:top_menu, %ARGS &>. The .top_menu_filter component would look something like this:

```
<%def .top_menu_filter>
% my $text = $m->content;
% my $uri = $r->uri;
% $text =~ s,<a href="\Q$uri\E[^"]*">([^<]+)</a>,<b>$1</b>,;
<% $text %>
</%def>
```

This looks more or less like any other <%filter> block, but with two main differences. First, the body of a <%filter> block contains plain Perl code, but since .top_menu_filter is a subcomponent, it contains Mason code. Second, we access the text to filter via a call to $m->content instead of in the $_ variable. The $m->content() method returns the evaluated output of the content block, which in this case is the output of the SELF:top_menu component.

Mason goes through some contortions in order to trick the wrapped portion of the component into thinking that it is still in the original component. If we had a component named *bob.html*, as shown in the example below:

```
<&| .uc &>
I am in <% $m->current_comp->name %>
</&>

<%def .uc>
<% uc $m->content %>
</%def>
```

we would expect the output to be:

```
I AM IN BOB.HTML
```

And indeed, that is what will happen. You can also nest these sorts of calls:

```
<&| .ucfirst &>
  <&| .reverse &>
I am in <% $m->current_comp->name %>
  </&>
</&>

<%def .reverse>
<% scalar reverse $m->content %>
</%def>
<%def .ucfirst>
<% join ' ', map {ucfirst} split / /, $m->content %>
</%def>
```

This produces:

```
Lmth.bob Ni Ma I
```

As you can see, the filtering components are called from innermost to outermost.

It may have already occurred to you, but this can actually be used to implement something in Mason that looks a lot like Java Server Page taglibs. Without commenting on whether the taglib concept is conducive to effective site management or not, we'll show you how to create a similar effect in Mason. Here's a simple SQL select expressed in something like a taglib style:

```
<table>
 <tr>
  <th>Name</th>
  <th>Age</th>
 </tr>
<&| /sql/select, query => 'SELECT name, age FROM User' &>
 <tr>
  <td>%name</td>
  <td>%age</td>
 </tr>
</&>
</table>
```

The idea is that the query argument specifies the SQL query to run, and the content block dictates how each row returned should be displayed. Fields are indicated here by a % and then the name of the field.

Now let's write the */sql/select* component.

```
<%args>
 $query
</%args>
<%init>
 my $sth = $dbh->prepare($query);
```

```
while ( my $row = $sth->fetchrow_hashref ) {
  my $content = $m->content;
  $content =~ s/%(\w+)/$row->{$1}/g;
  $m->print($content);
}
</%init>
```

Obviously, this example is grossly simplified (it doesn't handle things like bound SQL variables, and it doesn't handle extra embedded % characters very well), but it demonstrates the basic technique.

Seeing all this, you may wonder if you can somehow use this feature to implement control structures, again a taglib-esque idea. The answer is yes, with some caveats. We say "with caveats" because due to the way this feature is implemented, with closures, you have to jump through a few hoops. Here is something that will *not* work:

```
<&| /loop, items => ['one', 'two', 'three'] &>
<% $item %>
</&>
```

And in */loop*:

```
<%args>
 @items
</%args>
% foreach my $item (@items) {
<% $m->content %>
% }
```

Remember, the previous example will not work. The reason should be obvious. At no time is the variable $item declared in the calling component, either as a global or lexical variable, so a syntax error will occur when the component is compiled.

So how can this idea be made to work? Here is one way. Rewrite the calling component first:

```
% my $item;
<&| /loop, items => ['one', 'two', 'three'], item => \$item &>
<% $item %>
</&>
```

Then rewrite */loop*:

```
<%args>
 $item
 @items
</%args>
% foreach (@items) {
%    $$item = $_;
<% $m->content %>
% }
```

This takes advantages of how Perl treats lexical variables inside closures, but explaining this in detail is *way* beyond the scope of this book.

You can also achieve this same thing with a global variable. This next version assumes that $item has been declared using allow_globals:

```
<&| /loop, items => ['one', 'two', 'three'] &>
<% $item %>
</&>
```

And *loop* becomes this:

```
<%args>
@items
</%args>
% foreach $item (@items) {
<% $m->content %>
% }
```

This version is perhaps a little less funky, but it could lead to having more globals than you'd really like.

An in-between solution using Perl's special $_ variable can solve many of these problems. This variable is a global but is automatically localized by loop controls like foreach or while. So we can now write:

```
<&| /loop, items => ['one', 'two', 'three'] &>
<% $_ %>
</&>
```

And for *loop*:

```
<%args>
@items
</%args>
% foreach (@items) {
<% $m->content %>
% }
```

Magic. It isn't perfect, but it looks kind of neat.

In any case, Mason was designed to use Perl's built-in control structures, so we don't feel too bad that it's awkward to build your own.

Advanced Inheritance

In Chapter 3 we introduced you to the concept of component inheritance, and in this chapter we have discussed some of the ways you can use inheritance to create flexible, maintainable Mason sites. Now we show how inheritance interacts with other Mason features, such as multiple component roots and multiple autohandlers.

Inheritance and Multiple Component Roots

It is possible to tell Mason to search for components in more than one directory—in other words, to specify more than one component root. This is analogous to telling

Perl to look for modules in the various @INC directories or to telling Unix or Windows to look for executable programs in your PATH. In Chapters 6 and 7 you will learn more about how to configure Mason; for now, we will just show by example:

```
my $ah = HTML::Mason::ApacheHandler->new(
  comp_root => [
                [main => '/usr/http/docs'],
                [util => '/usr/http/mason-util'],
                ]
);
```

or, in an Apache configuration file:

```
PerlSetVar MasonCompRoot 'main => /usr/http/docs'
PerlAddVar MasonCompRoot 'util => /usr/http/mason-util'
```

This brings up some interesting inheritance questions. How do components from the two component roots relate to each other? For instance, does a component in */usr/http/docs* inherit from a top-level autohandler in */usr/http/mason-util*? With this setup, under what conditions will a component call from one directory find a component in the other directory? The answers to these questions are not obvious unless you know the rules.

The basic rule is that Mason always searches for components based on their component paths, not on their source file paths. It will be perfectly happy to have a component in one component root inherit from a component in another component root. When calling one component from another, you always specify only the path, not the particular component root to search in, so Mason will search all roots.

If it helps you conceptually, you might think of the multiple component roots as getting merged together into one big über-root that contains all the files from all the multiple roots, with conflicts resolved in favor of the earliest-listed root.

Let's think about some specific cases. Using the two component roots given previously, suppose you have a component named */dir/top_level.mas* in the main component root and a component named */dir/autohandler* in the util component root. */dir/top_level.mas* will inherit from */dir/autohandler* by default. Likewise, if */dir/top_level.mas* calls a component called *other.mas*, Mason will search for *other.mas* first in the main component root, then in the utils root. It makes no difference whether the component call is done by using the component path *other.mas* or */dir/other.mas*; the former gets transformed immediately into the latter by prepending the */dir/top_level.mas*'s dir_path.

If there are two components with the same path in the main and util roots, you won't be able to call the one in the util root by path no matter how hard you try, because the one in main overrides it.

This behavior is actually quite handy in certain situations. Suppose you're creating lots of sites that function similarly, but each individual site needs to have some small tweaks. There might be small differences in the functional requirements, or you might need to put a different "look and feel" on each site. One simple way to do this is to use multiple component roots, with each site having its own private root and a shared root:

```
my $interp = HTML::Mason::Interp->new(
    comp_root => [
                   [mine   => '/etc/httpd/sites/bobs-own-site'],
                   [shared => '/usr/local/lib/mason/common'],
                   ]
);
```

The shared root can provide a top-level autohandler that establishes a certain generic look and feel to the site, and the mine root can create its own top-level autohandler to override the one in shared.

Using this setup, any component call—no matter whether it occurs in a component located in the mine or shared component root—will look for the indicated component, first in mine, then in shared if none is found in mine.

An Advanced Inheritance Example

An example can help showcase several of the topics we've discussed in this chapter. The component in this section was originally written by John Williams, though we've removed a few features for the pedagogical purposes of this book. It implements an autohandler that allows you to run predefined SQL queries via a Mason component interface. For example, you might use the component as in Example 5-9.

Example 5-9. A calling component

```
<table>
<tr><th>Part Number</th><th>Quantity</th><th>Price</th><th>Total</th></tr>
<&| /query/order_items:exec, bind => [$OrderID] &>
<tr>
    <td><% $_->{PARTNUM} %></td>
    <td><% $_->{QUANTITY} %></td>
    <td><% $_->{PRICE} %></td>
    <td><% $_->{QUANTITY} * $_->{PRICE} %></td>
</tr>
</&>
</table>
```

Note that we're passing a content block to the /query/order_items:exec method call. The idea is that the method will repeat the content block for every database row returned by an SQL query, and the $_ variable will hold the data for each row, as returned by the DBI method fetchrow_hashref(). The query itself is specified in the */query/order_items* file, which could look like Example 5-10.

Example 5-10. /query/order_items

```
SELECT * FROM items WHERE order_id = ?
```

Yes, it's just one line. Where is the exec method we called earlier? It's in the parent component, which (since we didn't specify otherwise with an inherit flag) is *query/ autohandler*. This autohandler is the component that does all the work; see Example 5-11.

Example 5-11. /query/autohandler

```
<%flags>
 inherit => undef
</%flags>

<%method exec>
 <%args>
 @bind => ()
 </%args>

 <%init>
 local $dbh->{RaiseError} = 1;

 # Get the SQL from the base component
 my $sql = $m->scomp($m->base_comp, %ARGS);
 my $q = $dbh->prepare($sql);
 $q->execute(@bind);

 # Return now if called without content
 # (useful for insert/update/delete statements).
 return $dbh->rows unless defined $m->content;

 # Call the content block once per row
 local $_;
 while ($_ = $q->fetchrow_hashref('NAME_uc')) {
   $m->print( $m->content );
 }

 # Don't print any of the whitespace in this method
 return;
 </%init>
</%method>
```

Let's step our way through the autohandler. The only code outside the exec method ensures that this component is parentless. It's not strictly necessary, but we include it to make sure this example is isolated from any other interaction.

We access the database inside the exec method. Since we haven't declared the $dbh variable, it's assumed that it's already set up for us as a global variable, probably initialized in the site's top-level autohandler. The first thing we do is make sure that the code will throw an exception if anything goes wrong during the query, so we locally set $dbh->{RaiseError} to 1. Any exceptions thrown will be the responsibility of someone higher up the calling chain.

Next, we get the text of the SQL query. It's contained in our base component, which in our example was */query/order_items*. We call this component to get its output. Note that we also pass %ARGS to our base component, which lets us do additional substitutions into the SQL statement. For example, we could have a query that sorts by one of several different fields, using ORDER BY <% $ARGS{sort} %> inside the SQL statement.

After we fetch the SQL and prepare the query, we execute the query, passing any bound variables to the $q->execute() method. If there was no content block passed to us, then we're done—this allows the component to be used for INSERT/UPDATE/DELETE statements in addition to SELECT statements.

Finally, we iterate through the rows returned by the query, storing the data for each row in $_. Note that we localize $_ before using it, since blowing away any value that's already in there would be extremely impolite.

Be sure to notice that the $m->content body is reexecuted for each row. Because of this, its execution happens within the scope of the current $_ variable. This is really the only way this all could work, but it's subtle enough that we had to point it out.

The advantage of using inheritance this way is that you capture the complicated parts of a task in a single component, and then all the rest of the components become very simple. If you get familiar with Mason's inheritance model, you can create very sophisticated applications with a minimum of redundancy and hassle.

Subrequests

Once in a while you may want to call one component from another as if it were a top-level component, having it go through the full content-wrapping and dhandler-checking process. This is what *subrequests* are for, and the manner in which they work is similar to how subrequests work in Apache. Subrequests were introduced in Mason Version 1.10.

When executing a subrequest, you may simply execute it via the request object's subexec() method, or you may first create the object via make_subrequest() and then execute it via exec(). The subexec() method takes the same arguments as the comp() method:

```
Calling /some/comp:
% $m->subexec( '/some/comp', foo => 1 );
```

The output of the subrequest goes to the same place as normal component output, but can be captured in a variable fairly easily by using make_subrequest() to provide explicit arguments when creating the request:

```
<%perl>
my $output;
my $req = $m->make_subrequest
    ( comp => '/some/comp', args => [ foo => 1 ], out_method => \$output );
```

```
  $req->exec;
  $output =~ s/something/something else/g;
</%perl>
/some/comp produced:
<% $output %>
```

As this illustrates, one of the interesting things you can do with a subrequest is override some of the parameters provided by its parent request. So we can do:

```
Calling /some/comp:
<%perl>
 my $req = $m->make_subrequest
     ( comp => '/some/comp', autoflush => 1 );
 $req->exec;
</%perl>
```

In both cases, the request object created by the make_subrequest method inherits its parameters from the parent request, except for those that are explicitly overridden.

A Caution About Autohandler Inheritance

Remember that Mason determines the default parent of every component but that you can always specify a different parent using the special inherit flag in the <%flags> section. This applies not just to regular components, but to autohandlers too: any component, including the top-level autohandler, can inherit from a component of your choosing.

However, specifying an autohandler's inheritance explicitly can easily lead to an infinite inheritance chain if you're not careful. Suppose you set the parent of the top-level autohandler to a component called /syshandler. In setting up the inheritance chain at runtime, Mason will attempt to find the parent of /syshandler, and the default is (you guessed it) autohandler in the same directory. So unless you've overridden /syshandler's parent, you'll have /autohandler inheriting from /syshandler, and /syshandler inheriting from /autohandler. Not a good situation: it will cause a fatal runtime error due to the inheritance loop. The solution is to set the inherit flag for /syshandler to undef, terminating the inheritance chain. Yes, this sounds a bit like SCSI; perhaps someday someone will invent the equivalent of USB in the Mason world. Until then, just make sure you don't create any loops.

CHAPTER 6

The Lexer, Compiler, Resolver, and Interpreter Objects

Now that you're familiar with Mason's basic syntax and some of its more advanced features, it's time to explore the details of how the various pieces of the Mason architecture work together to process components. By knowing the framework well, you can use its pieces to your advantage, processing components in ways that match your intentions.

In this chapter we'll discuss four of the persistent objects in the Mason framework: the Interpreter, Resolver, Lexer, and Compiler. These objects are created once (in a mod_perl setting, they're typically created when the server is starting up) and then serve many Mason requests, each of which may involve processing many Mason components.

Each of these four objects has a distinct purpose. The Resolver is responsible for all interaction with the underlying component source storage mechanism, which is typically a set of directories on a filesystem. The main job of the Resolver is to accept a component path as input and return various properties of the component such as its source, time of last modification, unique identifier, and so on.

The Lexer is responsible for actually processing the component source code and finding the Mason directives within it. It interacts quite closely with the Compiler, which takes the Lexer's output and generates a Mason component object suitable for interpretation at runtime.

The Interpreter ties the other three objects together. It is responsible for taking a component path and arguments and generating the resultant output. This involves getting the component from the resolver, compiling it, then caching the compiled version so that next time the interpreter encounters the same component it can skip the resolving and compiling phases.

Figure 6-1 illustrates the relationship between these four objects. The Interpreter has a Compiler and a Resolver, and the Compiler has a Lexer.

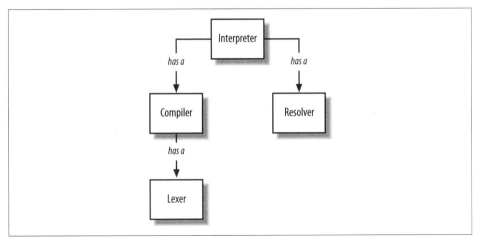

Figure 6-1. The Interpreter and its cronies

Passing Parameters to Mason Classes

An interesting feature of the Mason code is that, if a particular object contains another object, the containing object will accept constructor parameters intended for the contained object. For example, the Interpreter object will accept parameters intended for the Compiler or Resolver and do the right thing with them. This means that you often don't need to know exactly where a parameter goes. You just pass it to the object at the top of the chain.

Even better, if you decide to create your own Resolver for use with Mason, the Interpreter will take any parameters that your Resolver accepts—not the parameters defined by Mason's default Resolver class.

Also, if an object creates multiple delayed instances of another class, as the Interpreter does with Request objects, it will accept the created class's parameters in the same way, passing them to the created class at the appropriate time. So if you pass the `autoflush` parameter to the Interpreter's constructor, it will store this value and pass it to any Request objects it creates later.

This system was motivated in part by the fact that many users want to be able to configure Mason from an Apache config file. Under this system, the user just sets a certain configuration directive (such as `MasonAutoflush`* to set the `autoflush` parameter) in her *httpd.conf* file, and it gets directed automatically to the Request objects when they are created.

---

* All initialization parameters have corresponding Apache configuration names, found by switching from lower_case_with_underscores to StudlyCaps and prepending "Mason."

The details of how this system works are fairly magical and the code involved is so funky its creators don't know whether to rejoice or weep, but it works, and you can take advantage of this if you ever need to create your own custom Mason classes. Chapter 12 covers this in its discussion of the Class::Container class, where all the funkiness is located.

The Lexer

Mason's built-in Lexer class is, appropriately enough, HTML::Mason::Lexer. All it does is parse the text of Mason components and pass off the sections it finds to the Compiler. As of Version 1.10, the Lexer doesn't actually accept any parameters that alter its behavior, so there's not much for us to say in this section.

Future versions of Mason may include other Lexer classes to handle alternate source formats. Some people—crazy people, we assure you—have expressed a desire to write Mason components in XML, and it would be fairly simple to plug in a new Lexer class to handle this. If you're one of these crazy people, you may be interested in Chapter 12 to see how to use objects of your own design as pieces of the Mason framework.

By the way, you may be wondering why the Lexer isn't called a Parser, since its main job seems to be to parse the source of a component. The answer is that previous implementations of Mason had a Parser class with a different interface and role, and a different name was necessary to maintain forward (though not backward) compatibility.

The Compiler

By default, Mason will use the HTML::Mason::Compiler::ToObject class to do its compilation. It is a subclass of the generic HTML::Mason::Compiler class, so we describe here all parameters that the ToObject variety will accept, including parameters inherited from its parent:

allow_globals

> You may want to allow access to certain Perl variables across all components without declaring or initializing them each time. For instance, you might want to let all components share access to a $dbh variable that contains a DBI database handle, or you might want to allow access to an Apache::Session %session variable.

> For cases like these, you can set the allow_globals parameter to an array reference containing the names of any global variables you want to declare. Think of it like a broadly scoped use vars declaration; in fact, that's exactly the way it's implemented under the hood. If you wanted to allow the $dbh and %session variables, you would pass an allow_globals parameter like the following:

```
allow_globals => ['$dbh', '%session']
```

Or in an Apache configuration file:

```
PerlSetVar MasonAllowGlobals $dbh
PerlAddVar MasonAllowGlobals %session
```

The allow_globals parameter can be used effectively with the Perl local() function in an autohandler. The top-level autohandler is a convenient place to initialize global variables, and local() is exactly the right tool to ensure that they're properly cleaned up at the end of the request:

```
# In the top-level autohandler:
<%init>
  # $dbh and %session have been declared using 'allow_globals'
  local $dbh = DBI->connect(...connection parameters...);
  local *session;  # Localize the glob so the tie() expires properly
  tie %session, 'Apache::Session::MySQL',
    Apache::Cookie->fetch->{session_id}->value,
    { Handle => $dbh, LockHandle => $dbh };
</%init>
```

Remember, don't go too crazy with globals: too many of them in the same process space can get very difficult to manage, and in an environment like Mason's, especially under mod_perl, the process space can be very large and long-lasting. But a few well-placed and well-scoped globals can make life nice.

default_escape_flags

This parameter allows you to set a global default for the escape flags in <% $substitution %> tags. For instance, if you set default_escape_flags to 'h', then all substitution tags in your components will pass through HTML escaping. If you decide that an individual substitution tag should not obey the default_escape_flag parameter, you can use the special escape flag 'n' to ignore the default setting and add whatever additional flags you might want to employ for that particular substitution tag.

```
in compiler settings:
default_escape_flags => 'h',
```

```
in a component:
You have <% $amount %> clams in your aquarium.
This is <% $difference |n %> more than your rival has.
<a href="emotion.html?emotion=<% $emotion |nu %>">Visit
 your <% $emotion %> place!</a>
```

```
acts as if you had written:
You have <% $amount |h %> clams in your aquarium.
This is <% $difference %> more than your rival has.
<a href="emotion.html?emotion=<% $emotion |u %>">Visit
 your <% $emotion |h %> place!</a>
```

use_strict

By default, all components will be run under Perl's strict pragma, which forces you to declare any Perl variables you use in your component. This is a very good feature, as the strict pragma can help you avoid all kinds of programming slip-ups that may lead to mysterious and intermittent errors. If, for some sick reason you want to turn off the strict pragma for all your components, you can set the use_strict parameter to a false value and watch all hell get unleashed as you shoot your Mason application in the foot.

A far better solution is to just insert no strict; into your code whenever you use a construct that's not allowed under the strict pragma; this way your casual usage will be allowed in only the smallest enclosing block (in the worst case, one entire component). Even better would be to find a way to achieve your goals while obeying the rules of the strict pragma, because the rules generally enforce good programming practice.

in_package

The code written in <%perl> sections (or other component sections that contain Perl code) must be compiled in the context of some package, and the default package is HTML::Mason::Commands.* To specify a different package, set the in_package compiler parameter. Under normal circumstances you shouldn't concern yourself with this package name (almost everything in Mason is done with lexically scoped my variables), but for historical reasons you're allowed to change it to whatever package you want.

Related settings are the Compiler's allow_globals parameter/method and the Interpreter's set_global() method. These let you declare and assign to variables in the package you specified with in_package, without actually needing to specify that package again by name.

You may also want to control the package name in order to import symbols (subroutines, constants, etc.) for use in components. Although the importing of subroutines seems to be gradually going out of style as people adopt more strict object-oriented programming practices, importing constants is still quite popular, and especially useful in a web context, where various numerical values are used as HTTP status codes. The following example, meant for use in an Apache server configuration file, exports all the common Apache constants so they can be used inside the site's Mason components.

```
PerlSetVar MasonInPackage My::Application
<Perl>
  {
  package My::Application;
  use Apache::Constants qw(:common);
  }
</Perl>
```

comp_class

By default, components created by the compiler will be created by calling the HTML::Mason::Component class's new() method. If you want the components to be

---

* This package name is purely historical; it may be changed in the future.

objects of a different class, perhaps one of your own creation, you may specify a different class name in the comp_class parameter.

lexer
lexer_class

As of Release 1.10 you can redesign Mason on the fly by subclassing one or more of Mason's core classes and extending (or reducing, if that's your game) its functionality. In an informal sense, we speak of Release 1.10 as having made Mason more "pluggable."

By default, Mason creates a Lexer object in the HTML::Mason::Lexer class. By passing a lexer parameter to the Compiler, you can specify a different Lexer object with different behavior. For instance, if you like everything about Mason except for the syntax it uses for its component files, you could create a Lexer object that lets you write your components in a format that works well with your favorite WYSIWYG HTML editor, in a Python-esque whitespace soup, or however you like.

The lexer parameter should contain an object that inherits from the HTML::Mason::Lexer class. As an alternative to creating the object yourself and passing it to the Compiler, you may instead specify a lexer_class parameter, and the Compiler will create a new Lexer object for you by calling the specified package's new() method. This alternative is often preferable when it's inconvenient to create new Perl objects, such as when you're configuring Mason from a web server's configuration file. In this case, you should also pass any parameters that are needed for your Lexer's new() method, and they will find their way there.

Altering Every Component's Content

Several access points let you step in to the compilation process and alter the text of each component as it gets processed. The preprocess, postprocess_perl, postprocess_text, preamble, and postamble parameters let you exert a bit of ad hoc control over Mason's processing of your components.

Figure 6-2 illustrates the role of each of these five parameters.

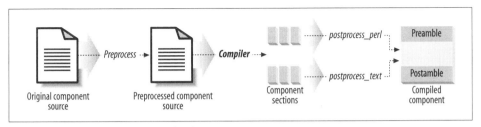

Figure 6-2. Component processing hooks

preprocess

With the preprocess parameter, you may specify a reference to a subroutine through which all components should be preprocessed before the compiler gets hold of them. The compiler will pass your subroutine the entire text of the component in a scalar reference. Your subroutine should modify the text in that reference directly—any return value will be ignored.

postprocess_perl
postprocess_text

The sections of a Mason component can be coarsely divided into three categories: Perl sections (%-lines, <%init> blocks, and so on), sections for special Mason directives (<%args> blocks, <%flags> blocks, and so on), and plain text sections (anything outside the other two types of sections). The Perl and text sections can become part of the component's final output, whereas the Mason directives control how the output is created.

Similar to the preprocess directive, the postprocess_perl and postprocess_text directives let you step in and change a component's source before it is compiled. However, with these directives you're stepping into the action one step later, after the component source has been divided into the three types of sections just mentioned. Accordingly, the postprocess_perl parameter lets you process Perl sections, and the postprocess_text parameter lets you process text sections. There is no corresponding hook for postprocessing the special Mason sections.

As with the preprocess directive, the postprocess directives should specify a subroutine reference. Mason will pass the component source sections one at a time (again, as a scalar reference) to the subroutine you specify, and your subroutine should modify the text in-place.

preamble

If you specify a string value for the preamble parameter, the text you provide will be prepended to every component that gets processed with this compiler. The string should contain Perl code, not Mason code, as it gets inserted verbatim into the component object after compilation. The default preamble is the empty string.

postamble

The postamble parameter is just like the preamble parameter, except that the string you specify will get appended to the component rather than prepended. Like the preamble, the default postamble is the empty string.

One use for preamble and postamble might be an execution trace, in which you log the start and end events of each component.

One potential gotcha: if you have an explicit return statement in a component, no further code in that component will run, including code in its postamble. Thus it's not necessarily a good place to run cleanup code, unless you're positive you're never going to use return statements. Cleanup code is usually better

---

placed in an autohandler or similar location. An alternate trick is to create objects in your preamble code and rely on their `DESTROY` methods to tell you when they're going out of scope.

Compiler Methods

Once an `HTML::Mason::Compiler::ToObject` object is created, the following methods may be invoked. Many of them simply return the value of a parameter that was passed (or set by default) when the Compiler was created. Some methods may be used by developers when building a site, while other methods should be called only by the various other pieces in the Mason framework. Though you may need to know how the latter methods work if you start plugging your own modules into the framework, you'll need to read the Mason documentation to find out more about those methods, as we don't discuss them here.

The compiler methods are `comp_class()`, `in_package()`, `preamble()`, `postamble()`, `use_strict()`, `allow_globals()`, `default_escape_flags()`, `preprocess()`, `postprocess_perl()`, `postprocess_text()`, and `lexer()`.

Each of these methods returns the given property of the Compiler, which was typically set when the Compiler was created. If you pass an argument to these methods, you may also change the given property. One typically doesn't need to change any of the Compiler's properties after creation, but interesting effects could be achieved by doing so:

```
% my $save_pkg = $m->interp->compiler->in_package;
% $m->interp->compiler->in_package('MyApp::OtherPackage');
<& /some/other/component &>
% $m->interp->compiler->in_package($save_pkg);
```

The preceding example will compile the component */some/other/component*—and any components it calls—in the package `MyApp::OtherPackage` rather than the default `HTML::Mason::Commands` package or whatever other package you specified using in_package.

Of course, this technique will work only if */some/other/component* actually needs to be compiled at this point in the code; it may already be compiled and cached in memory or on disk, in which case changing the `in_package` property (or any other Compiler property) will have no effect. Because of this, changing Compiler properties after the Compiler is created is neither a great idea nor officially supported, but if you know what you're doing, you can use it for whatever diabolical purposes you have in mind.

The Resolver

The default Resolver, `HTML::Mason::Resolver::File`, finds components and their meta-information (for example, modification date and file length) on disk. The Resolver is a pretty simple thing, but it's useful to give it its own place in the pluggable Mason framework because it allows a developer to use whatever storage mechanism she wants for her components.

The `HTML::Mason::Resolver::File` class accepts only one parameter:

comp_root

> The `comp_root` parameter is Mason's component root. It specifies where components may be found on disk. It is roughly analogous to Perl's `@INC` array or the shell's `$PATH` variable. You may specify `comp_root` as a string containing the directory in which to search for components or as an array reference of array references like so:
>
> ```
> my $comp_root = [
>                  [web    => '/usr/local/httpd/documents'],
>                  [shared => '/usr/local/mason/comps'],
>                  [custom => '/home/ken/my_components'],
>                 ];
> my $resolver = HTML::Mason::Resolver::File->new(comp_root => $comp_root);
> ```
>
> Every time the Resolver is asked to find a component on disk, it will search these three directories in the given order, as discussed in Chapter 5.
>
> After a Resolver has been created, you may call its `comp_root()` method, which returns the value of the `comp_root` parameter as it was set at creation time.

If you don't provide a `comp_root` parameter, it defaults to something reasonably sensible. In a web context it defaults to the server's `DocumentRoot`; otherwise, it defaults to the current working directory.

The Interpreter

The Interpreter is the center of Mason's universe. It is responsible for coordinating the activities of the Compiler and Resolver, as well as creating Request objects. Its main task involves receiving requests for components and generating the resultant output of those requests. It is also responsible for several tasks behind the scenes, such as caching components in memory or on disk. It exposes only a small part of its object API for public use; its primary interface is via its constructor, the `new()` method.

The `new()` method accepts lots of parameters. It accepts any parameter that its Resolver or Compiler (and through the Compiler, the Lexer) classes accept in their `new()` methods; these parameters will be transparently passed along to the correct constructor. It also accepts the following parameters of its own:

autohandler_name

> This parameter specifies the name that Mason uses for autohandler files. The default name is "autohandler."

code_cache_max_size

This parameter sets the limit, in bytes, of the in-memory cache for component code. The default is 10 megabytes (10 * 1024 * 1024). This is not the same thing as the on-disk cache for component code, which will keep growing without bound until all components are cached on disk. It is also different from the data caches, the sizes of which you control through the $m->cache and $m->cache_self methods.

data_dir

This parameter specifies the directory under which Mason stores its various data, such as compiled components, cached data, and so on. This cannot be changed after the Interpreter is created.

ignore_warnings_expr

Normally, warnings issued during the loading of a component are treated as fatal errors by Mason. Mason will ignore warnings that match the regular expression specified in this parameter. The default setting is qr/Subroutine .* redefined/i. If you change this parameter, you will probably want to make sure that this particular warning continues to be ignored, as this allows you to declare named subroutines in the <%once> section of components and not cause an error when the component is reloaded and the subroutine is redefined.

preloads

This parameter takes a list of components to be preloaded when the Interpreter is created. In a mod_perl setting this can lead to substantial memory savings and better performance, since the components will be compiled in the server's parent process and initially shared among the server children. It also reduces the amount of processing needed during individual requests, as preloaded components will be standing at the ready.

The list of components can either be specified by listing each component path individually or by using glob()-style patterns to specify several component paths.

static_source

Passing a true value for this parameter causes Mason to execute in "static source" mode, which means that it will compile a source file only once, ignoring subsequent changes. In addition, it will resolve a given path only once, so adding or removing components will not be noticed by the interpreter.

If you do want to make changes to components when Mason is in this mode, you will need to delete all of Mason's object files and, if you are running Mason under mod_perl, restart the Apache server.

This mode is useful in order to gain a small performance boost on a heavily trafficked site when your components don't change very often. If you don't need the performance boost, then don't bother turning this mode on, as it just makes for extra administrative work when you change components.

compiler
compiler_class
resolver
resolver_class

As we mentioned before, each Interpreter object creates a Compiler and a Resolver object that it works with to serve requests. You can substantially alter the compilation or resolution tasks by providing your own Compiler or Resolver when creating the Interpreter, passing them as the values for the `compiler` or `resolver` parameters. Alternatively, you may pass `compiler_class` or `resolver_class` parameters (and any arguments required by those classes' `new( )` methods) and allow the Interpreter to construct the Compiler or Resolver from the other parameters you specify:

```
my $interp = HTML::Mason::Interpreter->new
  (
   resolver_class => 'MyApp::Resolver',
   compiler_class => 'MyApp::Compiler',
   comp_root => '/home/httpd/docs',  # Goes to resolver
   default_escape_flags => 'h',      # Goes to compiler
  );
```

By default, the Compiler will be an `HTML::Mason::Compiler::ToObject` object, and the Resolver will be an `HTML::Mason::Resolver::File` object.

Request Parameters Passed to the Interpreter

Besides the Interpreter's own parameters, you can pass the Interpreter any parameter that the Request object accepts. These parameters will be saved internally and used as defaults when making a new Request object.

The parameters that can be set are: `autoflush`, `data_cache_defaults`, `dhandler`, `error_mode`, `error_format`, and `out_method`.

Besides accepting these as constructor parameters, the Interpreter also provides get/set accessors for these attribute. Setting these attributes in the interpreter will change the attribute for all future Requests, though it will *not* change the current Request.

## CHAPTER 7

Using Mason with mod_perl

While Mason can be used in any text generation context, it is most frequently used to create dynamic web sites. As you probably know, executing Perl (or anything else for that matter) as a CGI can be very slow. Mason, because it is not a small amount of code, can be sluggish when run as a CGI under heavy loads.

To that end, Mason has been designed to play nice when run under mod_perl. In fact, Mason has quite a number of features that make it nicely suited to running under mod_perl.

This chapter assumes that you are familiar with Apache, particularly Apache's configuration files, and with mod_perl. If you're not, here's a teaser: mod_perl embeds a Perl interpreter inside the Apache web server. Because Perl is already loaded, no external processes need to be launched to serve Perl-generated content. mod_perl also allows many server tasks to be configured and executed using Perl, which can be a great convenience.

More information on Apache can be found via the Apache web site at *http://httpd. apache.org/*, as well as in O'Reilly's *Apache: The Definitive Guide*, 3rd Edition (Ben and Peter Laurie, 2003).

For more information on mod_perl, the mod_perl site at *http://perl.apache.org/* is useful, as is Stas Bekman's fabulous mod_perl guide, which can be found at the same location. Also useful is *Writing Apache Modules with Perl and C* (the "Eagle Book") by Lincoln Stein and Doug MacEachern, also published by O'Reilly.* Despite the title, it is really primarily about mod_perl.

A recent book from Sams Publishing, *The mod_perl Developer's Cookbook* by Geoffrey Young, Paul Lindner, and Randy Kobes, is also an extremely valuable resource for anyone who's going to spend a significant amount of time working with mod_perl. It fills a different niche in the developer's mental toolkit.

---

* They told us we get extra royalties every time we mention one of their other books.

With Apache 2.0 and `mod_perl` 2.0 on the horizon as this is being written, please note that this chapter assumes that you are using Apache 1.3.x and `mod_perl` 1.22 or greater. In addition, your `mod_perl` should have been compiled with `PERL_METHOD_HANDLERS=1` and `PERL_TABLE_API=1`, or with `EVERYTHING=1`.

We expect Mason to work immediately under the 1.x compatibility layer that `mod_perl` 2.0 will provide. And of course, once `mod_perl` and Apache 2.0 are out, we hope to find new features for Mason to exploit.

Configuring Mason

Mason can be configured under `mod_perl` in two different ways. The easiest of the two merely requires that you add a few directives to Apache's configuration files. This method is very easy to use and is appropriate for most uses of Mason. It's commonly called "configuration via *httpd.conf*," though many configuration directives can be placed anywhere Apache will see them, such as in an *.htaccess* file.

The other way is to write a custom piece of Perl code to bind Mason and `mod_perl` together, which you instruct `mod_perl` to use when handling requests. This method is very flexible but is a bit more complicated. It is not usually necessary, but it can be useful for a particularly complex or dynamic configuration. This configuration method is commonly called "configuration via a *handler.pl*," though the *handler.pl* file can be called anything you like.

For simplicity's sake, we always refer to the *httpd.conf* and *handler.pl* files throughout the book.

Configuration via httpd.conf

To make Mason work under `mod_perl`, we need to set up a few Mason configuration variables and then tell `mod_perl` to use Mason as a `PerlContentHandler`. Here is the simplest possible configuration:

```
SetHandler    perl-script
PerlHandler   HTML::Mason::ApacheHandler
```

The `SetHandler` directive just tells Apache to use `mod_perl` for this request. The `PerlHandler` directive is provided by `mod_perl`, and it tells Apache that the given module is a content handler. This means that the module will respond to the request and generate content to be sent to the client.

Putting the previous snippet in your configuration file will cause every file your web server processes to be handled by Mason. This is probably not what you want most of the time, so let's narrow it down a bit:

```
<Location /mason>
   PerlSetVar    MasonCompRoot   /path/to/doc/root/mason
   SetHandler    perl-script
```

```
    PerlHandler  HTML::Mason::ApacheHandler
  </Location>
```

This tells Apache that only requests that have a path starting with *mason* will be handled by Mason. We've narrowed down the component root correspondingly, though this is not required. In fact, it's important to realize that component root and document root are *not* the same thing. There will be more on this later.

Alternately, we might want to specify that only certain file extensions will be handled by Mason:

```
AddType  text/html  .mhtml
<FilesMatch "\.mhtml$">
  SetHandler  perl-script
  PerlHandler  HTML::Mason::ApacheHandler
</FilesMatch>
```

The first directive tells Apache that files ending with *.mhtml* have a content-type of text/html. The FilesMatch section says that files ending with *.mhtml* will be handled by Mason. This configuration is convenient if you want to intermix Mason components with other types of content, such as static HTML or image files, in the same directory. You want Mason to process only the Mason components, as having it process images or CSS is both a waste of time and a possible source of errors. Who knows what Mason will make of an image's binary data? You probably don't want to find out.

By default Mason will use the server's document root for the resolver's comp_root parameter. Mason also needs a data directory to store things like compiled components and cache files. By default, this will be a subdirectory called *mason* under your server's ServerRoot. It is important that this directory be writable by the user or group ID that the Apache children run as, though the ApacheHandler will ensure that this happens if your server is started as the root user.

Both of these defaults can easily be overridden.

```
  PerlSetVar  MasonCompRoot  /var/www/comps
  PerlSetVar  MasonDataDir   /var/mason-data-dir
```

The PerlSetVar directive sets variables that are accessible by Perl modules via the Apache API. Mason uses this API internally to get at these settings.

All of the Interp, Compiler, and Lexer parameters that were discussed in Chapter 6 can be set from the configuration file. A full listing of all the variables that can be set via PerlSetVar directives can be found in Appendix B.

You also may have multiple Mason configurations for different parts of your web server:

```
<VirtualHost 1.2.3.4>
  ServerName  www.example.com
  DocumentRoot  /home/example/htdocs/
  PerlSetVar  MasonCompRoot  /home/example/htdocs
```

```
PerlSetVar  MasonDataDir    /home/example/mason-data

<FilesMatch "\.mhtml$">
 SetHandler   perl-script
 PerlHandler  HTML::Mason::ApacheHandler
</FilesMatch>
</VirtualHost>

<VirtualHost 1.2.3.4>
 ServerName  hello-kitty-heaven.example.com
 DocumentRoot  /home/hello-kitty/htdocs/
 PerlSetVar  MasonCompRoot  /home/hello-kitty/htdocs/mason
 PerlSetVar  MasonDataDir   /home/hello-kitty/mason-data

<FilesMatch "\.mhtml$">
 SetHandler   perl-script
 PerlHandler  HTML::Mason::ApacheHandler
</FilesMatch>
</VirtualHost>
```

In this case, Mason will find the relevant configuration directives when asked to handle a request.

When you have only a single Mason configuration for your server, Mason will attempt to create the objects it needs as early as possible, during the initial server startup.

Doing this increases the amount of shared memory between Apache processes on most systems. The reason is that memory that is not modified after a process forks can be shared between a parent and any children it spawns, at least with some operating systems.

Configuration via Custom Code

When simple configuration variables aren't enough, when you simply must do it the hard way, Mason has an alternative. Write your own code. This method gives you complete control over how Mason handles requests at the cost of a bit of extra code to maintain.

The simplest external script that would work might look something like this:

```
package MyMason::MyApp;

use strict;
use HTML::Mason::ApacheHandler;
use Apache::Request;

my $ah =
  HTML::Mason::ApacheHandler->new
    ( comp_root => '/home/httpd/html',
      data_dir  => '/home/httpd/mason' );
```

```
sub handler {
    my $r = shift;  # Apache request object;

    return $ah->handle_request($r);
}
```

Assume that this file is saved in the Apache configuration directory as *handler.pl*.

Then you'd add a few configuration directives to your Apache configuration file:

```
PerlRequire  handler.pl

<FilesMatch "\.mhtml$">
  SetHandler   perl-script
  PerlHandler  MyMason::MyApp
</FilesMatch>
```

Notice the lack of `PerlSetVar` directives this time. Also note that the value given to the `PerlHandler` directive is now the package you declared in the *handler.pl* file. This combination of script and Apache configuration would give us the exact same results as in the previous section.

Let's go through this in more detail to understand exactly what it is doing. Starting with the Apache configuration piece, we see that we set `PerlHandler` to `MyMason::MyApp`. This tells `mod_perl` to look for a subroutine called `handler()` in the `MyMason::MyApp` namespace. Mason does not include any such thing, so we have to write it ourselves, which is what the script does.

The choice of naming it `MyMason::MyApp` is completely arbitrary. You might prefer something that identifies the project you're working on, like `GooberCorp::WebEmail::Mason` or something like that. It doesn't even need to have the word `Mason` in it, though it will probably improve the clarity of your *httpd.conf* file if it does.

Why are we declaring ourselves as being in the `MyMason::MyApp` namespace? Look at our `PerlHandler` directive. It indicates that the handler subroutine will be found in that same namespace.

The first few lines of the script are simple. The only module that *must* be loaded is `HTML::Mason::ApacheHandler`.

To save some memory, we load `Apache::Request` in this file. Mason would load this for us when it was needed, but we want to make sure it gets loaded during the server startup so memory can be shared.

Then we create the `HTML::Mason::ApacheHandler` object. This object takes an Apache request object and figures out how to dispatch it to Mason.

This object contains an `HTML::Mason::Interp` object. As we discussed in the previous chapter, when a Mason object contains another Mason object, you can pass parameters to the containing object's constructor that are intended for the contained object(s).

This means that parameters that are intended for the Interpreter object's constructor can be passed to the ApacheHandler's new() method. In addition, since the Interpreter contains a Resolver, Compiler, and so forth, you can also pass parameters for those objects to the ApacheHandler constructor.

The handler() subroutine itself is quite simple. The Apache request object is always passed to any handler subroutine by mod_perl. This object is then passed to the ApacheHandler object's handle_request() method. The handle_request() method does all the real work and makes sure that content is sent to the client. Its return value is a status code for the request and the handler() subroutine simply returns this status code to mod_perl, which passes it onto Apache, which handles it however it is configured to do so.

If this were all we did with a handler subroutine it would be awfully pointless. Let's examine a more complicated scenario.

We can rewrite the earlier virtual hosting example to use an external script:

```
PerlRequire  handler.pl

<VirtualHost 1.2.3.4>
 ServerName  www.example.com

 <FilesMatch "\.mhtml$">
  SetHandler   perl-script
  PerlHandler  MyMason::MyApp
 </FilesMatch>
</VirtualHost>

<VirtualHost 1.2.3.4>
 ServerName  hello-kitty-heaven.example.com

 <FilesMatch "\.mhtml$">
  SetHandler   perl-script
  PerlHandler  MyMason::MyApp
 </FilesMatch>
</VirtualHost>
```

That takes care of the Apache configuration file; now the script:

```
package MyMason::MyApp;

use strict;

use HTML::Mason::ApacheHandler;

use Apache::Request;

my %host_to_comp_root =
    ( 'www.example.com' => '/home/example/htdocs',
      'hello-kitty-heaven.example.com' => '/home/hello-kitty/htdocs' );

my %ah;
```

```
sub handler {
    my $r = shift;  # Apache request object;

    my $host = $r->hostname; # tells us what server was requested;
    my $comp_root = $host_to_comp_root{$host};

    # create a new object for this host if none exists yet.
    $ah{$host} ||=
        HTML::Mason::ApacheHandler->new( comp_root => $comp_root );

    return $ah{$host}->handle_request($r);
}
```

This is a rather simple example and doesn't necessarily justify writing a script rather than just configuring via the Apache configuration file. However, let's imagine that we also had the script check in each home directory for extra Mason configuration directives, which could be stored either as pure Perl or in a specified format.

How about if you had to do virtual hosting for 200 domain names? Then some sort of scripted solution becomes more appealing. Of course, you could always write a script to generate the Apache configuration directives too. It really depends on what your needs are. But Mason gives you the flexibility to handle it in the way you think best.

Document Root Versus the Component Root

Apache's document root is what defines the top level web directory of your Apache configuration. For example purposes, let's assume a document root of */home/httpd/ htdocs*. If you request the document */index.html* via your web browser, Apache will look for the file */home/httpd/htdocs/index.html*. If *index.html* contains an HREF to */some/ file.html*, you would have to place a file at */home/httpd/htdocs/some/file.html* for the link to be resolved properly.

Mason has a component root, which is somewhat similar. If Mason's component root is */home/httpd/htdocs/mason*, and a component makes a component call with an absolute path of */some/component*, Mason will look for a file at */home/httpd/htdocs/ mason/some/component*.

It can be confusing when the component root and the document root are not the same because this means that the path for an HREF and a component path, though they may appear to be the same, can point to two different files.

For example, with the preceding configuration, we have the following:

```
<a href="/some/file.html">resolves to /home/httpd/htdocs/some/file.html</a>.
```

```
<& /some/file.html &> resolves to /home/httpd/htdocs/mason/some/file.html.
```

Do you see the difference?

Be sure to keep this in mind while working on your components. To avoid dealing with this problem, you could simply make your document root and component root the same directory and decide whether or not something is a component based on its file extension.

This is generally a bit easier on the brain and is definitely what we recommend for first-time Mason users.

Not OK

By default, if a component does not give an explicit return code, the ApacheHandler object will assume that the request was error free and that the status it should return is OK. But sometimes things are just not OK.

For example, we may want to give an authorization error or a document not found error. There are several ways of doing this.

The first is to have the component that is called return the desired status code. Inside the handle_request() method, the ApacheHandler object checks to see if the component that it called returned a value. If so, it uses this as the status code for the request.

If you try to do this, remember that with autohandler wrapping, the last component executed is not necessarily the first one called. For example, let's assume a component called /give_up.html:

```
<%init>
 # I give up!
 use Apache::Constants qw(NOT_FOUND);
 return NOT_FOUND;
</%init>
```

This component could be wrapped by an /autohandler like this:

```
<html>
<head>
<title>My wonderful site</title>
</head>

<body>
% $m->call_next(%ARGS);
</body>
</html>
```

In this case the return code from the /give_up.html component ends up being ignored.

A better way to do this is to use the Mason request object's abort() method, which we covered in Chapter 4. Using the abort() method, we could rewrite /give_up.html like this:

```
<%init>
 # I give up!
 use Apache::Constants qw(NOT_FOUND);
 $m->abort(NOT_FOUND);
</%init>
```

Any value passed to abort() will eventually be passed to the client. But this still might not work. The problem is the text content in the /autohandler that is generated before /give_up.html is called. Mason sees this before abort() is called and will try to send it to the client. This may be a problem for some non-OK codes, particularly for redirects. We need to clear Mason's buffer in order to make sure that the client doesn't see any output before the error is generated.

```
<%init>
 # I really give up!
 use Apache::Constants qw(NOT_FOUND);
 $m->clear_buffer;
 $m->abort(NOT_FOUND);
</%init>
```

This will work just fine for all return codes, though some may need additional manipulation of the Apache object, $r, depending on the status code being returned.

$r

Every component that is run under Apache via the ApacheHandler module has access to a global variable called $r. This variable is the Apache request object for the current request. Using this variable gives you access to the full Apache API, including the ability to set HTTP headers, send messages to the Apache logs, access Apache configuration information, and much more.

If you used the Apache::Request module to processing incoming arguments, which is Mason's default, then $r will actually be an Apache::Request object.

Documenting what you can do with this object is outside the scope of the book, but do not despair. The mod_perl resources mentioned at the beginning of this chapter, as well as the Apache object's documentation (run perldoc Apache, and if you set args_method to mod_perl, also perldoc Apache::Request), can tell you everything you need to know. It's worth looking at the documentation to get an idea of what kinds of things it's capable of doing.

ApacheHandler Parameters

The ApacheHandler object can take several parameters to its constructor; all of them are optional:

args_method => 'mod_perl' or 'CGI'

> This tells the object what module you would like it to use for parsing incoming query string and POST parameters. CGI indicates that you want to use CGI.pm and mod_perl indicates that you want to use Apache::Request. Apache::Request is faster, uses less memory, and is the default.
>
> You may choose to use CGI.pm if you want to take advantage of its form element generation features or if you cannot use Apache::Request on your operating system.

decline_dirs => *$boolean*

> By default, requests that match directories under a Location or Directory section served by Mason are declined, returning a status code of DECLINED (-1) so that Apache will handle directory requests as it normally does. If you would like to handle these requests with Mason, presumably via a dhandler, you should set this to false.
>
> Obviously, if you told Apache to serve Mason requests based only on a file extension, this parameter is not likely to be meaningful.

apache_status_title => *$string*

> The ApacheHandler object will register itself with mod_perl's Apache::Status module if possible. This registration involves giving Apache::Status a unique title for the registered object. This defaults to "HTML::Mason status" but if you have multiple ApacheHandler objects you may want to give each one a unique title. Otherwise, only one will be visible under the Apache::Status display.

The ApacheHandler module provides a special subclass of the Request object $m. This object has an additional constructor parameter besides those available to normal requests:

auto_send_headers => *$boolean*

> This tells Mason whether or not you'd like it to automatically send the HTTP headers before sending content to a client. By default, this is true, and Mason will call $r->send_http_header() before sending output to the client. If you turn this off, you will need to send the headers yourself.
>
> If you do call the send_http_header() method yourself before Mason has a chance to do so, Mason will not send extra headers, regardless of the value of this variable.

Remember, you can simply pass this value to the ApacheHandler object when you create it, or you can set MasonAutoSendHeaders in your *httpd.conf* file.

To Autoflush or Not to Autoflush

In Chapter 4 we saw that autoflushing can be turned on and off for a request. Whether or not autoflushing is turned on has a big impact on what kind of things you can do while running under Apache.

With autoflush off, you can easily start generating content, have your code throw it away halfway through, and then issue a redirect. This will simply not work with autoflushing on.

For a redirect to work, it has to have a chance to set the headers. Since content is sent as soon as it is created when autoflushing, any redirects that happen after content is generated will happen after the headers have already been sent. This makes it harder to have a flexible application with autoflushing on, and for this reason most people do not use it.

Turning autoflush on can make the response time appear quicker, since the initial output gets to the client sooner. To get the best of both worlds, leave autoflushing off and send quick status reports with `$m->flush_buffer` on the pages that need it.

Generating Something Besides HTML

Eventually you may want to have Mason generate things besides HTML, such as plain text pages, MP3 playlists, or even images. This is quite easy to do. Here's a simple component that generates plain text:

```
I am a piece of plain text.  So boring.  This will not be <b>bold</b>.

<%init>
 $r->content_type('text/plain');
</%init>
```

If you want to generate binary data, you have to be careful to make sure that no extraneous snippets of text sneak into it:

```
<%args>
 $type => 'jpeg'
</%args>

<%init>
 use Apache::Constants qw(OK);

 $m->clear_buffer; # avoid extra output (but it only works when autoflush is off)

 my $img = make_image( type => $type ); # magic hand-waving ...

 $r->content_type("image/$type");
 $r->send_http_header;

 $m->print($img);
```

```
    $m->abort(OK);  # make sure nothing else gets sent
</%init>
```

This component does two things to ensure that nothing corrupts the image's binary data. First, it clears the buffer, because if this component was wrapped by an autohandler there could be some text in the buffer when it is called. Of course, if you've turned on autoflushing, the clear_buffer() method doesn't actually do anything, so you'd have to be extra careful in that situation.

Then, after sending the image, the component flushes the buffer to make sure that output gets sent and then aborts to make sure that nothing gets sent afterward. By passing the OK status code to the abort() method, we make sure that the correct status code makes its way to the client. The abort() method does not prevent output from being sent to the client, so the image is sent as we'd expect.

We put all this code in an <%init> block to make sure that it gets executed right away, before any whitespace from the rest of the component could be processed as output.

Note that Mason's templating capabilities aren't exactly taking center stage in this example. You may ask why Mason is being used in this situation at all. Indeed, without context, it's difficult to see a good reason; however, people have done just this kind of thing in order to take advantage of Mason's other features like dhandlers or to integrate the dynamically generated image into an existing Mason site.

Apache::Status and Mason

As was mentioned earlier, Mason can cooperate with the Apache::Status module to display information about itself. To enable this module is relatively simple. For example, if you'd like the module to be accessible at the URL /perl-status, you could add this to your Apache configuration:

```
<Location /perl-status>
  SetHandler perl-script
  PerlHandler Apache::Status
</Location>
```

Apache::Status provides information about mod_perl in general and allows other modules to provide their own status hooks. Mason provides a basic status report on the ApacheHandler and Interp objects, as well as a list of which components are currently in the code cache.

## CHAPTER 8

Building a Mason Site

This chapter covers, in detail, a full-fledged working web application. Our application is the Perl Apprenticeship site at *http://apprentice.perl.org/*. Back at O'Reilly's 2001 Open Source Conference, Adam Turoff suggested that the Perl community needed a site where people who had project ideas, but either not enough time or not enough expertise, could hook up with other programmers who could supply the missing pieces.

An experienced developer with a really neat idea and not nearly enough time to do it can post a project idea and offer to mentor a less experienced developer in its implementation. Conversely, a less experienced developer with a really neat idea who isn't quite sure how to go forward on it can look for a mentor to help him bring that idea to life.

This is a pretty basic database-backed web application, the kind of thing that Mason gets used for all the time. It didn't require anything too terribly complicated, but it shows off a number of Mason's features quite well, including how components can be used to isolate individual site elements, autohandlers and dhandlers, and a simple use of <%method> blocks.

One thing worth noting is that for database access we chose to use Alzabo, which is a project created and maintained by Dave Rolsky. Alzabo is a database-to-object mapper built on top of the DBI. It allows us to easily create Perl objects representing things in our database, like users or projects. We will not be going into detail on our schema or our Alzabo-related code here, as this is largely incidental to the goal of this chapter. Our hope is that if you don't understand any particular piece of the Alzabo functionality, you can just treat it as pseudocode.*

More information on Alzabo is available online at *http://www.alzabo.org/*. Alzabo is also available from the CPAN.

---

* Or pseudopseudocode, since it's actually code.

The code for the site is available at this book's site, *http://www.masonbook.com/*. This includes an installer that should help you get the site up and running without too much trouble.*

Functionality

The first issue at hand is determining what sort of functionality the site has to have in order to be useful. Our site is fairly simple. It needs to implement the following features:

Index page

> The index page will have a welcome message, site news, and a featured project selected by the site administrator.

Consistent and context-sensitive menu

> The lefthand side of the site is a navigation menu that is context-sensitive. Logged-in users see different options than guest users. Users with site admin options see an additional set of options. However, these options remain the same from page to page.

> Underneath the menu the site shows the five most recent projects entered into the system.

User information

> Some user information will be publicly viewable. This will be users' usernames and email addresses (displayed in an altered form to protect them from robots) and the list of projects with which they are involved. Their real names are not displayed.

Project browsing

> Since we do not anticipate an extremely large number of submissions, at least initially, we decided not to create any complicated search mechanism. The two ways to find projects will be to view a list of all the projects in the system or to browse the projects by category. The user can click on any displayed project to see more detailed information about it.

User accounts

> Users need to be able to create new accounts, retrieve a forgotten password, log in, and log out. In addition, we'd like to let them edit their own accounts.

> Users have the following properties:

> - Username
> - Password
> - Real name

---

* Famous last words, no doubt. Bug reports are always welcome, of course.

- Email address
- Status—available, semi-available, or busy
- Admin flag—is this user a site administrator?

Project editing

Logged-in users should be able to add a new project and edit an existing one for which they have admin privileges. This includes the ability to add and remove project members.

Projects have the following properties:

- Name
- Description
- Creation date
- Difficulty—from one to ten
- Project status—idea or active
- Support level—a lot, some, or a little. If the project is created by a mentor, this is how much support they can provide. If the project is created by an apprentice, this is how much support they think they need.
- Links—each link has a URL and an optional description
- Categories—a project has one or more categories such as database, GUI, and so on.
- Members—a project member is either a mentor or an apprentice. Any project member may be given project admin access.

Site administration

Site administrators should be able to edit any user or project. In addition, site admins can also edit the list of categories available for projects.

Security

A careful reader will notice that passwords are stored in the database in plain text form. This means that someone who hacks into the system where the data is stored won't have to do any extra work to get all the passwords.

In our opinion, this is OK for several reasons. Even if we stored hashed passwords, anyone sophisticated enough to be able to hack the operating system is going to be capable of running a dictionary attack against these passwords once they are retrieved from the database.

Furthermore, we like being able to send people their actual passwords via email when they request it, which is a choice we made in light of the fact that this is a relatively low security site. There is always a trade-off between security and convenience. But don't give us the same password you use for your bank account, OK?

Directory Layout

Because of the nature of Mason's autohandler feature, directory layout is actually an important consideration when designing a site. Of course, you can always override a component's inheritance and inherit from any other component, but it makes sense to come up with a directory layout that minimizes the need to do this.

In the case of the Apprenticeship site, we only have one "skin" we want to apply to all components. This is done in the top-level autohandler. Our subdirectories are then used to implement access controls and dhandlers. Table 8-1 shows our directory layout.

Table 8-1. Apprentice site layout

Directory	Purpose
/	Contains most of the components that can be viewed by any user.
/users	Contains components related to user accounts such as new user sign-up.
/project	Contains a single dhandler that displays a project.
/logged_in	Contains components accessible only to logged-in users such as new project creation.
/admin	Contains components accessible only by site administrators.
/lib	Contains components used by other components. These are not called as top-level components.

File Extensions

We decided to use several different extensions for our components. Files ending in *.html* are top-level components processed by Mason, like */index.html*. Files ending in *.mas* are called only by other components and are not accessible from a browser. In addition, we have a file ending in *.css* that is processed by Mason. This is our stylesheet.

The site has no images, so we don't need to worry about making sure they are served properly.

Apache Configuration

Our Apache configuration will assume that our document root and component root are the same directory, */home/apprentice/htdocs*. This is the simplest solution and is appropriate for a single-purpose web server.

Our configuration in *httpd.conf* begins as follows:

```
PerlModule Apprentice
```

The Apprentice.pm module loads all the Perl modules used by this application, including various Apache::* modules, Digest::SHA1, Time::Piece, and others.

```
PerlSetVar  MasonCompRoot        /home/apprentice/htdocs
PerlSetVar  MasonDataDir         /var/mason

PerlSetVar  MasonAllowGlobals  $Schema
PerlAddVar  MasonAllowGlobals  $User
```

These two objects will be used throughout almost all of the components of our site. Rather than passing them as arguments to every component, which can become extremely tedious, we will create them in our top-level autohandler and limit their lifetime via the use of local().

```
PerlModule HTML::Mason::ApacheHandler

<Directory /home/apprentice/htdocs>
 <FilesMatch "(\.html|\.css)$">
  SetHandler  perl-script
  PerlHandler HTML::Mason::ApacheHandler
 </FilesMatch>
</Directory>
```

As mentioned before, any file ending with *.html* or *.css* should be handled by Mason.

```
<FilesMatch "(\.mas|handler)$">
 SetHandler perl-script
 PerlModule  Apache::Constants
 PerlHandler "sub { return Apache::Constants::NOT_FOUND }"
</FilesMatch>
```

There's no reason to let anyone see our *.mas* components or our autohandlers and dhandlers, so in the interests of security we block them out. We return a NOT FOUND status so that a curious script kiddie won't even know that these files exist.

That's all we need in our Apache configuration to get this site up and running.

The Components

Now that the preliminaries are out of the way, it is time to look at the components that make up this site. We will not be looking at them in line-by-line detail, since this would be excruciatingly dull for all of us. In addition, since a number of components are conceptually similar to one another, we will not show the source for every component, instead saying something along the lines of "this one is mostly like that other one we looked at back there." But if you don't believe us, fear not, because this site's full source code is available at *http://www.masonbook.com/*.

It is worth noting that this site does not use all of Mason's features. Trying to create a site that did that would result in a monstrosity of biblical proportions (and that's big!). Instead, we created a clean, working site that is as elegantly designed as possible. We've tried to err on the side of brevity and pedagogy—we could certainly add more features.

We have done our best to make the HTML in these components compliant with the latest HTML 4.01 Transitional Standard, with one major exception. This standard forbids the presence of forms embedded inside tables, but our design would have been grossly complicated by following this restriction, so we ignored it. Yes, we know this is wrong and bad and that we'll burn in web standards hell for this, but we are lazy and we don't care.

We did our best to keep the HTML in this site relatively simple. For text colors and fonts, we have a simple stylesheet. For layout, we have used the nested tables approach. This produces ugly HTML, but CSS positioning doesn't work with Netscape 4.x or other early browsers. In general, we will not be explaining the HTML portions of the components we examine, since we want to talk about programming with Mason, not how to make nice HTML.

One rule we did follow is that any table or portion of a table, such as a <tr> or <td> tag, must start and end in the same component, because it can be extremely confusing when one component starts a table that another component finishes.

In addition, we have tried to make individual components self-contained whenever possible, so individual components often consist of one or more complete tables. Since tables can be embedded in other tables' cells, this makes it safe to call components from within a single table cell.

The Unrestricted Parts

A good place to start with the site is the index page and the other pages that are viewable by anybody without logging in.

Here are the components, in the order we'll discuss them:

/syshandler	/news.mas	/project/dhandler
/autohandler	/featured_project.mas	/users/new_user.html
/apprentice.css	/all_projects.html	/users/user_form.mas
/left_side_menu.mas	/search_results.mas	/users/new_user_submit.html
/lib/url.mas	/lib/paging_controls.mas	/users/login_submit.html
/latest_projects.mas	/lib/redirect.mas	/users/logout.html
/lib/format_date.mas	/lib/set_login_cookie.mas	/users/forgot_password.html
/index.html	/user.html	/users/forgot_password_submit.html
/welcome.mas	/login_form.html	/show_category.html
		/browse.html

These components form the bulk of the site, with the remainder being those pieces intended for logged-in users and site administrators.

/syshandler

> This is a component from which the top-level autohandler, /autohandler, inherits. Its job is to create a few objects that are used on almost every page. While some components don't inherit from the autohandler, they still inherit from this

component in order to be able to use these objects. This is useful because some of our components don't need the look and feel wrapping provided by the top-level autohandler.

The component itself is fairly simple. In the <%once> section, we create our schema object, $Schema, which is our point of entry for access to the database and therefore needed in almost every component. It is analogous to a DBI database handle, but at a higher level of abstraction. Since we need it everywhere and there is no point in re-creating it for each request, it is simply a global.

The $User object represents the currently logged-in user or a guest user. Since the API for these two types of users is the same, the components don't need to care about whether or not a user has logged in when using the $User object.

The bit that deals with the cookie is simply checking to see if the user is who she claims to be, using a MAC (Message Authentication Code) generated by the SHA1 algorithm.

This is a fairly common authentication technique. When a user logs in, we use the Digest::SHA1 module to generate a unique string based on the user's user ID and a secret stored on the server (in our case the secret is a phrase). We then send the user a cookie containing this user ID and the generated MAC.

When the user returns to the site, we simply regenerate the MAC based on the user ID that the cookie claims to represent. If the MAC matches what we would expect, we know that it is a valid cookie. If not, either the cookie got corrupted or someone is trying to trick us. This component only checks the cookie's value; it doesn't generate it. The cookie is generated in a different component that we will discuss later.

We place the call to the row_by_pk() method in an eval{} block because the method will throw an exception if the row doesn't exist, and we want to ignore this failure. This technique is used throughout the site.

Once we have some sort of user object, representing either a guest or a real user, we simply call the next component. In most cases, this will be the autohandler located at /autohandler.

We use the inherit flag to explicitly turn off inheritance for this component in order to prevent an inheritance loop between this component and the /autohandler component.

Although we promised not to spend too much time on Alzabo, we will point out that methods ending in _t return table objects, and that methods ending in _c return column objects, just in case you were curious.

```
<%once>
 $Schema = Apprentice::Data->schema;
</%once>
<%init>
 my %cookies = Apache::Cookie->fetch;
```

```
# A "potential row" is an object that looks like something from the
# database but that does not really exist.  However, it has the
# same interface so it is handy for things like a generic "guest"
# user.
my $guest = $Schema->User_t->potential_row( values => { username => 'Guest' } );
my $user;
if ( exists $cookies{apprentice_user_login} )
{
    my %user_info = $cookies{apprentice_user_login}->value;

    if ( $user_info{user_id} && $user_info{MAC} )
    {
        # This method of using a MAC to make sure a cookie is valid
        # is discussed in the Eagle Book.
        my $MAC = Digest::SHA1::sha1_hex
                    ( $user_info{user_id}, $Apprentice::Secret );

        # If the cookie's MAC matches the one we generate, we know
        # that the cookie has not been tampered with.
        if ( $user_info{MAC} eq $MAC )
        {
            # This will be a _real_ row object, representing an
            # actual entry in the User table
            $user = eval { $Schema->User_t->row_by_pk
                            ( pk => $user_info{user_id} ) };
        }
    }
}

local $User = $user || $guest;

$m->call_next;
</%init>
<%flags>
 inherit => undef
</%flags>
```

/autohandler

This component establishes the look of the site though most of the work is dele-
gated to other components and methods. The call to SELF:title allows individual components to override or add to the basic title of "The Perl Apprenticeship
Site," the default title.

We start a basic table, stick a title banner on the top of the page, and make a few
component calls. The first component called, *left_side_menu.mas*, generates a
menu down the left side of the page. This menu is part of every page.

The next component, *latest_projects.mas*, lists the five most recently created
projects. This is a nice way to show what's new on the site.

Finally, we invoke the call_next() method of the request object to pass control
onto the next component.

The Screen shot of the index page in Figure 8-1 shows how this looks in practice.

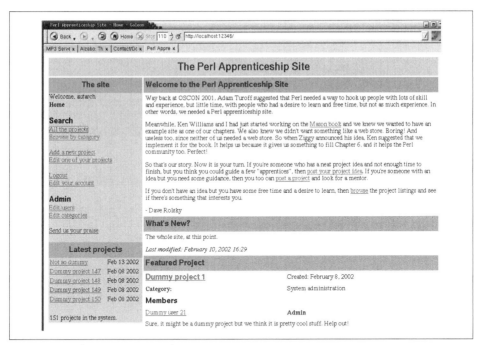

Figure 8-1. Perl Apprentice site index page

The parts handled by the autohandler are the title across the top that says "The Perl Apprenticeship Site," and everything down the left side. These portions of the page remain more or less the same on every page of the site. The pieces in the right two-thirds of the page are generated by the page specified by the client's request (see Figure 8-2). In this case, that part of the page was generated by the */index.html* component.

As noted before, this */autohandler* component inherits from the */syshandler* component.

```
<!DOCTYPE HTML PUBLIC "-//W3C//DTD HTML 4.01 Transitional//EN">
<html>
<head>
<meta http-equiv="Content-Type" content="text/html; charset=utf-8">
<title><& SELF:title, %ARGS &></title>
<link rel="stylesheet" href="<& /lib/url.mas, path => '/apprentice.css' &>"
    type="text/css">
</head>

<body bgcolor="#FFFFFF">

<table width="100%" cellspacing="3" cellpadding="0">
 <tr valign="middle">
  <td colspan="3" bgcolor="#CCCCCC" align="center">
   <h1 class="headline">The Perl Apprenticeship Site</h1>
  </td>
```

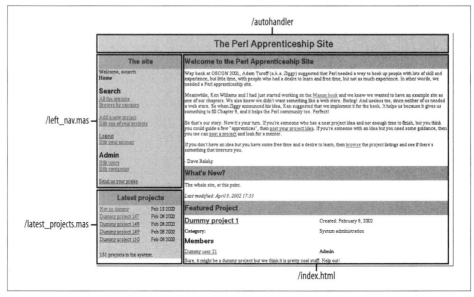

Figure 8-2. Perl Apprentice site divided into pieces

```
  </tr>
  <tr valign="top">
   <td width="240">
<& left_side_menu.mas, %ARGS &>
<& latest_projects.mas &>
   </td>
   <td>
% $m->call_next;
   </td>
  </tr>
 </table>

</body>
</html>
<%flags>
 inherit => '/syshandler'
</%flags>
<%method title>
 Perl Apprenticeship Site
</%method>
```

/apprentice.css

Mason doesn't have to be used just to generate HTML. This component generates a stylesheet for the site. It is dynamic because we want to have a smaller
body font if the browser is Internet Explorer. Other than that, it is just standard
text. This stylesheet is based in part on one created by Ask Bjørn Hansen for the
perl.org sites, including *http://dev.perl.org/* and *http://jobs.perl.org/*.

Setting the inherit flag to undef ensures that this component is not wrapped by any autohandler.

```
/* Netscape 4 doesn't inherit from the body class so we need to
   specify everything. */
body, table, td, p, span, ul
{
  color: black; font-size: <% $font_size %>; font-family: serif
}

h1
{ font-size: 16pt;
  font-weight: bold;
  font-family: sans-serif
}

h1.headline
{ color: #003366;
  line-height: 200%;
  font-size: 16pt;
  font-weight: bold;
  font-family: sans-serif
}

h2
{ font-size: 13pt;
  font-weight: bold;
  font-family: sans-serif
}

h2.headline
{
  color: #003399;
  line-height: 150%;
  font-size: 13pt;
  font-weight: bold;
  font-family: sans-serif
}

h3
{
  font-size: 12pt;
  font-weight: bold;
  font-family: sans-serif
}

td.heading
{
  background-color: #AAAAAA
}

.error
{
  color: #CC3333;
```

```
      font-size: 10pt
    }

    a:vlink
    { color: #690020 }

    a:active
    { color: #003600 }

    a:hover
    { color: #696040 }

    a:link
    { color: #900000 }

    <%init>
     $r->content_type('text/css');

     # For some reason IE seems to make fonts look bigger.
     my $font_size = "10pt";
     $font_size = "9pt" if $r->header_in("User-Agent") =~ m/MSIE/;
    </%init>
    <%flags>
     inherit => undef
    </%flags>
```

/left_side_menu.mas

This component is longer than any of the previous ones, but not significantly more complicated. Several features are worth noting here.

The first is that the menu changes based on whether or not the return value from $User->is_logged_in() is true. The $User object was generated in the */syshandler* component and may represent either a guest user or a real logged-in user.

If a user has logged in, she sees options that allow her to create a new project, edit any projects for which she may have editing access, change her user account information, and log out. The link to edit projects appears only if she actually has editing access to one or more projects.

Note that we construct all URLs using the */lib/url.mas* component, which we will examine later. This component handles the construction of properly escaped URLs of arbitrary complexity. Using this component for all URLs would make it easy to add in something like URL-based sessions later on.

For the Logout URL, we are regenerating the URL, and query string, if any, for the current page. We do this because the component that handles logouts, */users/logout.html*, will redirect the client back to the page where she clicked on the Logout link.

Getting back to the menu component, we can see that if the user is not logged in, we generate a form that POSTs to the */user/login_submit.html* component. Again, we will be passing in the current URL and query string parameters to the login component so that it can send the user back where she came from, with either a cookie indicating a successful login or an error message. That error message is handled just above where the form starts, where we check the variable $login_error.

We take advantage of the fact that a POST request can also have a query string in order to put the %caller_args hash into the query string, where we can be sure that keys and values will be received by the server in the right order. If we put the keys and values in the form itself as hidden fields, there is no guarantee that the browser will submit them in the order we specify.

A bit further on, we see that if the $User->is_admin() method returns true we add a few extra links for the site administrators.

The <%filter> section for this component shows a common application of filtering. We first determine the URL for our current page. Then, if there is a link in the menu that matches that page, we replace the anchor tag (<a>) with a bold tag (<b>).

We need to special-case the URL *index.html* because the link for this particular page is simply <a href="/">. We do this with a regular expression so that it'll work properly if we decide to add links to other directories here in the future.

```
<table width="100%" bgcolor="#CCCCCC" cellspacing="0" cellpadding="5">
 <tr>
  <td colspan="2" align="center" class="heading">
   <h2 class="headline">The site</h2>
  </td>
 </tr>
</table>
<table width="100%" bgcolor="#CCCCCC" cellspacing="0" cellpadding="1">
 <tr>
  <td colspan="2">Welcome, <% $User->username %></td>
 </tr>
 <tr>
  <td colspan="2"><a href="<& /lib/url.mas, path => '/' &>">Home</a></td>
 </tr>
 <tr>
  <td colspan="2"> </td>
 </tr>
 <tr>
  <td colspan="2"><h3>Search</h3></td>
 </tr>
 <tr>
  <td colspan="2">
   <a href="<& /lib/url.mas,
             path => '/all_projects.html' &>">All the projects</a>
  </td>
 </tr>
 <tr>
  <td colspan="2">
   <a href="<& /lib/url.mas, path => '/browse.html' &>">Browse by category</a>
  </td>
 </tr>
```

```
% if ( $User->is_logged_in ) {
 <tr>
  <td colspan="2"> </td>
 </tr>
 <tr>
  <td colspan="2">
   <a href="<& /lib/url.mas,
              path => '/logged_in/new_project.html' &>">Add a new project</a>
  </td>
 </tr>
%   if ( $User->has_projects ) {
 <tr>
  <td colspan="2">
   <a href="<& /lib/url.mas,
              path => '/logged_in/editable_project_list.html' &>">
    Edit one of your projects</a>
  </td>
 </tr>
%   }
% }
 <tr>
  <td colspan="2"> </td>
 </tr>
% if ( $User->is_logged_in ) {
 <tr>
  <td colspan="2">
   <a href="<& /lib/url.mas,
              path => '/users/logout.html',
              query => { caller_url  => $r->uri,
                         caller_args => \%query_args },
            &>">Logout</a></td>
 </tr>
 <tr>
  <td colspan="2">
   <a href="<& /lib/url.mas,
              path => '/logged_in/edit_self.html' &>">Edit your account</a>
  </td>
 </tr>
% } elsif ( $r->uri !~ m,/login_form, ) {
 <tr>
  <td colspan="2"><h3>Login</h3></td>
 </tr>
%   if ($login_error) {
 <tr>
  <td colspan="2"><span class="error"><% $login_error | h %></td>
 </tr>
%   }
 <form action="<& /lib/url.mas,
                  path => '/users/login_submit.html',
                  query => { caller_url  => $r->uri,
                             caller_args => \%query_args }
                &>" method="POST">
 <tr>
  <td>Username:</td>
```

```
 <td><input type="text" name="username"></td>
</tr>
<tr>
 <td>Password:</td>
 <td><input type="password" name="password"></td>
</tr>
<tr>
 <td colspan="2"><input type="submit" value="Submit"></td>
</tr>
</form>
<tr>
 <td colspan="2">
  <a href="<& /lib/url.mas,
             path => '/users/forgot_password.html' &>">Forgot my password</a>
 </td>
</tr>
<tr>
 <td colspan="2">
  <a href="<& /lib/url.mas, path => '/users/new_user.html' &>">New user</a>
 </td>
</tr>
% }
% if ($User->is_admin) {
 <tr>
  <td colspan="2"> </td>
 </tr>
 <tr>
  <td colspan="2"><h3>Admin</h3></td>
 </tr>
 <tr>
  <td colspan="2">
   <a href="<& /lib/url.mas, path => '/admin/user_list.html' &>">Edit users</a>
  </td>
 </tr>
 <tr>
  <td colspan="2">
   <a href="<& /lib/url.mas,
              path => '/admin/edit_categories.html' &>">Edit categories</a>
  </td>
 </tr>
% }
 <tr>
  <td colspan="2"> </td>
 </tr>
 <tr>
  <td colspan="2">
   <a href="mailto:dave@perl.org">Complaints / Compliments?</a>
  </td>
 </tr>
 <tr>
  <td colspan="2"> </td>
 </tr>
</table>
<%args>
```

```
  $username => ''
  $login_error => ''
</%args>
<%init>
 my %query_args = $m->request_args;

 # These arguments are intended for use on this page and do not need
 # to be passed through to the login_submit.html component
 delete @query_args{ 'username', 'login_error' };
</%init>
<%filter>
 (my $url = $r->uri) =~ s/index\.html$//;
 $url = $m->scomp( '/lib/url.mas', path => $url );

 s{<a href="$url">([^<]+)</a>}
  {<b>$1</b>};
</%filter>
```

/lib/url.mas

The purpose of this component is to construct a properly escaped and formatted query string based on the parameters it receives.

It would not be able to handle nested data structures or objects as values of the
%query hash. For these, it would be necessary for us to use a session mechanism
rather than trying to pass them around in the URL.*

Because the URI object's query_form( ) method doesn't allow hash references, we
convert any hash references we find in the %query values to array references
before passing %query to the query_form( ) method.

While right now we are not taking advantage of most of the parameters this
component allows us to pass, these were easy to implement and may come in
handy in the future.

The backslash at the end of the last line is there to ensure that we don't accidentally add a new line to the URL.

```
<%args>
 $scheme   => 'http'
 $username => undef
 $password => ''
 $host     => undef
 $port     => undef
 $path
 %query    => ()
 $fragment => undef
</%args>
<%init>
 my $uri = URI->new;

 if ($host) {
```

---

* See Chapter 11 for some session code examples.

```
    $uri->scheme($scheme);

    if (defined $username) {
      $uri->authority( "$username:$password" );
    }

    $uri->host($host);
    $uri->port($port) if $port;
}

# Sometimes we may want to path in a query string
# but the URI module will escape the question mark.
my $q;

if ( $path =~ s/\?(.*)$// ) {
    $q = $1;
}

$uri->path($path);

# If there was a query string, we integrate it into the query
# parameter.
if ($q) {
    %query = ( %query, split /[&=]/, $q );
}

# $uri->query_form doesn't handle hash ref values properly
while ( my ( $key, $value ) = each %query ) {
    $query{$key} = ref $value eq 'HASH' ? [ %$value ] : $value;
}

$uri->query_form(%query) if %query;

$uri->fragment($fragment) if $fragment;
</%init>
<% $uri->canonical | n %>\
```

/latest_projects.mas

With this component, we display the five most recently added projects. These projects are then displayed with their names and their creation dates. The date, which is returned from MySQL in the format of 'YYYY-MM-DD', is formatted via the */lib/format_date.mas* component.

This is the first time we have seen a project link. All project links are of the form */project/<project id number>.html*. Obviously, we do not actually have files with names like */project/10012491.html*. These URLs are intercepted by a dhandler instead. Underneath these links we show the total count of projects in the system.

Since we want this site to work properly from the moment it is made live, we also have to handle the case in which we have *no* projects in the system. Hopefully, this code path will not be followed for very long, but it is important.

```
<table width="100%" bgcolor="#CCCCCC" cellspacing="0" cellpadding="5">
 <tr>
  <td colspan="2" align="center" class="heading">
   <h2 class="headline">Latest projects</h2>
  </td>
 </tr>
</table>
<table width="100%" bgcolor="#CCCCCC" cellspacing="0" cellpadding="3">
% if ($count) {
%   while (my $project = $projects->next) {
 <tr>
  <td>
   <a href="<& /lib/url.mas,
              path => '/project/' . $project->project_id . '.html' &>">
    <% $project->name | h %></a>
  </td>
  <td>
   <& /lib/format_date.mas, date => $project->creation_date, short => 1 &>
  </td>
 </tr>
%   }
 <tr>
  <td colspan="2"> </td>
 </tr>
 <tr>
  <td colspan="2">
   <% $count %> project<% $count > 1 ? 's' : '' %> in the system.
  </td>
 </tr>
% } else {
 <tr>
  <td colspan="2">No projects in the system.</td>
 </tr>
% }
</table>
<%init>
 my $count = $Schema->Project_t->row_count;

 # This grabs a list of the five most recent projects, sorted first
 # by descending creation date, and then by name in ascending.
 my $projects = $Schema->Project_t->all_rows
   ( order_by => [ $Schema->Project_t->creation_date_c, 'desc',
                   $Schema->Project_t->name_c,          'asc' ],
     limit => 5,
   );
</%init>
```

/lib/format_date.mas

This simple component takes a date as returned by MySQL and turns it into a friendlier format. It can produce either a short ("Feb 24, 1970") or long ("February 24, 1970") date.

The particular formats used were chosen because they are understandable to (English-reading) users around the world. A purely numeric format such as

"02/10/2002" can be ambiguous, depending on whether you are expecting the American or European ordering of the date components.

A smarter site might allow users to specify their preference as part of their account.

```
<%args>
 $date
 $short => 0
</%args>
<%init>
 my $format;

 if ( $short ) {
     $format = '%b %d, %Y';
 } else {
     $format = '%B %e, %Y';
 }

 # remove time if it exists
 $date =~ s/ .*$//;
</%init>
<% Time::Piece->strptime( $date, '%Y-%m-%d' )->strftime($format) %>\
```

/index.html

Hey, there's nothing there!

Our index page simply calls a number of other components and provides almost nothing of its own. It does override the title method defined in the /*autohandler* component. The <& PARENT:title &> method call will call the title method in the /*autohandler* component which, as we saw previously, simply produced the string "Perl Apprenticeship Site". After this we add " - Home" to identify the page.

So now we should examine the components that actually make up our index page.

```
<& welcome.mas &>
<& news.mas &>
<& featured_project.mas &>

<%method title>
 <& PARENT:title &> - Home
</%method>
```

/welcome.mas

This component contains exactly one piece of code. In the course of our paragraph encouraging participation in the site, we want to offer context-appropriate links. Guest users should be encouraged to log in if they have an account or to create a new account. But a user who has already logged in should see links to create a new project.

This was something we did just because we could. It makes the site a little smarter and was easy to do with Mason.

```
<table width="100%" cellspacing="0" cellpadding="5">
 <tr>
  <td class="heading">
   <h2 class="headline">Welcome to the Perl Apprenticeship Site</h2>
  </td>
 </tr>
 <tr>
  <td>
   <p>
   Way back at OSCON 2001, Adam Turoff (a.k.a. Ziggy) suggested that
   Perl needed a way to hook up people with lots of skill and
   experience, but little time, with people who had a desire to
   learn and free time, but not as much experience.  In other words,
   we needed a Perl apprenticeship site.
   </p>

   <p>
   Meanwhile, Ken Williams and I had just started working on the <a
   href="http://www.masonbook.com/">Mason book</a> and we knew we
   wanted to have an example site as one of our chapters.  We also
   knew we didn't want something like a web store.  Boring!  And
   useless too, since neither of us needed a web store.  So when Ziggy
   announced his idea, Ken suggested that we implement it for the
   book.  It helps us because it gives us something to fill Chapter 8,
   and it helps the Perl community too.  Perfect!
   </p>

   <p>
   So that's our story.  Now it's your turn.  If you're someone who
   has a neat project idea and not enough time to finish, but you
   think you could guide a few 'apprentices', then
% if ($User->is_logged_in) {
   <a href="<& /lib/url.mas, path => '/logged_in/new_project.html' &>">
   post your project idea</a>.
   If you're someone with an idea but you need some guidance, then you
   too can <a href="<& /lib/url.mas, path => '/logged_in/new_project.html' &>">
   post a project</a>
   and look for a mentor.
% } else {
   log in over in the left menu or
   <a href="<& /lib/url.mas, path => '/users/new_user.html' &>">create
   a new account</a>
% }
   </p>

   <p>
   If you don't have an idea but you have some free time and a desire
   to learn, then <a href="<& /lib/url.mas, path => '/browse.html' &>">
   browse</a> the project
   listings and see if there's something that interests you.
   </p>

   <p>
   - Dave Rolsky
```

```
        </p>
      </td>
    </tr>
  </table>
```

/news.mas

New features of the site will be displayed with this component simply by editing its text.

We get the last modified time for the component by calling stat() on the component file. We figure that the only time this component will be changed is when there is new news. For now, the whole site is new, so there is not much news other than that.

```
<table width="100%" cellspacing="0" cellpadding="5">
  <tr>
    <td class="heading"><h2 class="headline">What's New?</h2></td>
  </tr>
  <tr>
    <td>
      <p>
      The whole site, at this point.
      </p>

      <p>
      <em>Last modified: <% $last_mod %></em>
      </p>
    </td>
  </tr>
</table>
<%init>
  my $comp_time = (stat $m->current_comp->source_file)[9];
  my $last_mod =
      Time::Piece->strptime( $comp_time, '%s' )->strftime( '%B %e, %Y %H:%M' );
</%init>
```

/featured_project.mas

This component is something that can be used to feature a particular project if one catches the eye of the site admins. An admin can simply edit the value of the $project_id variable in the <%init> section. If this value is set to zero or undef, the component will simply return before generating any text, which gives us a way to not feature any project at all.

We could have stored information on the featured project in the database, and in the future we may go that route. But for now we decided to keep it simple and just assume that this task can be done by someone with access to component files on the web server.

Of course, this particular method of storing the featured project would not scale well if the site were served by multiple web servers.

It is also worth noting that we can easily feature more than one project. Imagine that the <%init> section started thusly:

```
my @ids = (1, 3, 129, 440);
my $project_id = $ids[ rand @ids ];
```

Now each time the page is generated, one of the four project IDs in the @ids variable will be chosen as the featured project. Simple.

```
<table width="100%" cellspacing="0" cellpadding="5">
 <tr>
  <td class="heading" colspan="2">
   <h2 class="headline">Featured Project</h2>
  </td>
 </tr>
 <tr>
  <td>
   <h2><a href="<& /lib/url.mas,
                   path => "/project/$project_id.html" &>">
    <% $project->name | h %></a></h2>
  </td>
  <td>Created: <& /lib/format_date.mas, date => $project->creation_date &></td>
 </tr>
 <tr>
  <td><b>Categor<% @categories > 1 ? 'ies' : 'y' %>:</b></td>
  <td><% join ', ', @categories %></td>
 </tr>
 <tr>
  <td colspan="2"><h3>Members</h3></td>
 </tr>
% while ( my $user = $members->next ) {
 <tr>
  <td>
   <a href="<& /lib/url.mas,
               path  => '/user.html',
               query => { user_id => $user->user_id } &>">
    <% $user->username | h %></a>
  </td>
  <td>
%   if ($project->user_is_admin($user)) {
<b>Admin</b>
%   } else {
 
%   }
  </td>
 </tr>
% }
 <tr>
  <td colspan="2">
   <% HTML::FromText::text2html ( $project->description, paras => 1 ) %>
  </td>
 </tr>
 <tr>
  <td colspan="2">
   <p>
   Sure, it might be a dummy project but we think it is pretty cool
   stuff.  Help out!
   </p>
```

```
    </td>
   </tr>
  </table>
  <%init>
   my $project_id = 1;

   return unless $project_id;

   my $project = eval { $Schema->Project_t->row_by_pk( pk => $project_id ) }
        || return;

   # This grabs all of the project's members, ordered by their admin
   # status and then their username.
   my $members =
       $Schema->join( select => $Schema->User_t,
                      join   =>
                      [ $Schema->tables( 'ProjectMember', 'User' ) ],
                      where  =>
                      [ $Schema->ProjectMember_t->project_id_c, '=', $project_id ],
                      order_by =>
                      [ $Schema->ProjectMember_t->is_project_admin_c, 'desc',
                        $Schema->User_t->username_c, 'asc' ] );

   my @categories =
       map { $_->name }
       $project->Categories( order_by => $Schema->Category_t->name_c )->all_rows;
  </%init>
```

We used the handy HTML::FromText module (available on CPAN) to take the text description of the project and turn it into HTML. We tell it that the text is "paragraph-oriented" via the paras => 1 parameter so that it will turn line breaks into the proper HTML tags.

/all_projects.html

This component actually delegates most of its work to the /search_results.mas component. All this component does is create a cursor representing the rows of interest for this query. In this case, the query is simply 'all projects'. We take advantage of the limit and offset features of MySQL in order to select only those rows we are interested in. As we shall see in a moment, the /search_results.mas component displays paged results, 20 per page.

In addition, this component needs to get a count of how many rows this query *would* get without the limit. It also creates a textual description of the search it is doing so that this can be displayed to the user.

The $start and $limit arguments are part of the results paging system, and any component that implements a search query must accept them in order for the paging system to work.

```
<& search_results.mas,
   count => $count,
   projects => $projects,
   summary => $summary,
```

```
     start => $start,
     limit => $limit,
     %ARGS
   &>
  <%args>
  $start => 0
  $limit => 20
  </%args>
  <%init>
  my $summary = 'all projects';

  my $count = $Schema->Project_t->row_count;

  my $projects =
      $Schema->Project_t->all_rows
         ( order_by =>
           [ $Schema->Project_t->creation_date_c, 'desc',
             $Schema->Project_t->name_c,          'asc' ],
           limit => [ $limit, $start ],
         );
  </%init>
  <%method title>
  <& PARENT:title &> - All projects
  </%method>
```

/search_results.mas

This is where the actual work of displaying results is done. This component is currently used by just two other components, but it is designed so that if we add more search options, such as a keyword search, it can handle those as well.

This component takes the $summary and $count arguments and uses them to tell the user what kind of search he just did (in case he forgot) and how many results there were in total.

If there are more results than can be shown on one page, it calls the */lib/paging_controls.mas* component to do the work of generating links to all the other pages of results.

Finally, if there were results, it loops through the cursor and displays information about each project in turn.

```
<table width="100%" cellspacing="0" cellpadding="5">
 <tr>
  <td class="heading" colspan="4">
   <h2 class="headline">Search Results</h2>
  </td>
 </tr>
 <tr>
  <td colspan="4">
   You searched for <% $summary | h %>.
   There <% $count == 1 ? 'is' : 'are' %> <% $count %>
   result<% $count != 1 ? 's' : '' %>.
  </td>
 </tr>
```

```
% if ($count > $limit) {
 <tr>
  <td colspan="4">
<& /lib/paging_controls.mas, %ARGS &>
  </td>
 </tr>
% }
% if ($count) {
 <tr>
  <td width="40%"><b>Name</b></td>
  <td width="30%"><b>Created on</b></td>
  <td width="15%"><b>Difficulty</b></td>
  <td width="15%"><b>Project status</b></td>
 </tr>
%    while (my $project = $projects->next) {
 <tr>
  <td>
   <a href="<& /lib/url.mas,
               path => '/project/' . $project->project_id . '.html' &>">
    <% $project->name | h %></a>
  </td>
  <td><& /lib/format_date.mas, date => $project->creation_date &></td>
  <td><% $project->difficulty %></td>
  <td><% $project->status %></td>
 </tr>
%    }
% }
</table>
<%args>
 $count
 $projects
 $summary
 $start
 $limit
</%args>
```

/lib/paging_controls.mas

Generating paged search results is a common need in web applications. If you have a database of hundreds, thousands, or more searchable items, you need a way to handle large result sets. The usual way to do this is to break the results into multiple pages, showing a certain number per page with links to other pages.

This component generates the links to the others pages, which look something like this:

```
<< 1 2 3 4 5 6 7 8 >>
```

The "<<" link moves one page back while the ">>" link moves one page forward. The page the user is currently viewing is marked with bold text instead of being a link. If the user is on the first or last page, the previous or next page links are not shown.

This is all fine until you have something like 100 pages. At that point you need another level of navigation, so we will end up with something like this:

    ... << 21 22 23 24 25 26 27 28 29 30 >> ...

The first "..." link will move back to the last page of the previous group of 10, in this case page 20. The end "..." link will move to the beginning of the next group of 10, in this case, page 31.

This design is capable of handling a large number of pages gracefully, although if you anticipated that you would often be generating result sets consisting of thousands of items, you might want to add additional navigation links that allowed the user to jump forward and backward in larger chunks.

One interesting aspect of this component is how it generates its links. Instead of requiring that a URL be passed in to the component, we use the Apache request object's uri() method to determine the current URL. To find out what arguments were passed to the page, we use the $m->request_args() method. We do this because we just want to reproduce the arguments passed in by the client, not any generated by component calls earlier in the call stack. We delete the limit and start arguments since we will be overriding them for each link.

```
<table width="100%">
 <tr>
  <td>Displaying results <% $start + 1 %> - <% $last_shown %>.</td>
 </tr>
</table>
<table width="100%">
 <tr>
  <td width="7%">
% if ( $previous_tenth >= 10 ) {
    <a href="<& /lib/url.mas,
               path => $r->uri,
               query => { start => ($previous_tenth - 1) * $limit,
                          limit => $limit,
                          %query }
             &>">...</a>
% } else {
     
% }
  </td>
  <td width="7%">
% if ( $current_page > 1 ) {
    <a href="<& /lib/url.mas,
               path => $r->uri,
               query => { start => $start - $limit,
                          limit => $limit,
                          %query }
             &>">&lt;&lt;</a>
% }
  </td>
% foreach  my $page ( ($previous_tenth + 1)..($next_tenth - 1) ) {
%   if ( $page <= $total_pages ) {
```

```
   <td width="7%">
%      if ( $page != $current_page ) {
   <a href="<& /lib/url.mas,
             path => $r->uri,
             query => { start => ($page - 1) * $limit,
                        limit => $limit,
                        %query }
          &>"><% $page %></a>
%      } else {
   <b><% $page %></b>
%      }
%   } else {
    
%   }
% }
   </td>
   <td width="7%">
% if ( $current_page < $total_pages ) {
   <a href="<& /lib/url.mas,
             path => $r->uri,
             query => { start => $start + $limit,
                        limit => $limit,
                        %query }
          &>">&gt;&gt;</a>
% } else {
    
% }
   </td>
   <td width="7%">
% if ( $next_tenth <= $total_pages ) {
   <a href="<& /lib/url.mas,
             path => $r->uri,
             query => { start => ($next_tenth - 1) * $limit,
                        limit => $limit,
                        %query }
          &>">...</a>
% } else {
    
% }
   </td>
  </tr>
</table>
<%args>
 $start
 $limit
 $count
</%args>
<%init>
 my %query = $m->request_args;
 delete @query{ 'start', 'limit' };

 my $total_pages = int( $count / $limit );
 $total_pages++ if $count % $limit;
```

```
    my $current_page = ( $start / $limit ) + 1;

    my $previous_tenth =
        $current_page -
        ( $current_page % $limit ? $current_page % $limit : $limit );

    my $next_tenth = $previous_tenth + 11;

    my $last_shown = $start + $limit > $count ? $count : $start + $limit;
</%init>
```

/browse.html

This page simply iterates through all the different project categories. If a category has projects, then we generate a link to browse that category.

```
<table width="100%" cellspacing="0" cellpadding="5">
 <tr>
  <td class="heading"><h2 class="headline">Browse by Category</h2></td>
 </tr>
% while (my $category = $categories->next) {
 <tr>
  <td>
%   if (my $count = $category->project_count) {
   <a href="<& /lib/url.mas,
             path  => 'show_category.html',
             query => { category_id => $category->category_id } &>">
    <% $category->name | h %></a>
    (<% $count %> project<% $count > 1 ? 's' : '' %>)
%   } else {
    <% $category->name | h %> (No projects)
%   }
  </td>
 </tr>
% }
</table>
<%init>
 my $categories =
     $Schema->Category_t->all_rows( order_by => $Schema->Category_t->name_c );
</%init>
<%method title>
 <& PARENT:title &> - Browse by category
</%method>
```

/show_category.html

This is what */browse.html* links to for each category. This code is quite similar to what we saw in */all_projects.html* and uses the same component, */search_results. mas*, to do all the real work.

One feature new to this component is that the title method dynamically adds the category name to the page title. We used a <%shared> section here in order to avoid creating the same category object twice. If the category ID we are given is invalid, then we simply redirect the user back to the home page. It's lazy but it's better than simply showing an error message.

```
<& search_results.mas,
   count => $count,
   projects => $projects,
   summary => $summary,
   start => $start,
   limit => $limit,
   %ARGS
&>
<%shared>
 my $category =
     eval { $Schema->Category_t->row_by_pk
                 ( pk => $m->request_args->{category_id} ) }
         || $m->comp( '/lib/redirect.mas', path => '/' );
</%shared>
<%args>
 $start => 0
 $limit => 20
 $category_id
</%args>
<%init>
 my $summary = 'projects in the "' . $category->name . '" category';

 my $count = $category->project_count;

 my $projects =
     $Schema->join( select => $Schema->Project_t,
                    join   =>
                    [ $Schema->tables( 'Project', 'ProjectCategory' ) ],
                    where  =>
                    [ $Schema->ProjectCategory_t->category_id_c, '=',
                      $category_id ],
                    order_by =>
                    [ $Schema->Project_t->creation_date_c, 'desc',
                      $Schema->Project_t->name_c,          'asc' ],
                    limit => [ $limit, $start ],
                  );
</%init>

<%method title>
 <& PARENT:title &> - <% $category->name | h %> projects
</%method>
```

/user.html

This is our user info display component. There's not much here that we haven't seen before. Make some objects, display some information from the objects. Been there, done that.

Note that this isn't actually duplicating code from other components, though. It's just similar to them.

/project/dhandler

This component is quite similar to the */user.html* component but instead of being called with a query string, is called with a URL like */project/77.html*, where

77 is the project ID. Using a dhandler here was an arbitrary choice, but it lets us have nice, search-engine-friendly URLs.

```
<table width="100%" cellspacing="0" cellpadding="5">
 <tr>
  <td class="heading" colspan="2">
   <h2 class="headline"><% $project->name | h %></h2>
  </td>
 </tr>
 <tr>
  <td colspan="2">
   Created: <& /lib/format_date.mas, date => $project->creation_date &>
  </td>
 </tr>
 <tr>
  <td colspan="2">
   <% HTML::FromText::text2html ( $project->description, paras => 1 ) %>
  </td>
 </tr>
 <tr>
  <td><b>Categor<% @categories > 1 ? 'ies' : 'y' %>:</b></td>
  <td><% join ', ', @categories %></td>
 </tr>
 <tr>
  <td><b>Project status:</b></td>
  <td><% $project->status | h %></td>
 </tr>
 <tr>
  <td><b>Support level:</b></td>
  <td><% $project->support_level | h %></td>
 </tr>
 <tr>
  <td colspan="2"><h3>Members</h3></td>
 </tr>
% while (my $user = $members->next) {
 <tr>
  <td>
   <a href="<& /lib/url.mas,
              path  => '/user.html',
              query => { user_id => $user->user_id } &>">
    <% $user->username | h %></a>
  </td>
  <td>
%   if ($project->user_is_admin($user)) {
<b>Admin</b>
%   } else {
 
%   }
  </td>
 </tr>
% }
% if ( $Schema->ProjectLink_t->row_count
%         ( where => [ $Schema->ProjectLink_t->project_id_c, '=', $project_id ]
% ) ) {
```

```
 <tr>
  <td colspan="2"> </td>
 </tr>
 <tr>
  <td colspan="2"><h3>Links</h3></td>
 </tr>
%   while (my $link = $links->next) {
 <tr>
  <td colspan="2">
   <a href="<% $link->url %>"><% $link->description | h %></a>
  </td>
 </tr>
%   }
% }
% if ($User->is_admin || $User->is_project_admin($project)) {
 <tr>
  <td colspan="2"> </td>
 </tr>
 <tr>
  <td colspan="2">
   <a href="<& /lib/url.mas,
               path  => '/logged_in/edit_project.html',
               query => { project_id => $project->project_id } &>">
   Edit this project</a>
  </td>
 </tr>
% }
</table>
<%shared>
  my ($project_id) = $m->dhandler_arg =~ /(\d+).html/;
  my $project = eval { $Schema->Project_t->row_by_pk( pk => $project_id ) }
      || $m->comp( '/lib/redirect.mas', path => '/' );
</%shared>
<%init>
 my $links = $project->Links( order_by => $Schema->ProjectLink_t->url_c );

 my $members =
     $Schema->join( select => $Schema->User_t,
                    join   =>
                    [ $Schema->tables( 'ProjectMember', 'User' ) ],
                    where  =>
                    [ $Schema->ProjectMember_t->project_id_c, '=', $project_id ],
                    order_by =>
                    [ $Schema->ProjectMember_t->is_project_admin_c, 'desc',
                      $Schema->User_t->username_c,                  'asc' ] );

 my @categories =
     map { $_->name }
     $project->Categories( order_by => $Schema->Category_t->name_c )->all_rows;
</%init>

<%method title>
 <& PARENT:title &> - <% $project->name | h %>
</%method>
```

/login_form.html

This is a simple login form that forwards various parameters it receives, like $success_url and %success_args, to the */users/login_submit.html* component.

```
<table width="100%" cellspacing="0" cellpadding="5">
 <tr>
  <td class="heading" colspan="2"><h2 class="headline">Login</h2></td>
 </tr>
% if ($message) {
 <tr>
  <td colspan="2"><% $message | h %></td>
 </tr>
% }
% if ($login_error) {
 <tr>
  <td colspan="2"><% $login_error | h %></td>
 </tr>
% }
 <form action="<& /lib/url.mas,
                  path => '/users/login_submit.html',
                  query => { caller_url    => $r->uri,
                             success_url  => $success_url,
                             success_args => \%success_args }
              &>" method="POST">
 <tr>
  <td>Username:</td>
  <td><input type="text" name="username" value="<% $username | h %>"></td>
 </tr>
 <tr>
  <td>Password:</td>
  <td><input type="password" name="password"></td>
 </tr>
   <tr>
  <td colspan="2"><input type="submit" value="Submit"></td>
 </tr>
 </form>
</table>
<%args>
 $message => undef
 $login_error => undef
 $success_url => '/'
 %success_args => ()
 $username => ''
</%args>

<%method title>
 <& PARENT:title &> - Login
</%method>
```

/users/new_user.html

This component delegates most of its work to the */users/user_form.mas* component, which will do the actual work of generating the form.

The $new_user object represents a "potential" database row, which is an object that has the same API as a real user object. However, a potential row does not correspond to any actual data in the database. This simplifies creating the */users/ user_form.mas* component, as that component can simply use the row object API whether we are creating a new user or editing an existing one.

The $available_status object represents the row from the UserStatus table where the status is 'Available'. We fetch this rather than hard-coding that column's id value.

```
<table width="100%" cellspacing="0" cellpadding="5">
 <tr>
  <td class="heading" colspan="2"><h2 class="headline">New User</h2></td>
 </tr>
 <& user_form.mas, submit_to => 'new_user_submit.html', user => $new_user, %ARGS
 &>
 </table>
 <%init>
  my $available_status =
      $Schema->UserStatus_t->one_row
          ( where =>
           [ $Schema->UserStatus_t->column('status'), '=', 'Available' ] );

  my $new_user =
      $Schema->User_t->potential_row
          ( values =>
            { username       => '',
              password       => '',
              real_name      => '',
              email_address  => '',
              user_status_id => $available_status->user_status_id,
            } );
 </%init>
 <%method title>
  <& PARENT:title &> - New user
 </%method>
```

/users/user_form.mas

This form is used for both creating new users and editing existing ones. To pre-populate the form fields, it first looks at the %ARGS hash. If there are values for these fields here, it assumes that these have priority because the only way for %ARGS to have such values is if the form was submitted but then rejected for a data validation error, in which case the browser is redirected back to the submitting page. When that happens, we want to show the user the rejected values that were just entered into the form. If there is nothing in %ARGS, then we look at the $user object for these values.

Unless the user for whom this page is being generated is an admin user, we don't bother showing the checkbox that allows them to turn on the admin flag for a user since that checkbox is respected only when a site administrator submits the form.

The $submit_to variable is used to set the form's action attribute. This allows us to use this form for both creating new users and editing existing ones.

The $return_to value is simply passed through the form to the component that handles the form submission, which will use it to determine where to send the browser if the form submission is successful.

```
% foreach my $err (@errors) {
 <tr>
  <td colspan="2"><span class="error"><% $err | h %></td>
 </tr>
% }
 <form action="<& /lib/url.mas, path => $submit_to &>" method="POST">
 <input type="hidden" name="return_to" value="<% $return_to %>">
% if ($user->user_id) {
 <input type="hidden" name="user_id" value="<% $user->user_id %>">
% }
 <tr>
  <td>Username:</td>
  <td>
   <input type="text" name="username"
          value="<% $form_vals{username} | h %>" size="20" maxlength="30">
  </td>
 </tr>
 <tr>
  <td>Password:</td>
  <td>
   <input type="password" name="password"
          value="<% $form_vals{password} | h %>" size="20" maxlength="100">
  </td>
 </tr>
 <tr>
  <td>Confirm password:</td>
  <td>
   <input type="password" name="password2"
          value="<% $form_vals{password2} | h %>" size="20" maxlength="100">
  </td>
 </tr>
 <tr>
  <td>Real name:</td>
  <td>
   <input type="text" name="real_name"
          value="<% $form_vals{real_name} %>" size="20" maxlength="75">
  </td>
 </tr>
 <tr>
  <td>Email address:</td>
  <td>
   <input type="text" name="email_address"
          value="<% $form_vals{email_address} %>" size="20" maxlength="150">
  </td>
 </tr>
 <tr>
  <td>How available are you?</td>
```

```
    <td>
      <select name="user_status_id">
% while (my $status = $user_statuses->next) {
        <option value="<% $status->user_status_id %>"
          <% $form_vals{user_status_id} == $status->user_status_id ?
'selected="selected"' : ''%>>
          <% $status->status | h %>
        </option>
% }
      </select>
    </td>
  </tr>
% if ($User->is_admin) {
  <tr>
   <td>Site admin:</td>
   <td>
    <input type="checkbox" name="is_admin"
          value="1" <% $form_vals{is_admin} ? 'checked="checked"': '' %>
   </td>
  </tr>
% }
  <tr>
   <td colspan="2"><input type="submit" value="Submit"></td>
  </tr>
  <form>
<%args>
 $submit_to
 $return_to => '/'
 $user
 @errors => ()
</%args>
<%init>
 my $user_statuses =
     $Schema->UserStatus_t->all_rows
        ( order_by => $Schema->UserStatus_t->status_c );

 my %form_vals;
 foreach my $field ( qw( username password real_name email_address
                         user_status_id is_admin ) ) {
     $form_vals{$field} =
         exists $ARGS{$field} ? $ARGS{$field} : $user->$field();
 }

 $form_vals{password2} =
     exists $ARGS{password2} ? $ARGS{password2} :
     exists $ARGS{password} ? $ARGS{password} :
     $user->password;
</%init>
```

/users/new_user_submit.html

Because data validation is handled by our module code, this component doesn't have much to do. If the insert succeeds, we set the cookie used to indicate a successful login and redirect the client to whatever path is in the $return_to variable.

Note that we will never set the is_admin flag to true unless the submitting user is a site administrator.

One style point: this component calls a few other components, but it uses $m->comp() instead of <& &> tags to do so. This is partly just because it was convenient to call the components from within the <%init> section, but it also emphasizes the fact that those particular components don't generate any HTML output.

```
<%args>
$return_to
</%args>
<%init>
# When inserting a new row, data validation checks are performed and an
# exception is thrown if any of the checks fail.
my $user =
    eval { $Schema->User_t->insert
              ( values =>
                { ( map { $_ => $ARGS{$_} }
                    qw( username password password2
                        real_name email_address
                        user_status_id ) ),
                  is_admin => $User->is_admin ? $ARGS{is_admin} : 0,
                }
              );
         };

# One or more data validation checks failed
$m->comp( '/lib/redirect.mas',
          path => 'new_user.html', query => { %ARGS, errors => $@->errors } )
    if $@ && UNIVERSAL::isa( $@, 'Apprentice::Exception::DataValidation' );

# Some other unforeseen error happened
die $@ if $@;

$m->comp( '/lib/set_login_cookie.mas', user => $user );

$m->comp( '/lib/redirect.mas', path => $return_to );
</%init>
<%flags>
inherit => '/syshandler'
</%flags>
```

/lib/redirect.mas

With Mason's built-in redirect() method, this component is trivially simple. We use the scomp() method to get a URL in the form of a string from the */lib/url. mas* component, then pass that to the redirect() method, which will generate the proper headers and send them to the client.

```
<%init>
my $url = $m->scomp( '/lib/url.mas', %ARGS );
```

```
    $m->redirect($url);
    </%init>
```

/users/login_submit.html

This component is the target for the login form we saw back in */left_side_menu. mas*, as well as */login_form.html* page.

We check the given username to make sure it exists and that the password given matches the password in the database. If this is not the case, we simply redirect the user back to the calling page with an error.

Otherwise, we set the cookie that marks a successful login and issue a redirect to the URL specified in $success_url.

This is a common pattern in web applications. You have a URL that handles form submissions that needs to redirect the browser to a different page, so you make the submission-receiving component capable of taking a parameter indicating where to redirect the client.

```
<%args>
$username
$password
$caller_url
%caller_args => ()
$success_url => undef
%success_args => ()
</%args>
<%init>
my $user =
    $Schema->User_t->one_row
        ( where => [ $Schema->User_t->username_c, '=', $username ] );

unless ( $user && $password eq $user->password ) {
    $m->comp( '/lib/redirect.mas',
              path  => $caller_url,
              query => { caller_args => \%caller_args,
                         username => $username,
                         login_error => 'Invalid login.' },
            );
}

$m->comp( '/lib/set_login_cookie.mas', user => $user );

# By default, we just send them back to the calling page.
$success_url = $caller_url unless defined $success_url && length $success_url;
%success_args = %caller_args unless %success_args;

$m->comp( '/lib/redirect.mas', path => $success_url, query => \%success_args );
</%init>
<%flags>
 inherit => '/syshandler'
</%flags>
```

/lib/set_login_cookie.mas

We discussed using a MAC for authentication in our explanation of the */syshandler* component. This is the flip side of that process. Here we simply set a cookie containing the user's user ID and a MAC based on that user ID.

A component that affects the headers sent to the client, such as this one, must be called *before* headers are sent. Since this site runs with autoflushing turned off, this is not a problem, because headers won't be sent until after all the content is generated.

```
<%args>
$user
</%args>
<%init>
Apache::Cookie->new
    ( $r,
      -name  => 'apprentice_user_login',
      -value => { user_id => $user->user_id,
                  MAC =>
                  Digest::SHA1::sha1_hex
                      ( $user->user_id, $Apprentice::Secret ) },
      -path    => '/',
      -domain  => 'apprentice.perl.org',
      -expires => '+1M',
    )->bake;
</%init>
```

/users/logout.html

Here we remove the login cookie set by the */lib/set_login_cookie.mas* component by setting a cookie with an expiration date in the past, which removes the cookie from the browser.

```
<%args>
$caller_url
%caller_args => ()
</%args>
<%init>
Apache::Cookie->new
    ( $r,
      -name  => 'apprentice_user_login',
      -value => '',
      -path  => '/',
      -domain  => 'apprentice.perl.org',
      -expires => '-1d',
    )->bake;

$m->comp( '/lib/redirect.mas', path => $caller_url, query => \%caller_args );
</%init>
<%flags>
inherit => '/syshandler'
</%flags>
```

/users/forgot_password.html

This is a simple form for users who forgot their password. A user enters her username, and the system sends her an email.

/users/forgot_password_submit.html

This component does the actual sending of email for forgotten passwords. Assuming that there is a username matching that entered by the user, we generate a simple email telling her her password.

We use the $r->register_cleanup() method to delay sending email until after output has been sent to the client. This technique is useful for any sort of operation that might take a long time, but the downside is that if the callback fails, there is no easy way to communicate this to the user. If this is a problem, you will simply have to do this while the client waits for output.

The $r->register_cleanup() method is documented in the Apache module documentation as well as the books mentioned in the beginning of Chapter 7.

```
<%args>
$username
</%args>
<%init>
my $user =
    $Schema->User_t->one_row
        ( where => [ $Schema->User_t->username_c, '=', $username ] );

unless ( $user ) {
    $m->comp( '/lib/redirect.mas',
            path => 'forgot_password.html',
            query => { error => 'Invalid username.' } );
}

my $body = "Your password is:\n\n" . $user->password .
            "\n\nwebmaster\@apprentice.perl.org";

$r->register_cleanup
    ( sub { Apprentice::send_email
                ( to   => $user->email_address,
                  from => 'webmaster@apprentice.perl.org',
                  subject => 'Your password for apprentice.perl.org',
                  body => $body ) } );

$m->comp( '/lib/redirect.mas',
        path => '/index.html',
        query => { login_error => 'Your password has been mailed to you.' } );
</%init>
<%flags>
inherit => '/syshandler'
</%flags>
```

Components with Access Controls

The components we just looked at are available to anybody who comes to the site, with no login required. The rest of the components are divided into two directories: one for logged-in users and the other for site administrators. We will start with the components available for logged-in users only. They are:

/logged_in/autohandler
/lib/check_access_level.mas
/logged_in/edit_self.html
/logged_in/edit_user_submit.html
/logged_in/new_project.html
/logged_in/project_form.mas
/logged_in/new_project_submit.html
/logged_in/editable_project_list.html
/logged_in/edit_project.html
/logged_in/check_access_to_project.mas
/logged_in/edit_project_submit.html
/logged_in/edit_members.html
/logged_in/add_project_member.html
/logged_in/remove_project_member.html
/logged_in/delete_project.html

These components are all about editing things on the site. Let's take a look.

/logged_in/autohandler

All this component does is implement access checking for the directory. If you are not a logged-in user, you cannot look at any components in this directory.

```
<%init>
 $m->comp( '/lib/check_access_level.mas', level => 'is_logged_in' );

 $m->call_next;
</%init>
```

/lib/check_access_level.mas

This component simply redirects the user to the login form if he does not meet the access-level requirement. If the user logs in successfully, he'll be redirected back to the component he was originally prevented from accessing.

```
<%args>
 $level
</%args>
<%init>
 my $requested_url = $r->uri;
 my %query_args = $m->request_args;

 my $level_description = $level eq 'is_logged_in' ? 'a logged-in' : 'an admin';

 $m->comp( '/lib/redirect.mas',
```

```
                    path => '/login_form.html',
                    query => { message => "This area requires $level_description user.",
                               success_url  => $requested_url,
                               success_args => \%query_args,
                             } )
         unless $User->$level();
    </%init>
```

/logged_in/edit_self.html

Editing a user simply uses the handy */users/user_form.mas* component we saw previously, this time with a different action attribute for the form, set via the submit_to parameter. It doesn't get any easier than that.

```
<table width="100%" cellspacing="0" cellpadding="5">
 <tr>
  <td class="heading" colspan="2">
   <h2 class="headline">Edit Your Account</h2>
  </td>
 </tr>
 <& /users/user_form.mas,
    submit_to => 'edit_user_submit.html',
    return_to => $r->uri,
    user => $User,
    %ARGS
 &>
</table>

<%method title>
 <& PARENT:title &> - Edit your account
</%method>
```

/logged_in/edit_user_submit.html

This component implements an additional access check. We want to make sure that the user submitting this form is either a site administrator or the owner of the account being edited. Otherwise, we simply send her away.

As with creating a new user, we always set the is_admin flag to a false value unless the submitting user is a site administrator.

```
<%args>
$user_id
$return_to
</%args>

<%init>
$m->comp( '/lib/redirect.mas', path => '/' )
    unless $User->is_admin or $User->user_id == $user_id;

my $user =
    eval { $Schema->User_t->row_by_pk( pk => $user_id ) }
        || $m->comp( '/lib/redirect.mas', path => '/' );

eval {
    $user->update( ( map { $_ => $ARGS{$_} }
                    qw( username password password2
```

```
                              real_name email_address
                              user_status_id ) ),
                     is_admin  => $User->is_admin ? $ARGS{is_admin} : 0,
                 );
     };

     $m->comp( '/lib/redirect.mas',
             path => $return_to, query => { %ARGS, errors => $@->errors } )
         if $@ && UNIVERSAL::isa( $@, 'Apprentice::Exception::DataValidation' );

     die $@ if $@;

     $m->comp( '/lib/redirect.mas', path => $return_to );
     </%init>

     <%flags>
      inherit => '/syshandler'
     </%flags>
```

/logged_in/new_project.html

The project creation and editing pages are very similar to the pages for creating and adding users. In both cases, we were able to take advantage of Mason's component system to achieve a high level of reuse.

/logged_in/project_form.mas

This page is closely analogous to /users/user_form.mas. Once again, we need to handle prepopulating the form with existing values when editing projects or with defaults for new projects. We also need to take into account that we may have come here as the result of an error in data validation, in which case we want to preserve the values submitted by the user.

Once again, we take a $submit_to parameter to set the form's action attribute, just as with the user form component.

This component has more code simply because projects are more complicated than users. Projects can have multiple categorizations, zero or more links each with an optional description, and so on.

The manner in which links are handled is interesting. We need a way to distinguish between editing or deleting an existing link and adding a new one. We do this by giving the form fields different names. For existing links, the fields contain the link IDs, which we also store separately so that we can iterate over them in the /logged_in/edit_project_submit.html component, discussed later.

```
% foreach my $err (@errors) {
  <tr valign="top">
   <td colspan="2"><span class="error"><% $err | h %></td>
  </tr>
% }
  <form action="<& /lib/url.mas, path => $submit_to &>" method="POST">
% if ($project->project_id) {
  <input type="hidden" name="project_id" value="<% $project->project_id %>">
% }
```

```
  <tr valign="top">
   <td>Name:</td>
   <td>
    <input type="text" name="name"
           value="<% $form_vals{name} | h %>" size="20" maxlength="30">
   </td>
  </tr>
  <tr valign="top">
   <td>Description:</td>
   <td>
    <textarea name="description" rows="5" cols="40">\
<% $form_vals{description} | h %>\
</textarea>
   </td>
  </tr>
  <tr valign="top">
   <td>Categories<br>(1 or more):</td>
   <td>
    <select name="category_ids" multiple="1" size="4">
% while (my $category = $categories->next) {
     <option value="<% $category->category_id %>"
       <% $current_categories{ $category->category_id } ?
          'selected="selected"' : '' %>>
      <% $category->name | h %>
     </option>
% }
    </select>
   </td>
  </tr>
  <tr valign="top">
   <td>Difficulty:</td>
   <td>
    <select name="difficulty">
% foreach (1..10) {
     <option value="<% $_ %>"
       <% $form_vals{difficulty} == $_ ? 'selected="selected"' : '' %>>
      <% $_ %>
     </option>
% }
    </select>
   </td>
  </tr>
  <tr valign="top">
   <td>Status:</td>
   <td>
    <select name="project_status_id">
% while (my $status = $statuses->next) {
     <option value="<% $status->project_status_id %>"
       <% $status->project_status_id == $form_vals{project_status_id} ?
          'selected="selected"' : '' %>>
      <% $status->status %>
     </option>
% }
    </select>
```

```
    </td>
   </tr>
% unless ($member_count) {
 <tr valign="top">
  <td>
  My role will be:</td>
  <td>
   <select name="role_id">
%   while (my $role = $roles->next) {
    <option value="<% $role->role_id %>"
     <% $form_vals{role_id} == $role->role_id ? 'selected="selected"': '' %>>
     <% $role->role | h %>
    </option>
%   }
  </td>
 </tr>
% }
 <tr valign="top">
  <td colspan="2">
   <p>
   If you chose the 'Mentor' role, then this is the
   support level you will provide.  If you chose the
   'Apprentice' role, then this is the support level you
   think you require.
   </p>
  </td>
 </tr>

 <tr valign="top">
  <td>Support level:</td>
  <td>
   <select name="project_support_level_id">
% while (my $level = $support_levels->next) {
    <option value="<% $level->project_support_level_id %>"
     <% $level->project_support_level_id ==
        $form_vals{project_support_level_id} ?
        'selected="selected"' : '' %>>
     <% $level->support_level %>
    </option>
% }
   </select>
  </td>
 </tr>
 <tr valign="top">
  <td colspan="2">
   <table width="100%" cellpadding="0">
    <tr valign="top">
     <td colspan="2"><h3>Links</h3></td>
    </tr>
    <tr valign="top">
     <td>URL</td>
     <td>Description</td>
    </tr>
% foreach my $link (@links) {
```

```
      <input type="hidden" name="project_link_ids" value="<% $link->{id} %>">
%     next unless defined $link->{url};
      <tr valign="top">
       <td>
        <input type="text" name="url<% $link->{id} %>"
               value="<% $link->{url} | h %>" size="30" maxlength="200">
       </td>
       <td>
        <input type="text" name="description<% $link->{id} %>"
               value="<% $link->{description} | h %>" size="50" maxlength="200">
       </td>
      </tr>
% }
% foreach (1..2) {
      <tr valign="top">
       <td>
        <input type="text" name="new_url<% $_ %>"
               value="<% $ARGS{"new_url$_"} || '' | h %>"
               size="30" maxlength="200">
       </td>
       <td>
        <input type="text" name="new_description<% $_ %>"
               value="<% $ARGS{"new_description$_"} || '' | h %>"
               size="50" maxlength="200">
       </td>
      </tr>
% }
   </table>
  </td>
 </tr>
 <tr valign="top">
  <td colspan="2"><input type="submit" value="Submit"></td>
 </tr>
 <form>

<%args>
 $submit_to
 $project
 @category_ids => ()
 @errors => ()
</%args>

<%init>
 my $statuses =
     $Schema->ProjectStatus_t->all_rows
         ( order_by => $Schema->ProjectStatus_t->status_c );

 my $support_levels =
     $Schema->ProjectSupportLevel_t->all_rows
         ( order_by =>
           $Schema->ProjectSupportLevel_t->project_support_level_id_c );

 my $categories =
     $Schema->Category_t->all_rows
```

```
                  ( order_by => $Schema->Category_t->name_c );

        my $links = $project->Links;

        my @links;
        while (my $link = $links->next) {
            my $id = $link->project_link_id;
            # the link was deleted but we've returned to this page because
            # of some error.
            if (exists $ARGS{"url$id"} && ! length $ARGS{"url$id"}) {
                push @links, { id => $id, url => undef };
            } elsif (exists $ARGS{"url$id"} && length $ARGS{"url$id"}) {
                push @links, { id => $id,
                               url => $ARGS{"url$id"},
                               description => $ARGS{"description$id"} };
            } else {
                push @links, { id => $id,
                               url => $link->url,
                               description => $link->description };
            }
        }

        my %current_categories;
        if (@category_ids) {
            %current_categories = map { $_ => 1 } @category_ids;
        } else {
            %current_categories =
                map { $_->category_id => 1 } $project->Categories->all_rows;
        }

        my $member_count =
            $Schema->ProjectMember_t->row_count
                ( where =>
                  [ $Schema->ProjectMember_t->project_id_c,
                    '=', $project->project_id ] );

        my %form_vals;
        foreach my $field ( qw( name description difficulty
                                project_status_id project_support_level_id ) ) {

            $form_vals{$field} =
                exists $ARGS{$field} ? $ARGS{$field} : $project->$field();
        }

        $form_vals{role_id} = $ARGS{role_id} || 0;

        # Only used if a project has no members (i.e. a new project)
        my $roles;
        $roles =
            $Schema->Role_t->all_rows( order_by => $Schema->Role_t->role_id_c )
                unless $member_count;
</%init>
```

/logged_in/new_project_submit.html

Here we handle creating a new project, along with its associated members, categories, and links. It looks fairly similar to */users/new_user_submit.html*.

Since this is a new project, we give it a single member, which is the submitting user. This user is flagged as having administrative access to the project, meaning that they can edit the project.

/logged_in/editable_project_list.html

This component is used to display a list of projects for which the current user has administrative privileges. It provides links to edit each project's data and membership as well as a project deletion link.

/logged_in/edit_project.html

There is nothing here that we haven't seen before. Let's move on, shall we?

/logged_in/check_access_to_project.mas

This is a helper component that is called from several places in order to confirm that a user should be allowed to edit a given project. Basically, the user must be a site administrator or have administrative privileges for the project in question.

```
<%args>
 $project
</%args>

<%init>
 unless ($User->is_admin || $User->is_project_admin($project)) {
     $m->comp( '/lib/redirect.mas', path => '/' );
 }
</%init>
```

/logged_in/edit_project_submit.html

While similar to the component used to edit users, this one is a bit more complicated. To detect the fact that a project should no longer be in a category, we need to check the project's current list of categories in the database against those submitted to this component. Similarly, we need to check the submitted list to see if there are any categories not already assigned to the project.

For links, we delete any existing link where the URL was erased from the text editing box. For others we simply update them. Then if new links were given, we add them to the database.

```
<%args>
 $project_id
 @project_link_ids => ()
 @category_ids => ()
</%args>

<%init>
 my $project =
     eval { $Schema->Project_t->row_by_pk( pk => $project_id ) }
         || $m->comp( '/lib/redirect.mas', path => '/' );
```

```
$m->comp( 'check_access_to_project.mas', project => $project );

eval {
    $project->update
        ( name => $ARGS{name},
          description => $ARGS{description},
          difficulty => $ARGS{difficulty},
          project_status_id => $ARGS{project_status_id},
          project_support_level_id => $ARGS{project_support_level_id},
        );
};

$m->comp( '/lib/redirect.mas',
          path => '/logged_in/edit_project.html',
          query => { %ARGS, errors => $@->errors } )
    if $@ && UNIVERSAL::isa( $@, 'Apprentice::Exception::DataValidation' );

my %current_categories =
    map { $_->category_id => 1 } $project->Categories->all_rows;

foreach my $id (@category_ids) {
    $Schema->ProjectCategory_t->insert( values => { project_id => $project_id,
                                                    category_id => $id } )
        unless exists $current_categories{$id};
}

{
    # This is the categories selected on the project editing page.
    my %selected_categories = map { $_ => 1 } @category_ids;

    # These are categories the project currently has which were
    # _not_ selected on the editing page.
    my @to_delete;
    foreach my $id (keys %current_categories) {
        push @to_delete, $id unless $selected_categories{$id};
    }

    if (@to_delete) {
        foreach ( $Schema->ProjectCategory_t->rows_where
                    ( where =>
                      [
                        [ $Schema->ProjectCategory_t->project_id_c,
                          '=',  $project_id ],
                        [ $Schema->ProjectCategory_t->category_id_c,
                          'IN', @to_delete  ]
                      ]
                    )->all_rows ) {
            $_->delete;
        }
    }
}

{
```

```
# This is basically the same logic as was used for categories
# except that if a link wasn't deleted, we may need to update
# it.
my @to_delete;
foreach my $id (@project_link_ids) {
    if ( defined $ARGS{"url$id"} && length $ARGS{"url$id"} ) {
        my $link =
            eval { $Schema->ProjectLink_t->row_by_pk( pk => $id ) }
                || next;
        $link->update( url => $ARGS{"url$id"},
                       description => $ARGS{"description$id"} );
    } else {
        push @to_delete, $id
    }
}

if (@to_delete) {
    foreach ( $Schema->ProjectLink_t->rows_where
                    ( where =>
                    [ $Schema->ProjectLink_t->project_link_id_c,
                      'IN', @to_delete ] )->all_rows ) {
        $_->delete;
    }
}
}

# Finally, insert any new links from the previous page.
foreach (1..2) {
    if (exists $ARGS{"new_url$_"} && length $ARGS{"new_url$_"}) {
        $Schema->ProjectLink_t->insert
            ( values =>
              { project_id => $project->project_id,
                url => $ARGS{"new_url$_"},
                description =>
                defined $ARGS{"new_description$_"} ?
                $ARGS{"new_description$_"} : $ARGS{"new_url$_"},
              }
            );
    }
}

$m->comp( '/lib/redirect.mas',
          path => '/logged_in/edit_project.html',
          query => { project_id => $project_id } );
</%init>

<%flags>
inherit => '/syshandler'
</%flags>
```

/logged_in/edit_members.html

Because the project editing screen already had enough on it, we decided to give
project member editing its own distinct page in order to avoid interface overload.

We intentionally do not allow a user to give or take away administrative privileges from an existing member. It would have complicated the interface with another button, and it is easy enough to simply remove the member and re-add them with changed privileges.

We also don't allow a user to remove himself from the project, because this is more likely to be something someone does by accident than intentionally. And if a user removes himself, he could end up leaving the project with no one capable of editing it other than the site admins.

```
<table width="100%" cellspacing="0" cellpadding="5">
 <tr>
  <td class="heading" colspan="5">
   <h2 class="headline">Edit Project Members</h2>
  </td>
 </tr>
 <tr>
  <td colspan="2">
   <a href="<& /lib/url.mas,
             path  => '/logged_in/edit_project.html',
             query => { project_id => $project->project_id } &>">
    Edit project</a>
  </td>
 </tr>
 <tr>
  <td colspan="5"><h3>Current members for <% $project->name | h %></h3></td>
 </tr>
% while (my $member = $members->next) {
 <tr>
  <td><% $member->username | h %></td>
  <td><% $member->role %></td>
  <td>
%   if ($member->is_project_admin) {
   <b>Project admin</b>
%   } else {
    
%   }
  </td>
%   if ( $member->username eq $User->username ) {
  <td colspan="2"> </td>
%   } else {
  <form action="<& /lib/url.mas,
                  path => 'remove_project_member.html' &>" method="POST">
   <input type="hidden" name="project_id" value="<% $project_id %>">
   <input type="hidden" name="user_id" value="<% $member->user_id %>">
   <td colspan="2"><input type="submit" value="Remove"></td>
  </form>
%   }
 </tr>
% }
 <tr>
  <td colspan="5"><h3>Add a new member</h3></td>
 </tr>
```

```
% if ($error) {
 <tr>
  <td colspan="5"><span class="error"><% $error | h %></span></td>
 </tr>
% }
 <form action="<& /lib/url.mas,
                 path => 'add_project_member.html' &>" method="POST">
  <input type="hidden" name="project_id" value="<% $project_id %>">
  <tr>
   <td><input type="text" name="username" value="<% $username | h %>"></td>
   <td>
    <select name="role_id">
%    while (my $role = $roles->next) {
     <option value="<% $role->role_id %>"
      <% $role_id == $role->role_id ? 'selected="selected"': '' %>>
      <% $role->role | h %>
     </option>
%    }
   </td>
   <td>
    As admin?
    <input type="checkbox" name="is_project_admin"
           value="1" <% $is_project_admin ? 'checked="checked"': '' %>>
   </td>
   <td><input type="submit" value="Add"></td>
  </tr>
 </form>
</table>
<%shared>
my $project =
    eval { $Schema->Project_t->row_by_pk
              ( pk => $m->request_args->{project_id} ) }
        || $m->comp( '/lib/redirect.mas', path => '/' );
</%shared>
<%args>
 $project_id
 $username => ''
 $role_id => 0
 $is_project_admin => 0
 $error => ''
</%args>

<%init>
 $m->comp( 'check_access_to_project.mas', project => $project );

 my $members =
     $Schema->join( select => $Schema->ProjectMember_t,
                    join   =>
                    [ $Schema->tables( 'ProjectMember', 'User' ) ],
                    where  =>
                    [ $Schema->ProjectMember_t->project_id_c, '=', $project_id ],
                    order_by => $Schema->User_t->username_c );
```

```
    my $roles = $Schema->Role_t->all_rows( order_by => $Schema->Role_t->role_id_c );
    </%init>

    <%method title>
    <& PARENT:title &> - Members of <% $project->name | h %>
    </%method>
```

/logged_in/add_project_member.html

This component makes sure that the submitted username actually exists and, assuming it does, inserts a new row into the ProjectMember table.

/logged_in/remove_project_member.html

This component checks access, deletes a row from the database, and redirects.

/logged_in/delete_project.html

This is much like the component used to remove a project member. The main difference here is that we try to be intelligent in determining where to redirect the user after deleting the project. If she still has projects, we send her back to her list of projects. Otherwise, we simply send her to the top-level page.

```
    <%args>
    $project_id
    $redirect_to => undef
    </%args>
    <%init>
    my $project = $Schema->Project_t->row_by_pk( pk => $project_id );

    $m->comp( 'check_access_to_project.mas', project => $project );

    $project->delete;

    unless ($redirect_to) {
        $redirect_to =
            $User->has_projects ? '/logged_in/editable_project_list.html' : '/';
    }

    $m->comp( '/lib/redirect.mas', path => $redirect_to );
    </%init>
    <%flags>
    inherit => '/syshandler'
    </%flags>
```

The last components we have to look at are in the */admin* directory. These are:

/admin/autohandler

This is almost identical to */logged_in/autohandler* but with a different access check and title method.

/admin/user_list.html

This component presents a paged list of users for site administrators to browse through. A link for each user allows the admin to edit that user.

/admin/edit_user.html

This one is almost identical to the */logged_in/edit_self.html* component except that it takes a $user_id parameter in order to allow any user to be edited. It uses the */users/user_form.mas* component, like other user editing components.

/admin/edit_categories.html

This component provides a form that allows categories to be edited, deleted, or added.

/admin/alter_category.html

An admin can alter a category's name.

/admin/add_category.html

This one adds a new category.

/admin/delete_category.html

This component deletes an existing category.

All Done

And that is our site. Putting this site together took maybe 30–40 person-hours from start to finish, which is not too bad. Plenty of that time was spent fiddling with HTML, since that is not our strongest area. Doing this as a traditional CGI application without Mason would probably have either taken much longer to achieve a similar level of code reuse or just ended up as a sloppier application.

Further Directions

As we mentioned at the beginning of this chapter, we wanted to make this site small enough to show you in a single chapter (albeit a rather long chapter), and we sometimes avoided using some features of Alzabo that could have simplified some of the code in order to avoid getting sidetracked into an Alzabo how-to. When you're designing your own sites, you won't have these constraints. Here are some things you might try adding to this site:

More inheritance

Note that the final three components, */admin/add_category.html*, */admin/alter_ category.html*, and */admin/delete_category.html*, all share certain properties, like the fact that they redirect to the same place and all inherit from */syshandler*. It would be possible to encapsulate this common behavior in a component that all of them could inherit from.

Use Alzabo more effectively

Since Alzabo is able to provide metadata about the database (such as column names, types, lengths, etc.), we could have made form widget components to create form elements with the proper size and maxlength attributes for a given column. In fact, Alzabo includes Mason components for this purpose in its distribution, but in the interest of not turning this into an Alzabo tutorial, we chose not to use them.

Two-level component root

If you plan to replicate this kind of site in more than one location, you have two options. The first is to install the components and modules separately in each location. The second is to create a common set of shared components for all sites in one component root, overriding only the portions you need to override in another component root. This creates a more portable site framework. See the discussion of "Inheritance and Multiple Component Roots" in Chapter 5.

One way to start creating such a framework is to move all our components to a shared component root and override only the parts you need to override in your site-specific root. This approach will take some reengineering as you go, but it's a fairly painless approach to the problem of generalizing a site that was designed as a one-off.

## CHAPTER 9

Mason and CGI

Although mod_perl is pretty cool, it's not the only way to use Mason to build a web site. In fact, plenty of times it's more advisable to use CGI than mod_perl, as we describe in this chapter. If you find yourself in such a situation, you're in luck— Mason works just fine under CGI, and special care has gone into making sure the cooperation is smooth. The HTML::Mason::CGIHandler module provides the glue necessary to use Mason in most common CGI environments.

CGI-Appropriate Situations

Before we get into the details of how to set up Mason under CGI, let's think about *why* you might want to use this setup. After all, isn't mod_perl supposed to be *better* than CGI? Well, yes and no. As in most things, context is everything. The following factors may conspire to make you choose clunky old CGI over clunky new mod_perl in a particular situation:

Need instant gratification

Installing mod_perl can be somewhat difficult if you've never done it before (heck, even if you *have* done it before), and it can take a while to get used to the peculiarities of developing in a mod_perl environment. If you want to try Mason out but don't want to spend time installing and configuring mod_perl (or you don't want to wait for the person who's going to come install it for you), you may be interested in using HTML::Mason::CGIHandler to start development, then switching over to mod_perl and HTML::Mason::ApacheHandler once you've gotten comfortable with mod_perl.

Must share hosting environments

Many organizations simply don't have the money to pay for their own server and staff to administer it, so they sign up with a cheap virtual hosting service that lets them run CGI scripts. The key word "virtual" means that several organizations, inevitably of varying scruples, share the same web server on the same machine.

Although some of these services say they offer mod_perl, you should not use it, because it is very insecure and very prone to catastrophic development errors.

It is insecure because all your code will run in the web server process, along with any other hooligan's code on your shared server. Unless you trust all those hooligans not to steal your passwords, harass your clients, delete your files, and plunder your village, you should avoid using mod_perl offered in a virtual hosting environment.

It is prone to development errors for the same reason: your code runs in the web server process, so if your Mason code accidentally gets into an infinite loop or hangs the server process, you bring the server down with you. Hosting services tend to dislike that. If you had enough money, you'd handle this problem by running separate servers for development and production, but you clearly don't have enough money for that, since you're using cheap virtual hosting.

Good old CGI, unpleasant as it is in other ways, provides a solution. Apache's ExecCGI mechanism (and its equivalent in other servers) can be configured to use a "setuid" execution mechanism to make sure that your CGI scripts run as the user that owns them—you. This means that you can make all your sensitive data files accessible only by you, that any files your scripts create are owned by you, and that if you make a big mistake, you don't anger the other people who share your server.

Of course, this argument is moot if your web hosting service doesn't support the ExecCGI model. Most good full-featured services do, and most crappy ones don't. Make sure you do the proper research.

Speed not critical

Alas, all the claims of the mod_perl crowd are true—CGI is slower than mod_perl, and it doesn't provide nearly as much control over the server process. However, sometimes you don't care. If request speed doesn't mean too much on your site, and you don't need to do anything fancy with mod_perl's various request phases and content management, then there are few, if any, reasons to use mod_perl. mod_perl itself isn't (necessarily) all that complicated, but the environment you deploy it in can be.

A strong factor in your decision should be rigorous benchmarking; if your site running under CGI can keep up with the amount of traffic you'll need to handle, then HTML::Mason::CGIHandler holds promise for you. As always, do the proper research.

Special memory usage situations

One of the particular constraints of mod_perl is that it can use a lot of memory. This is mainly due to the persistent nature of the embedded Perl interpreter; memory you allocate during one request may not get freed until many more requests are served and the child process is terminated. Even if you explicitly free the memory when you're done with it, using Perl's undef() function, most operating systems won't actually return the memory block to the general pool of free system memory; they'll just mark it as reusable within that same process. Because of this, mod_perl developers are often quite miserly with memory and will sometimes do convoluted things just to keep memory usage at a minimum.

The persistence of memory creates a problem when you need to have a large chunk of data resident in memory for processing. One of the most common instances of this is HTTP file uploads: if the user uploads a large file, that file will often end up in memory, creating a real problem in a mod_perl environment. However, if the user is uploading a large file, he'll typically have to wait around for the file to transfer over the network, which means that he won't really care (or notice) if the receiving script takes an extra half-second to execute. CGI can be useful in this situation, because any memory used during the request will be freed up immediately when the request is over.

Web server isn't Apache

Although Apache is a great and flexible web server with a huge support team and developer community, it's not the only web server on the planet. If you find yourself needing to use a server other than Apache, of course you won't be able to use mod_perl either. Since most web servers support a CGI mechanism of some sort, CGI may be the best way to use Mason in an environment like this.

In fact, even when your web server *is* Apache, you may want to use a different execution model like FastCGI. Mason's CGI support extends well into situations like these.

CGI-Inappropriate Situations

In some situations, CGI just won't do. Depending on who you ask, these situations might be characterized with terms ranging from "always" to "never." It's beyond the scope of this book to make all the arguments germane to the CGI versus mod_perl debate, but these factors might make choosing CGI impossible:

Startup cost too great

The most commonly encountered argument in favor of mod_perl is that it reduces the startup cost of each request by putting a Perl interpreter in resident memory, allowing various resources to be allocated once per server child rather than once per request. This is true, and important.

This resource allocation scheme can produce tremendous speedups in several areas, most notably database connection time. Many modern dynamic sites rely on a database connection, and if you're using an industrial-strength database like Oracle that has to perform lots of tasks every time you connect, connections can take so long to obtain that connecting on every request is simply unacceptable. Other resources may suffer from this same constraint, so try to determine your needs before running full speed into the CGI camp.

Advanced mod_perl features too tantalizing

Let's face it, mod_perl is cool. It's a window into the most advanced web server in the world, using the most fun and versatile language in the world. If you simply can't live without some of the more advanced mod_perl features like content negotiation, server-side subrequests, and multiple request phase hooks, you're forever going to feel fettered by CGI's inherent limitations.

Creating a CGI-Based Site in Mason

You can get Mason and CGI to work together in several different ways. One model is to write traditional CGI scripts that use Mason as a templating language, executing Mason components from inside the CGI program. See "Using Mason Templates Inside Regular CGI Scripts" for how to set this up.

A better approach to building a Mason site under CGI is to let the components drive the site. You can configure your web server to invoke a CGI script of your choosing for certain requests, and that script can begin Mason processing on those files. In other words, you can have the same set of Mason components in your site you would have under mod_perl, but those components get executed under the CGI paradigm.

Your comrade in this endeavor is the HTML::Mason::CGIHandler module. Its role is similar to the HTML::Mason::ApacheHandler module, but since CGI is a bit clunkier than mod_perl and the CGIHandler is a bit younger than ApacheHandler, a bit more configuration is necessary. You'll need to combine four ingredients: directives in the server's configuration files (*httpd.conf* or *.htaccess* under Apache), a Mason wrapper CGI script, the Mason components themselves, and the HTML::Mason::CGIHandler module.

The necessary configuration directives are fairly straightforward. Here's an example for Apache:

```
Action html-mason /cgi-bin/mason_handler.cgi
<FilesMatch "\.html$">
 SetHandler html-mason
</FilesMatch>
```

Here, the *mason_handler.cgi* script can be located wherever you want, provided it's set up by the server to be run as a CGI script. The */cgi-bin* directory is already configured on most systems using the ScriptAlias directive, so that's a reasonable place to put the handler script, though it's certainly not the only place.

Instead of passing all *.html* files through Mason as in the previous example, you might configure the server to Masonize all files in a certain directory (use a <Directory> block for this or an *.htaccess* file in that directory), only certain specific files (use a <Files> block or a different <FilesMatch> pattern to select those files), or some more complicated scheme. See your server's documentation for more configuration help. Remember, each CGI request will take a highly nonzero time to execute, so don't process a file with Mason unless it's actually a Mason component. In particular, make sure you don't accidentally pass image files to Mason, because each web page typically contains many images, and the extra processing time for those images will be a big waste if you invoke Mason unnecessarily, not to mention that Mason may mangle those images when processing them.

Next, you need to create your *mason_handler.cgi* script. It should be located wherever the Action directive indicates in the server configuration. Here's a *mason_handler.cgi* that will serve nicely for most sites. It's fairly simple, since most of the real work is done inside the HTML::Mason::CGIHandler module.

```
#!/usr/bin/perl -w

use strict;
use HTML::Mason::CGIHandler;

my $h = HTML::Mason::CGIHandler->new
  (
    data_dir  => "$ENV{DOCUMENT_ROOT}/../mason-data",
    allow_globals => [qw(%session $user)],
  );

$h->handle_request;
```

The data_dir and allow_globals parameters should look familiar; they're just passed along to the Interpreter and Compiler, respectively. Note that the data_dir we use here may need to be changed for your setup. The main consideration is that your data_dir is somewhere outside the document root, so feel free to put it wherever makes sense for you.

Note that we didn't pass a comp_root parameter. If no comp_root is specified, HTML::Mason::CGIHandler will use $ENV{DOCUMENT_ROOT} as the document root.

With the server configuration and handler script in place, you're ready to use Mason. You can create a hierarchy of components for your site just as you would under a mod_perl setup.

Using Mason Templates Inside Regular CGI Scripts

We have argued several times against the traditional CGI model, in which the response to each web request is driven primarily by a Perl script (or other executable program*) that focuses on making all the logical decisions necessary for fulfilling that request. We tend to prefer template-based solutions driven by the content of the request, using concise sprinklings of programming to control the dynamic elements of the request. In other words, we prefer Mason components to CGI scripts.

---

* But who are we kidding, eh? Are you going to be writing these things in COBOL?

However, the world is a strange place. For some odd reason, managers may not always be persuaded by the well-reasoned arguments their programmers make in favor of using Mason in its traditional way. They may even want to take an existing functional site based on badly written CGI scripts and use some basic Mason-based templating techniques to achieve the timeless goal of separating logic from presentation. In these situations, you may be called upon to use Mason as if it were one of the lightweight solutions mentioned in Chapter 1.

Luckily, you won't be the first person to want such a thing. This path has been tread often enough that it's fairly easy to use Mason as a standalone templating language. To do this, you create a Mason Interpreter, then call the Interpreter's exec( ) method, passing it either a component path or component object as the first argument.

The CGI script in Example 9-1 is sort of the "Hello, World" of dynamic web programming. It lets the user enter text in an HTML form, submit the form, and see the resultant text in the server's response.

Example 9-1. Hello, World in Mason with traditional CGI

```perl
#!/usr/bin/perl -w

use strict;
use CGI;
use HTML::Mason;

# Create a new query object, and print the standard header
my $q = CGI->new;
print $q->header;

# Create a Mason Interpreter
my $interp = HTML::Mason::Interp->new();

# Generate a Component object from the given text
my $component = $interp->make_component(comp_source => <<'EOF');
<%args>
 $user_input => '(no input)'
</%args>

<HTML>
<HEAD><TITLE>You said '<% $user_input |h %>'</TITLE></HEAD>
<BODY>
You said '<% $user_input |h %>'.  Type some text below and submit the form.<BR>

<FORM ACTION="" METHOD="GET">
<INPUT NAME="user_input" value=""><br>
<INPUT TYPE="submit" VALUE="Submit">
</FORM>
</BODY>
</HTML>
EOF
```

Example 9-1. Hello, World in Mason with traditional CGI (continued)

```
my %vars = $q->Vars;
$vars{user_input} =~ s/^\s+|\s+$//g;   # Sanitize

# Execute the component, with output going to STDOUT
$interp->exec($component, %vars);
```

Notice a couple of things about the code. First, the Mason component is located in the middle of the code, surrounded by some fairly generic Perl code to fetch the query parameters and pass them to the component. Second, the Mason Interpreter is the main point of entry for most of the tasks performed. First we create an Interpreter, then we use the Interpreter's make_component() method to create a new Component object (see Chapter 5 for more on the make_component() method), then we call the Interpreter's exec() method to set the Mason wheels in motion.

Also, notice that the example code calls the CGI method Vars() to get at the query parameters. This is relatively convenient but doesn't properly handle multiple key/value pairs with the same key. To do this better, we'd either have to use the CGI param() method and parse out the multiple keys ourselves or split the Vars() values on ASCII \0 (thus disallowing \0 in our data). You're probably not jumping for joy at the prospect of dealing with these kinds of minutiae, but this is the kind of thing you'll find yourself dealing with in CGI environments.

If you don't actually need to examine or alter the query parameters yourself before invoking the Mason template, you can take advantage of the HTML::Mason::CGIHandler handle_comp() method, which will create a CGI object and parse out the query parameters, then invoke the component you pass it. Example 9-2 shows the previous example rewritten using the handle_comp() method.

Example 9-2. A lazier approach to Mason in CGI

```
#!/usr/bin/perl -w

use strict;
use HTML::Mason::CGIHandler;

# Create a new CGIHandler object
my $h = HTML::Mason::CGIHandler->new();

# Generate a Component object from the given text
my $component = $h->interp->make_component(comp_source => <<'EOF');
<%args>
 $user_input => '(no input)'
</%args>

<HTML>
<HEAD><TITLE>You said '<% $user_input %>'</TITLE></HEAD>
<BODY>
You said '<% $user_input %>'.  Type some text below and submit the form.<BR>
```

Example 9-2. A lazier approach to Mason in CGI (continued)

```
<FORM ACTION="" METHOD="GET">
<INPUT NAME="user_input" value=""><br>
<INPUT TYPE="submit" VALUE="Submit">
</FORM>
</BODY>
</HTML>
EOF

# Invoke the component, with output going to STDOUT
$h->handle_comp($component);
```

As you can see, this hides all the CGI argument processing, ensuring that you don't make a silly mistake (or get lazy) in handling the query parameters. It also handles sending the HTTP headers. This approach is usually preferable to the one shown in Example 9-1. Of course, if you're letting Mason handle all the details of the request, you have to wonder why you don't just use the Action directive with a generic CGI wrapper, as covered in "Creating a CGI-Based Site in Mason."

Design Considerations

If you start building a site in this way, with each CGI script invoking Mason as a templating engine, you're going to face some design decisions. For instance, if your code needs to do some argument processing or other decision making that alters the output, should those decisions happen inside or outside the Mason template? If you do a bunch of important stuff outside the template that alters the behavior inside the template, you can create lots of nonobvious logical dependencies that can be a nightmare to maintain. It's somewhat better to put this stuff inside the template, but you run the risk of obscuring the template's real purpose, which is to generate HTML output.

To really make the right kinds of decisions, direct yourself to Chapter 10, in which we try to convince you to use Mason for what Mason is good for and Perl modules for what Perl modules are good for. These design issues don't have much to do with the CGI approach per se, but as you can see from our example script, the flow is already a little convoluted even in the simplest of cases. Anything you can do to keep things tidy may save you a lot of pain later.

Differences Between Mason Under CGI and mod_perl

The main functional difference between the environments provided by HTML::Mason::CGIHandler and HTML::Mason::ApacheHandler is that $r, the Apache request object, is much more limited in functionality under CGI. In fact, under CGI it's not a real Apache request object at all; it just emulates a few of the more useful methods. It can't emulate some methods because they make sense only in a mod_perl environment. For example, you won't be able to access the Apache subrequest mechanism through lookup_uri() or lookup_file(), you won't be able to get at the client connection through the connection() method, and you can't get configuration parameters via dir_config().

However, $r does have methods to help you set headers in the outgoing response, including Location and Content-Type headers. This makes it relatively straightforward to send client-side redirects and to use Mason to generate plain text, XML, image data, or other formats besides the default HTML.

To set outgoing headers, you can use the $r->header_out() and $r->content_type() methods in your components. They are very similar to their mod_perl counterparts of the same names. The header_out() method takes two arguments, the name of a header and the value it should be set to. If you pass only one argument, the header's value won't be set, but the method will return the current value of the header, as set by a previous call to header_out().

The content_type() method is the "official" way to set the content type of the outgoing response. It's essentially just an abbreviation for passing Content-Type as the first argument to the header_out() method. If you pass an argument to content_type(), you'll set the outgoing content type. If you don't set the content type during the request, the CGI module will set the content type to text/html.

Under normal circumstances, header_out() and content_type() just pass along any headers you set to the CGI module's header() method. If you previously set a header that you want to unset, you can pass undef as the new value to header_out() or content_type(). Instead of setting the header's value to undef (which wouldn't make a lot of sense in the HTTP context), the header will be unset (i.e., removed from the table of headers to send to the client).

Like its cousin ApacheHandler, CGIHandler adds an $m->redirect() method to the request object $m, so you can redirect browsers to a URL of your choosing in the same way you would under mod_perl.

Finally, if you want to access the CGI query object for the current request, you may do so by calling the $m->cgi_object method. In general it's best to avoid using the query object directly, because doing so will lead to nonportable code and you most likely won't be taking advantage of Mason's argument-processing and content-generation techniques. However, as with most things Perl, you can always get enough rope, even if it means you might end up in a hopelessly tangled mess, dangling by an ankle from the gallows pole of your own code.

See the documentation for HTML::Mason::CGIHandler for more details.

## CHAPTER 10

Scalable Design

So now that you know how to do things with Mason, it's time to start thinking about how to do things cleanly, scalably, and maintainably. Mason is a good tool, but it is not magic, and you still need to think about design when you use it.

Modules Versus Components

Mason is a powerful tool for generating content. Its combination of easy templating syntax, powerful component structures, and features like autohandlers, dhandlers, and component inheritance all combine to make it much like Perl itself: it makes easy things easy, and difficult things possible.

However, exactly like Perl itself, the facilities it provides can make it all too tempting to do things the easy way, and Mason makes no attempt to enforce any sort of discipline in your design. Instead, this is your responsibility as a programmer and application designer. This is where the responsibility always lies, no matter what language or tool you are using.

Though Mason is at its core a text templating tool, it also provides much more functionality. One such piece of functionality is that individual components are almost exactly like subroutines. They can be called anywhere in your processing and they can, in turn, call other components, generate output, and/or return values to the caller. And, like Perl's subroutines, variables defined inside a component are lexically scoped to that component.

It is this similarity between components and subroutines that can lead to design trouble. As long-time Mason users, we have come to believe that Mason components should be used almost exclusively for generating output. For data processing, we believe that Perl modules are the better solution. In our experience, this division of labor leads to long-term benefits in maintainability and clarity of design.

When we say "generating output," we mean generating binary or text output of any sort (HTML, XML, plain text, images, etc.) to be sent somewhere (STDOUT, a web client, etc.). In a web environment, this includes things like sending redirect headers or custom error responses as well as HTML. When we say "data processing," we mean the work of retrieving data from an external data source such as a database, processing data and constructing useful objects or data structures, doing calculations, implementing business logic, or munging data.

Our exception to this rule is when the data processing is entirely part of the UI that Mason is generating. For example, in a web context, it may be necessary to do some munging of POSTed data or to translate data from the manner in which it is presented in the UI to a format suitable for your backend.

But Mason is not the right tool for all jobs, and it should not form the entire infrastructure of any project.

The rest of this discussion will assume a web environment, as that is Mason's primary domain, though this discussion can apply to any environment in which Mason could be used.

Another important goal is to minimize duplication of code. You will never eliminate this entirely, but this should always be your goal. Duplicated code leads to bugs when one piece changes and the other doesn't, increases the difficulty of understanding the entire code base, and increases implementation time for bug fixes and changes.

Obviously, the line between generating output and data processing is extremely blurry. Given that fact, perhaps the best goal is to reduce the data processing in Mason components to the minimal amount necessary to properly generate output. All other application logic should be placed in Perl modules and called from your components.

The line that needs to be drawn is one that makes the code flow in both your modules and your components as natural as possible. We don't want to go into impossible contortions in order to eliminate four lines of processing from a component, nor do we want to put knowledge about Mason or our components into our modules. Like all design tasks, there is as much art as skill involved.

For example, as mentioned before, we consider it entirely appropriate for Mason components to handle incoming request argument processing. A component could use these arguments to determine what library function to call or what object to instantiate. It might also use these arguments to change the way it generates output, for example if there were a parameter indicating that no images should be included on a page.

There is little reason to handle this particular processing task with a module. Indeed, this would be creating exactly the kind of dependency we believe is so problematic in using Mason for application logic. Your modules should be generically useful and if they depend on being called by Mason components, they are useless outside of the Mason environment.

What exactly is the danger of blurring these lines? Well, Mason is a fine system for generating HTML or other forms of output. However, let's assume that you plan to also provide your data via an email interface. A user may write an email to you with a specific body such as "fetch file 1," and your application will respond with the contents of file 1.

In a case such as this, you just want to execute some application logic to fetch a file and then spit it out to your mailer. It is unlikely that any of Mason's powerful features would be necessary in order to perform this task; in fact, Mason would probably get in the way.

Another example can illustrate this issue further. Let's assume we want to build an application to serve as the backend for a new web site focused on news about Hong Kong movies. Let's assume you intelligently decide to make a single component to generate a story box. A story box has a headline, an author, and the first 500 characters of the story. If there are more, it has a link to read the whole thing.

Here's the HTML-making portion of the component:

```
<h1><% $story{headline} | h %></h1>

<p>
written by <b><% $story{author} | h %></b>
</p>

<p>
<% substr ($story{body}, 0, 500) | h %>
</p>
% if ( length $story{body} > 500 ) {
<p>
<a href="full_story.html?story_id=<% $story{story_id} %>">
Read the full story
</a>
</p>
% }
```

Pretty simple, no? The component contains *some* application logic, of course. It checks the length of the story's body and changes the output depending on it. But the real question is where the %story hash comes from. Let's assume that we call another component to get it. So then we have this:

```
<%init>
 my %story = $m->comp('get_newest_story.mas');
</%init>
```

So what's the problem? Well, there is none as long as the only time you want to get the newest story is in a Mason environment. But what if you wanted to send out the top story anytime someone sent an email to you at *newest_story@hkmovienews.example.com*?

Hmm, let's write a quick program to do that:

```perl
#!/usr/bin/perl -w

use HTML::Mason::Interp;

my $outbuf;
my $interp = HTML::Mason::Interp->new( out_method => \$outbuf );

my %story = $interp->exec('/path/to/get_newest_story.mas');
send_story_mail(%story);

# imagine the mail is sent
```

Not so bad, we suppose. Here are some issues to consider:

- You just loaded a couple of thousand lines of Perl code in order to do a simple database fetch and then send an email. And because this email interface has become quite popular, it's happening a few times every minute. Your sysadmin is looking for you and she's carrying a big spiked club!

- The return value of $interp->exec() may not be what you'd expect. If the component you called did an $m->abort('something') internally, the return value will be 'something'. This works fine when using the Mason Apache-Handler code, but it isn't what you expected in this situation.

- If any component you call (or that it calls) references $r (the Apache request object), it will fail spectacularly. It's nice to feel free to access $r in your components, but if you were trying to make a multipurpose Mason system you'd have to be sure not to use $r in any component that might be used outside of a web context, and you would feel fettered and stifled.

Now imagine that you multiply this by 40 more data processing and application logic components. Then remember that if you try to do 'perldoc get_newest_story' from the command line, it won't do anything! And remember that you have 40 separate files, one per API call. Now imagine that you take advantage of Mason's inheritance and other fancy features in your data processing code. Now imagine trying to debug this later.

If, however, you put the 'get_newest_story' functionality into a module, you could call this module from both your component and your email sending program, looking something like this:

```perl
#!/usr/bin/perl -w

use MyApplication;

my %story = MyApplication->get_newest_story();
MyApplication->send_story_mail(%story);
```

The advantages include:

- You can easily preload your shared library code in the main Apache server at startup, resulting in a memory savings.

- Performancewise, calling a subroutine in a module is much more lightweight than calling a Mason component. A Mason component call involves calling a subroutine and also performing a bunch of overhead tasks like checking the age of the component file, checking required arguments and types, and so on.

- Perl modules have well-known mechanisms for documentation and regression testing. Psychologically, we feel that an API is more stable when we have a documented module that instantiates it. A tree of components feels more mutable, and we hate feeling as if we've built a shaky house of logic that we don't necessarily understand in the end.

The Other Side

However, that's not to say you don't lose anything. Here's a summary of a number of arguments we've heard on the possible advantages of using Mason components for data processing, along with our responses.

Data processing in Mason components provides developers with a unified way of writing both display and processing code. This is especially appreciated by less experienced developers not accustomed to writing modules.

Perl modules are one of the fundamental tools for writing reusable code and creating maintainable applications. It may be convenient to use Mason for data processing in the short term, but in the long term you'll be better served by moving to a more formalized approach involving separate mechanisms for processing and display.

For rapid development environments, it's hands-down faster to create a new component, and you are less likely to have a merge conflict with another person's work.

Once a module is created, adding a new function or method to it is fairly trivial, but the initial process does require some thought. And yes, merge conflicts are more likely when using version control because you will have fewer files, though in our experience this is not terribly common.

Mason has support for private versions of processing code. One person said that where they work everyone has a version of the site checked out from version control and views his version through TransHandler magic via <name>.dev.example.com. Developers can change their own version of the processing components and preview the changes. If the processing code were in modules, every developer would need his own Perl interpreter, thus a separate server.

It is *possible*, though not completely trivial, to provide every developer a unique copy of the modules in his own server. This can be more of a maintenance hassle, particularly when adding new developers, though some automation can eliminate the hassle. Again, this is a case of investing time up front as an investment in the future. This issue is discussed in Chapter 11.

For example, giving each developer his own Apache daemon is relatively easy, running it on a unique high-numbered port. Each developer's server can then use the developer's local copies of the code, modules, and components, so the developer can work in isolation and feel free to break things without slowing anyone else down.

Or, just as easily, each developer can run a daemon locally on his own computer, perhaps connecting to a central test database or even running a RDBMS locally.*

Most importantly, nothing can replace solid coding guidelines, development practices, and testing, coupled with tools like version control.

Components give you many fringe benefits over Perl subroutines: named argument passing and checking, result caching, a lightweight hierarchical naming structure, component logging, and so on.

We can't really argue with this. It's true. However, we have yet to find ourselves really wishing for this functionality when developing application logic. Named arguments are nice, but CPAN provides several nice solutions for validating named arguments, including `Params::Validate`, which Mason uses internally.

There have been times when shoving data processing into a Mason component was exactly what we've needed. The code sits there right next to the code that calls it, not off in *site_perl/*, which should usually have some tight controls over what gets put in it. In a matter of seconds you can try things out without worrying about module naming, namespace collisions, server restarts, and so forth. Then when you've had a chance to think about what a good interface should be like, you can migrate the code to a module. It's all well and good to extol the virtues of good planning, but the creative process is seldom very plannable unless you've done a similar task before.

On yet another hand, you can always maintain your own module directories and add them to Perl's search path via a quick use `lib`.

We are certainly not advocates of the "design everything and make sure it's perfect before coding" school of design. Our points are more about the end product than the development process itself. Your process should lead to the creation of clean, maintainable code. If you make a mess while writing it, we certainly won't criticize as long as it gets cleaned up in the end.

---

* Though a local RDBMS may be more trouble than it's worth with a high-maintenance RDBMS like Oracle.

Our summary is simple. Writing your application logic and data processing as Mason components is a shortcut that can bite you later. Like many design trade-offs, it speeds up initial time to release while guaranteeing maintenance pain in the future.

Components as Independent Units

Like subroutines in any language, Mason components are vulnerable to the disease known as "jumboitis." Symptoms of this disease include monstrous chains of `if-elsif` clauses as well as a general excess of code. This disease, untreated, can lead to developer confusion, application fragility, and apathetic mindset toward fixing bugs because "it doesn't matter, the code will still suck."

It is never a good idea to pack all your decisions into a single component. Even if you're not planning to reuse a particular piece of Mason code, it doesn't hurt to turn it into a separate component in order to demarcate pieces of code as having different functions. In some cases, you may prefer to use subcomponents instead of actually creating a separate file.

One practice that often leads to jumboitis is often seen in the CGI world. Quite commonly, a single CGI program starts off with a big chain of `if-elsif` clauses that basically try to figure out what the program is supposed to do. First it displays a form then it processes the form output, and then it might show the form again with errors marked, or it might show another page, then update the database, then show an index page, and then...

OK, we're out of breath and our brains are throbbing. This sort of code is scary though we've all probably written something just like it in the past.

It would be easy to do this with Mason, but there's no need. In a cleaner design, you'd have one component display the form. Then it would post to a component that would handle the form input, which can call another component or a module to do data validation. If the data has errors, it redirects back to the form component. Otherwise it might redirect to a component that shows a preview of the data. Then a Submit button could post the data to yet another component that updates the database (after doing data validation again, no doubt). As long as you've got smooth pathways for sharing data among components, you'll be able to design a component tree that makes sense and isn't a nightmare to maintain.

And don't forget about autohandlers and dhandlers, which can go a long way to reducing code duplication with very little effort. We saw this sort of pattern in Chapter 8 when we looked at the user and project editing components.

Component Layout

If you are working with other people on a Mason project, you should probably standardize the layout of code within your components, if for no other reason than consistency. You may find that putting all of the text generation at the top of the component, followed by other sections like <%args> and <%init>, is a good layout. This means that when HTML folks have to look at your components, they won't be overwhelmed by many lines of what is, to them, gibberish. Here is another possible component layout stardard:

- A <%doc> section describing what the component does. You can omit this section if it purpose is obvious—for some suitable strict definition of "obvious."
- The <%args> section.
- The <%flags> section.
- The <%attr> section.
- The text generation portion of the component, along with whatever embedded code it contains.
- The <%once> section.
- The <%shared> section.
- The <%init> section.
- The <%cleanup> section.
- The <%filter> section.
- All of the component's <%def> sections.
- All of the component's <%method> sections.

In turn, each subcomponent or method should follow the same ordering of sections as the main component.

The general aesthetic is that we first put sections that define the component's interface (<%doc>, <%args>, <%flags>, <%attr>), then the main body of the component, then any sections written in Perl. This tends to balance the needs of Perl developers, HTML developers, and code administrators.

Alternatively, you could place the <%args>, <%flags>, and <%attr> sections after the main body. You might do this if Mason components may be edited by nonprogramming web designers; they will probably prefer to see the text portions of the component first without being distracted by code sections that they may not understand anyway. This is the style we adopted for our sample site, in Chapter 8.

Of course, use a layout that makes sense in your specific situation. For instance, if a subcomponent is tiny enough, you might just put it near the code that calls it. Choose a layout that gives you inner peace.

File Naming and Directory Layout

As with your component layout, the most important aspect of naming is consistency. Give your components consistent names and file extensions. For example, components intended to be called by a client might end in *.html* or *.mhtml*, while components intended only for use by other components might end in *.mas*. Consistently naming your files will simplify your web server setup and lots of maintenance tasks as well as slightly lowering the barrier to entry for new developers.

One other consideration when determining your directory and file layout is how you plan to use autohandlers. One symptom of a bad layout is finding yourself frequently using the `inherit` flag to override a component's default inheritance. Even worse is when you have many components in a single directory, all with *different* `inherit` flags. That is a strong sign that you should consider grouping files together based on inheritance.

Of course, you can always use the `inherit` flag to change a component's parent, but if you can avoid it and simply use the closest autohandler file, that's one less complication to deal with and one less source of potential bugs.

Random Advice

Finally, we want to say a few things that don't justify their own section:

- Always put whitespace around the contents of a substitution tag. This looks nicer.
- Don't output content and return a value from the same component. This makes for a confusing API.
- Put as much code as possible in external modules, and try to stick as much of the rest into <%init>, <%once>, and <%shared> blocks. Don't litter your components with <%perl> blocks and Perl lines. Interspersing HTML (or other text) with lots of code makes for hard-to-read components.
- Use a period (.) as the first character of subcomponent names.

None of these rules are etched in stone, but they provide some good guidelines to your coding that may make your life, and your fellow coders' lives, a little more pleasant.

## CHAPTER 11

Recipes

No, we are not going teach you how to make a delicious tofu and soybean stew. But this is almost as good. This chapter shows how to do some common Mason tasks, some of them with more than one implementation.

Sessions

For many of our session examples, we will be using the `Apache::Session` module. Despite its name, this module doesn't actually require mod_perl or Apache, though that is the context in which it was born and in which it's most often used. It implements a simple tied hash interface to a persistent object.[*] It has one major gotcha: you must make sure that the session object gets cleaned up properly (usually by letting it go out of scope), so that it will be written to disk after each access.

Without Touching httpd.conf

Here is an example that doesn't involve changing any of your Apache configuration settings. The following code should be placed in a top-level autohandler. Any component that needs to use the session will have to inherit from this component, either directly or via a longer inheritance chain.

It uses cookies to store the session.

```
<%once>
 use Apache::Cookie;
 use Apache::Session::File;
</%once>
<%init>
 my %c = Apache::Cookie->fetch;
 my $session_id =
     exists $c{masonbook_session} ? $c{masonbook_session}->value : undef;
```

---

[*] If you are not familiar with Perl's tied variable feature, we suggest reading the perltie manpages (`perldoc perltie`).

First, it loads the necessary modules. Normally we recommend that you do this at server startup via a PerlModule directive in your *httpd.conf* file or in your *handler.pl* file to save memory, but we load them here just to show you which ones we are using. The component uses the `Apache::Cookie` module to fetch any cookies that might have been sent by the browser. Then we check for the existence of a cookie called `masonbook_session`, which if it exists should contain a valid session ID.

```
local *MasonBook::Session;

eval {
    tie %MasonBook::Session, 'Apache::Session::File', $session_id, {
        Directory => '/tmp/sessions',
        LockDirectory => '/tmp/sessions',
    };
};

if ($@) {
    die $@ unless $@ =~ /Object does not exist/;  # Re-throw

    $m->redirect('/bad_session.html');
}
```

The first line ensures that when this component ends, the session variable will go out of scope, which triggers `Apache::Session`'s cleanup mechanisms. This is quite important, as otherwise the data will never be written to disk. Even worse, `Apache::Session` may still be maintaining various locks internally, leading to deadlock. We use `local()` to localize the symbol table entry `*MasonBook::Session`; it's not enough to localize just the hash `%MasonBook::Session`, because the `tie()` magic is attached to the symbol table entry. It's also worth mentioning that we use a global variable rather than a lexical one, because we want this variable to be available to all components.

If the value in the `$session_id` variable is undef, that is not a problem. The `Apache::Session` module simply creates a new session ID. However, if `$session_id` is defined but does not represent a valid session, an exception will be thrown. This means either that the user's session has expired or that she's trying to feed us a bogus ID. Either way, we want to tell her what's happened, so we redirect to another page that will explain things. To trap the exception, we wrap the `tie()` in an eval `{}` block.

If an exception is thrown, we check `$@` to see whether the message indicates that the session isn't valid. Any other error is fatal. If the session isn't valid, we use the `redirect()` method provided by the request object.

Finally, we send the user a cookie:

```
Apache::Cookie->new( $r,
                     name => 'masonbook_session',
                     value => $MasonBook::Session{_session_id},
                     path => '/',
                     expires => '+1d',
                   )->bake;
```

This simply uses the Apache::Cookie module to ensure that a cookie will be sent to the client with the response headers. This cookie is called 'masonbook_session' and is the one we checked for earlier. It doesn't hurt to send the cookie every time a page is viewed, though this will reset the expiration time of the cookie each time it is set. If you want the cookie to persist for only a certain fixed length of time after the session is created, don't resend the cookie.

```
    $m->call_next;
    </%init>
```

This line simply calls the next component in the inheritance chain. Presumably, other components down the line may change the contents of %MasonBook::Session, and those modifications will be written to disk at the end of the request.

Example 11-1 shows the entire component.

Example 11-1. session-autohandler-Apache-Session.comp

```
<%once>
 use Apache::Cookie;
 use Apache::Session::File;
</%once>
<%init>
 my %c = Apache::Cookie->fetch;
 my $session_id =
     exists $c{masonbook_session} ? $c{masonbook_session}->value : undef;

 local *MasonBook::Session;

 eval {
     tie %MasonBook::Session, 'Apache::Session::File', $session_id, {
         Directory => '/tmp/sessions',
         LockDirectory => '/tmp/sessions',
     };
 };

 if ($@) {
     die $@ unless $@ =~ /Object does not exist/;  # Re-throw

     $m->redirect('/bad_session.html');
 }

 Apache::Cookie->new( $r,
                      name => 'masonbook_session',
                      value => $MasonBook::Session{_session_id},
                      path => '/',
                      expires => '+1d',
                     )->bake;

  $m->call_next;
</%init>
```

Predeclaring the Global via an httpd.conf File

It'd be nice to be able to simply use the global session variable without having to type the fully qualified name, %MasonBook::Session in every component. That can be done by adding this line to your *httpd.conf* file:

```
PerlSetVar MasonAllowGlobals %session
```

Of course, if you're running more than one Mason-based site that uses sessions, you may need to come up with a unique variable name.

Adding this to your *httpd.conf* means you can simply reference the %session variable in all of your components, without a qualifying package name. The %session variable would actually end up in the HTML::Mason::Commands package, rather than MasonBook.

Predeclaring the Global via a handler.pl Script

If you have a *handler.pl* script, you could also use the session-making code we just saw. If you wanted to declare a %session global for all your components, you'd simply pass the allow_globals parameter to your interpreter when you make it, like this:

```
my $ah =
    HTML::Mason::ApacheHandler->new( comp_root => ...,
                                     data_dir  => ...,
                                     allow_globals => [ '%session' ] );
```

You might also choose to incorporate the session-making code into your handler subroutine rather than placing it in a component. This would eliminate the need to make sure that all components inherit from the session-making component.

Using Cache::Cache for Sessions

Just to show you that you don't have to use Apache::Session, here is a simple alternate using Cache::Cache, which is integrated into Mason via the request object's cache() method.

This version also sets up the session in a top-level autohandler just like our first session example. It looks remarkably similar.

```
<%once>
 use Apache::Cookie;
 use Cache::FileCache;
 use Digest::SHA1;
</%once>
```

Again, for memory savings, you should load these modules at server startup.

```
<%init>
 my $cache =
     Cache::FileCache->new( namespace  => 'Mason-Book-Session',
                            cache_root => '/tmp/sessions',
```

```
default_expires_in   => 60 * 60 * 24, # 1 day
auto_purge_interval  => 60 * 60 * 24, # 1 day
auto_purge_on_set => 1 } );
```

This creates a new cache object that will be used to store sessions. Without going into too much detail, this creates a new caching object that will store data on the filesystem under */tmp/sessions*.* The namespace is basically equivalent to a subdirectory in this case, and the remaining options tell the cache that, by default, stored data should be purged after one day and that it should check for purgeable items once per day.

```
my %c = Apache::Cookie->fetch;

if (exists $c{masonbook_session}) {
    my $session_id = $c{masonbook_session}->value;
    $MasonBook::Session = $cache->get($session_id);
}

$MasonBook::Session ||=
    { _session_id => Digest::SHA1::sha1_hex( time, rand, $$ ) };
```

These lines simply retrieve an existing session based on the session ID from the cookie, if such a cookie exists. If this fails or if there was no session ID in the cookie, we make a new one with a randomly generated session ID. The algorithm used earlier for generating the session ID is more or less the same as the one provided by Apache::Session's Apache::Session::Generate::MD5 module, except that it uses the SHA1 digest module. This algorithm should provide more than enough randomness to ensure that there will never be two identical session IDs generated. It may *not* be enough to keep people from guessing possible session IDs, though, so if you want make sure that a session cannot be hijacked, you should incorporate a secret into the digest algorithm input.

```
Apache::Cookie->new( $r,
                     name => 'masonbook_session',
                     value => $MasonBook::Session->{_session_id},
                     path => '/',
                     expires => '+1d',
                   )->bake;
```

We then set a cookie in the browser that contains the session ID. This cookie will expire in one day. Again, this piece is identical to what we saw when using Apache::Session.

```
eval { $m->call_next };

$cache->set( $MasonBook::Session->{_session_id} => $MasonBook::Session );
```

---

* See the documentation accompanying the Cache::Cache modules for more detail.

Unlike with Apache::Session, we need to explicitly tell our cache object to save the data. This means we need to wrap the call to $m->call_next() in an eval {} block in order to catch any exceptions thrown in other components. Otherwise, this part looks almost exactly like our example using Apache::Session.

```
die $@ if $@;
</%init>
```

After saving the session, we rethrow any exception we may have gotten.

The entire component is shown in Example 11-2.

Example 11-2. session-autohandler-Cache-Cache.comp

```
<%once>
 use Apache::Cookie;
 use Digest::SHA1;
</%once>
<%init>
 my $cache =
     Cache::FileCache->new( namespace  => 'Mason-Book-Session',
                            cache_root => '/tmp/sessions',
                            default_expires_in  => 60 * 60 * 24, # 1 day
                            auto_purge_interval => 60 * 60 * 24, # 1 day
                            auto_purge_on_set => 1 } );

 my %c = Apache::Cookie->fetch;

 if (exists $c{masonbook_session}) {
     my $session_id = $c{masonbook_session}->value;
     $MasonBook::Session = $cache->get($session_id);
 }

 $MasonBook::Session ||=
     { _session_id => Digest::SHA1::sha1_hex( time, rand, $$ ) };

 Apache::Cookie->new( $r,
                      name => 'masonbook_session',
                      value => $MasonBook::Session->{_session_id},
                      path => '/',
                      expires => '+1d',
                    )->bake;

 eval { $m->call_next };

 $cache->set( $MasonBook::Session->{_session_id} => $MasonBook::Session );

 die $@ if $@;
</%init>
```

Sessions with `Cache::Cache` have these major differences from those with `Apache::Session`:

- The session itself is not a tied hash. Objects are faster than tied hashes but not as transparent.

- No attempt is made to track whether or not the session has changed. It is *always* written to the disk at the end of a session. This trades the performance boost of `Apache::Session`'s behavior for the assurance that the data is always written to disk.

  When using `Apache::Session`, many programmers are often surprised that changes to a nested data structure in the session hash, like:

  ```
  $session{user}{name} = 'Bob';
  ```

  are not seen as changes to the top-level %session hash. If no changes to this hash are seen, `Apache::Session` will not write the hash out to storage.

  As a workaround, some programmers may end up doing something like:

  ```
  $session{force_a_write}++;
  ```

  or:

  ```
  $session{last_accessed} = time();
  ```

  after the session is created. Using `Cache::Cache` and explicitly saving the session every time incurs the same penalty as always changing a member of an `Apache::Session` hash.

Putting the Session ID in the URL

If you don't want to, or cannot, use cookies, you can store the session ID in the URL. This can be somewhat of a hassle because it means that you have to somehow process all the URLs you generate. Using Mason, this isn't as bad as it could be. There are two ways to do this:

One would be to put a filter in your top-level autohandler that looks something like this:

```
<%filter>
s/href="([^"])+"/add_session_id($1)/eg;
s/action="([^"])+"/add_session_id($1)/eg;
</%filter>
```

The `add_session_id()` subroutine, which should be defined in a module, would look something like this:

```
sub add_session_id {
    my $url = shift;
    return $url if $url =~ m{^\w+://}; # Don't alter external URLs
    if ($url =~ /\?/) {
        $url =~ s/\?/?session_id=$MasonBook::Session{_session_id}&/;
    } else {
        $url .= "?session_id=$MasonBook::Session{_session_id}";
```

```
        }
        return $url;
    }
```

This routine accounts for external links as well as links with or without an existing query string. However, it doesn't handle links with fragments properly.

The drawback to putting this in the <%filter> is that it filters URLs only in the content body, not in headers. Therefore you'll need to handle those cases separately.

The other solution would be to create all URLs (including those intended for redirects) via a dedicated component or subroutine that would add the session ID. This latter solution is probably a better idea, as it handles redirects properly. The drawback with this strategy is that you'll have a Mason component call for every link, instead of just regular HTML.

We'll add a single line (bolded in Example 11-3) to the */lib/url.mas* component we saw in Chapter 8. Now this component expects there to be a variable named %UserSession.

Example 11-3. url-plus-session-id.mas

```
<%args>
 $scheme   => 'http'
 $username => undef
 $password => ''
 $host     => undef
 $port     => undef
 $path
 %query    => ()
 $fragment => undef
</%args>
<%init>
 my $uri = URI->new;

 if ($host) {
    $uri->scheme($scheme);
    if (defined $username) {
      $uri->authority( "$username:$password" );
    }

    $uri->host($host);
    $uri->port($port) if $port;
 }

 # Sometimes we may want to path in a query string as part of the
 # path but the URI module will escape the question mark.
 my $q;

 if ( $path =~ s/\?(.*)$// ) {
    $q = $1;
 }
```

Example 11-3. url-plus-session-id.mas (continued)

```
$uri->path($path);
# If there was a query string, we integrate it into the query
# parameter.

if ($q) {
    %query = ( %query, split /[&=]/, $q );
}

$query{session_id} = $UserSession{session_id};

# $uri->query_form doesn't handle hash ref values properly
while ( my ( $key, $value ) = each %query ) {
    $query{$key} = ref $value eq 'HASH' ? [ %$value ] : $value;
}

$uri->query_form(%query) if %query;

$uri->fragment($fragment) if $fragment;
</%init>
<% $uri->canonical | n %>\
```

Making Use of Autoflush

Every once in a while you may have to output a very large component or file to the client. Simply letting this accumulate in the buffer could use up a lot of memory. Furthermore, the slow response time may make the user think that the site has stalled.

Example 11-4 sends out the contents of a potentially large file without sucking up lots of memory.

Example 11-4. send_file-autoflush.comp

```
<%args>
 $filename
</%args>
<%init>
 local *FILE;
 open FILE, "< $filename" or die "Cannot open $filename: $!";
 $m->autoflush(1);
 while (<FILE>) {
     $m->print($_);
 }
 $m->autoflush(0);
</%init>
```

If each line wasn't too huge, you might just flush the buffer every once in a while, as in Example 11-5.

Example 11-5. send_file-flush-every-10.comp

```
<%args>
 $filename
</%args>
<%init>
 local *FILE;
 open FILE, "< $filename" or die "Cannot open $filename: $!";
 while (<FILE>) {
     $m->print($_);
     $m->flush_buffer unless $. % 10;
 }
 $m->flush_buffer;
</%init>
```

The `unless $. % 10` bit makes use of the special Perl variable $., which is the current line number of the file being read. If this number modulo 10 is equal to zero, we flush the buffer. This means that we flush the buffer every 10 lines. Replace the number 10 with any desired value.

User Authentication and Authorization

One problem that web sites have to solve over and over is user authentication and authorization. These two topics are related but not the same, as some might think. Authentication is the process of figuring out if someone is who he says he is, and usually involves checking passwords or keys of some sort. Authorization comes after this, when we want to determine whether or not a particular person is allowed to perform a certain action.

There are a number of modules on CPAN intended to help do these things under mod_perl. In fact, Apache has separate request-handling phases for both authentication and authorization that mod_perl can handle. It is certainly possible to use these modules with Mason.

You can also do authentication and authorization using Mason components (as seen in Chapter 8). Authentication will usually involve some sort of request for a login and password, after which you give the user some sort of token (either in a cookie or a session) that indicates that he has been authenticated. You can then check the validity of this token for each request.

If you have such a token, authorization simply consists of checking that the user to whom the token belongs is allowed to perform a given action.

Using Apache::AuthCookie

The `Apache::AuthCookie` module, available from CPAN, handles both authentication and authorization via mod_perl and can be easily hooked into Mason. Let's just skip all the details of configuring `Apache::AuthCookie`, which requires various settings in your server config file, and show how to make the interface to Mason.

`Apache::AuthCookie` requires that you create a "login script" that will be executed the first time a browser tries to access a protected area. Calling this a script is actually somewhat misleading since it is really a page rather than a script (though it could be a script that generates a page). Regardless, using a Mason component for your login script merely requires that you specify the path to your Mason component for the login script parameter.

We'll call this script *AuthCookieLoginForm-login.comp*, as shown in Example 11-6.

Example 11-6. AuthCookieLoginForm-login.comp

```
<html>
<head>
<title>Mason Book AuthCookie Login Form</title>
</head>
<body>
<p>
Your attempt to access this document was denied
(<% $r->prev->subprocess_env("AuthCookieReason") %>).  Please enter
your username and password.
</p>

<form action="/AuthCookieLoginSubmit">
<input type="hidden" name="destination" value="<% $r->prev->uri %>">
<table align="left">
 <tr>
  <td align="right"><b>Username:</b></td>
  <td><input type="text" name="credential_0" size="10" maxlength="10"></td>
 </tr>
 <tr>
  <td align="right"><b>Password:</b></td>
  <td><input type="password" name="credential_1" size="8" maxlength="8"></td>
 </tr>
 <tr>
  <td colspan="2" align="center"><input type="submit" value="Continue"></td>
 </tr>
</table>
</form>

</body>
</html>
```

This component is a modified version of the example login script included with the `Apache::AuthCookie` distribution.

The action used for this form, */AuthCookieLoginSubmit*, is configured as part of your AuthCookie configuration in your *httpd.conf* file.

That is about it for interfacing this module with Mason. The rest of authentication and authorization is handled by configuring mod_perl to use Apache::AuthCookie to protect anything on your site that needs authorization. A very simple configuration might include the following directives:

```
PerlSetVar MasonBookLoginScript /AuthCookieLoginForm.comp

<Location /AuthCookieLoginSubmit>
    AuthType MasonBook::AuthCookieHandler
    AuthName MasonBook
    SetHandler perl-script
    PerlHandler MasonBook::AuthCookieHandler->login
</Location>

<Location /protected>
    AuthType MasonBook::AuthCookieHandler
    AuthName MasonBook
    PerlAuthenHandler MasonBook::AuthCookieHandler->authenticate
    PerlAuthzHandler MasonBook::AuthCookieHandler->authorize
    require valid-user
</Location>
```

The MasonBook::AuthCookieHandler module would look like this:

```
package MasonBook::AuthCookieHandler;

use strict;

use base qw(Apache::AuthCookie);

use Digest::SHA1;

my $secret = "You think I'd tell you?  Hah!";

sub authen_cred {
    my $self = shift;
    my $r = shift;
    my ($username, $password) = @_;

    # implementing _is_valid_user() is out of the scope of this chapter
    if ( _is_valid_user($username, $password) ) {
        my $session_key =
          $username . '::' . Digest::SHA1::sha1_hex( $username, $secret );
        return $session_key;
    }
}

sub authen_ses_key {
    my $self = shift;
    my $r = shift;
    my $session_key = shift;

    my ($username, $mac) = split /::/, $session_key;
```

```
        if ( Digest::SHA1::sha1_hex( $username, $secret ) eq $mac ) {
            return $session_key;
        }
    }
```

This provides the minimal interface an Apache::AuthCookie subclass needs to provide to get authentication working.

Authentication Without Cookies

But what if you don't want to use Apache::AuthCookie? Your site may need to work
without using cookies.

First, we will show an example authentication system that uses only Mason and
passes the authentication token around via the URL (actually, via a session).

This example assumes that we already have some sort of session system that passes
the session ID around as part of the URL, as discussed previously.

We start with a quick login form. We will call this component *login_form.html*, as
shown in Example 11-7.

Example 11-7. login_form.html

```
<%args>
 $username => ''
 $password => ''
 $redirect_to => ''
 @errors => ()
</%args>
<html>
<head>
<title>Mason Book Login</title>
</head>

<body>

% if (@errors) {
<h2>Errors</h2>
%    foreach (@errors) {
<b><% $_ | h %></b><br>
%    }
% }

<form action="login_submit.html">
<input type="hidden" name="redirect_to" value="<% $redirect_to %>">
<table align="left">
 <tr>
  <td align="right"><b>Login:</b></td>
  <td><input type="text" name="username" value="<% $username %>"></td>
 </tr>
 <tr>
  <td align="right"><b>Password:</b></td>
```

Example 11-7. login_form.html (continued)

```
  <td><input type="password" name="password" value="<% $password %>"></td>
  </tr>
  <tr>
  <td colspan="2" align="center"><input type="submit" value="Login"></td>
  </tr>
</table>
</form>

</body>
</html>
```

This form uses some of the same techniques we saw in Chapter 8 to prepopulate the form and handle errors.

Now let's make the component that handles the form submission. This component, called *login_submit.html* and shown in Example 11-8, will check the username and password and, if they are valid, place an authentication token into the user's session.

Example 11-8. login_submit.html

```
<%args>
 $username
 $password
 $redirect_to
</%args>
<%init>
 if (my @errors = check_login($username, $password) {
     $m->comp( 'redirect.mas',
               path => 'login_form.html',
               query => { errors => \@errors,
                          username => $username,
                          password => $password,
                          redirect_to => $redirect_to } );
 }

 $MasonBook::Session{username} = $username;
 $MasonBook::Session{token} =
     Digest::SHA1::sha1_hex( 'My secret phrase', $username );

 $m->comp( 'redirect.mas',
           path => $redirect_to );
</%init>
```

This component simply checks (via magic hand waving) whether the username and password are valid and, if so, generates an authentication token that is added to the user's session. To generate this token, we take the username, which is also in the session, and combine it with a secret phrase. We then generate a MAC from those two things.

The authentication and authorization check looks like this:

```
if ( $MasonBook::Session{token} ) {
    if ( $MasonBook::Session{token} eq
        Digest::SHA1::sha1_hex( 'My secret phrase',
                                $MasonBook::Session{username} ) {

        # ... valid login, do something here
    } else {
        # ... someone is trying to be sneaky!
    }
} else { # no token
    my $wanted_page = $r->uri;

    # Append query string if we have one.
    $wanted_page .= '?' . $r->args if $r->args;

    $m->comp( 'redirect.mas',
              path => '/login/login_form.html',
              query => { redirect_to => $wanted_page } );
}
```

We could put all the pages that require authorization in a single directory tree and have a top-level autohandler in that tree do the check. If there is no token to check, we redirect the browser to the login page, and after a successful login the user will return, assuming she submitted valid login credentials.

Access Controls with Attributes

The components we saw previously assumed that there are only two access levels, unauthenticated and authenticated. A more complicated version of this code might involve checking that the user has a certain access level or role.

In that case, we'd first check that we had a valid authentication token and then go on to check that the user actually had the appropriate access rights. This is simply an extra step in the authorization process.

Using attributes, we can easily define access controls for different portions of our site. Let's assume that we have four access levels, Guest, User, Editor, and Admin. Most of the site is public and viewable by anyone. Some parts of the site require a valid login, while some require a higher level of privilege.

We implement our access check in our top-level autohandler, /autohandler, from which all other components *must* inherit in order for the access control code to be effective.

```
<%init>
my $user = get_user();  # again, hand waving

my $required_access = $m->base_comp->attr('required_access');

unless ( $user->has_access_level($required_access) ) {
    # ... do something like send them to another page
```

```
    }
   $m->call_next;
</%init>
<%attr>
   required_access => 'Guest'
</%attr>
```

It is crucial that we set a default access level in this autohandler. By doing this, we are saying that, by default, all components are accessible by all people, since every visitor will have at least Guest access.

We can override this default elsewhere. For example, in a component called */admin/ autohandler*, we might have:

```
<%attr>
   required_access => 'Admin'
</%attr>
```

As long as all the components in the */admin/* directory inherit from the */admin/ autohandler* component and don't override the required_access attribute, we have effectively limited that directory (and its subdirectories) to admin users only. If we for some reason had an individual component in the */admin/* directory that we wanted editors to be able to see, we could simply set the required_access attribute for that component to 'Editor'.

Co-Branding Color Schemes

One common business practice these days is to take a useful site and offer "cobranded" versions of it to other businesses. A co-branded site might display different graphics and text for each client while retaining the same basic layout and functionality across all clients.

Mason is extremely well-suited to this task. Let's look at how we might apply a new color scheme to each co-brand.

For the purpose of these examples, we're going to assume that the name of the co-brand has already been determined and is being passed to our components as a variable called $cobrand. This variable could be set up by including the co-brand in the query string, in a session, or as part of a hostname.

With Stylesheets

One way to do this is to use stylesheets for all of your pages. Each cobrand will then have a different stylesheet. However, since most of the stylesheets will be the same for each client, you'll probably want to have a parent stylesheet that all the others inherit from.

Of course, while it is *supposed* to be possible to inherit stylesheets, some older browsers like Netscape 4.x don't support that at all, so we will generate the stylesheet on the fly using Mason instead. This gives you all the flexibility of inheritance without the compatibility headaches.

The stylesheet will be called via:

```
<link rel="stylesheet" href="/styles.css?cobrand=<% $cobrand %>">
```

Presumably, this snippet would go in a top-level autohandler.*

The *styles.css* component might look something like Example 11-9.

Example 11-9. styles.css

```
% while (my ($name, $def) = each %styles) {
<% $name %> <% $def %>
% }
<%args>
 $cobrand
</%args>
<%init>
 my %styles;

 die "Security violation, style=$style" unless $cobrand =~ /^\w+$/;
 foreach my $file ('default.css', "$cobrand.css") {
     local *FILE;
     open FILE, "< /var/styles/$file"
         or die "Cannot read /var/styles/$file: $!";
     while (<FILE>) {
         next unless /(\S+) \s+ (\S.*)/x;
         $styles{$1} = $2;
     }
     close FILE;
 }

 $r->content_type('text/css');
</%init>
```

Of course, this assumes that each line of the stylesheet represents a single style definition, something like:

```
.foo_class { color: blue }
```

This isn't that hard to enforce for a project, but it limits you to just a subset of CSS functionality. If this is not desirable, check out the CSS and CSS::SAC modules on CPAN.

This component first grabs all the default styles from the *default.css* file and then overwrites any styles that are defined in the co-brand-specific file.

---

* The overachieving reader may want to imagine a dhandler-based solution with URLs like */styles/<cobrand>* *.css*.

One nice aspect of this method is that if the site designers are not programmers, they can just work with plain old stylesheets, which should make them more comfortable.

With Code

Another way to do this is to store the color preferences for each co-brand in a component or perhaps in the database. At the beginning of each request, you could fetch these colors and pass them to each component.

For example, in your top-level autohandler you might have:

```
<%init>
 my $cobrand = determine_cobrand(); # magic hand waving again

 my %colors = cobrand_colors($cobrand);

 $m->call_next(%ARGS, colors => \%colors);
</%init>
```

The cobrand_colors() subroutine could be made to use defaults whenever they were not overridden for a given co-brand.

Then the components might do something like this:

```
<%args>
 %colors
</%args>

<html>
<head>
<title>Title</title>
</head>

<body bgcolor="<% $colors{body_bgcolor} %>">
...
```

This technique is a bit more awkward, as it requires that you have a color set for every possibility ($colors{left_menu_table_cell}, $colors{footer_text}, ad nauseam). It also works *only* for colors, whereas stylesheets allow you to customize fonts and layouts. But if you're targeting browsers that don't support stylesheets or you don't know CSS, this is a possible alternative.

Developer Environments

Having a development environment is a good thing for many reasons. Testing potential changes on your production server is likely to get you fired, for one thing.

Ideally, you want each developer to have his own playground where changes he makes don't affect others. Then, when something is working, it can be checked into source control and everyone else can use the updated version.

Multiple Component Roots

A fairly simple way to achieve this goal is by giving each developer his own component root, which will be checked before the main root.

Developers can work on components in their own private roots without fear of breaking anything for anyone else. Once changes are made, the altered component can be checked into source control and moved into the shared root, where everyone will see it.

This means that one HTML::Mason::ApacheHandler object needs to be created for each developer. This can be done solely by changing your server configuration file, but it is easiest to do this using an external handler.

The determination of which object to use can be made either by looking at the URL path or by using a different hostname for each developer.

By path

This example checks the URL to determine which developer's private root to use:

```
use Apache::Constants qw(DECLINED);

my %ah;

sub handler {
    my $r = shift;
    my $uri = $r->uri;
    $uri =~ s,^/(\w+),,;  # remove the developer name from the path

    my $developer = $1 or return DECLINED;

    $r->uri($uri);  # set the uri to the new path

    $ah{$developer} ||=
      HTML::Mason::ApacheHandler->new
          ( comp_root => [ [ dev  => "/home/$developer/mason" ],
                           [ main => '/var/www' ] ],
            data_dir => "/home/$developer/data" );

    return $ah{$developer}->handle_request($r);
}
```

We first examine the URL of the request to find the developer name, which we assume will always be the first part of the path, like */faye/index.html*. We use a regex to remove this from the URL, which we then change to be the altered path.

If there is no developer name we simply decline the request.

The main problem with this approach is that it would then require that all URLs on the site be relative in order to preserve the developer's name in the path. In addition, some Apache features like index files and aliases won't work properly either. Fortunately, there is an even better way.

By hostname

This example lets you give each developer their own hostename:

```
my %ah;

sub handler {
    my $r = shift;

    my ($developer) = $r->hostname =~ /^(\w+)\./;

    $ah{$developer} ||=
      HTML::Mason::ApacheHandler->new
          ( comp_root => [ [ dev  => "/home/$developer/mason" ],
                           [ main => '/var/www' ] ],
            data_dir => "/home/$developer/data" );

    return $ah{$developer}->handle_request($r);
}
```

This example assumes that for each developer there is a DNS entry like dave.dev.
masonbook.com. You could also insert a CNAME wildcard entry in your DNS. The important part is that the first piece is the developer name.

Of course, with either method, developers will have to actively manage their development directories. Any component in their directories will block their access to a component of the same name in the main directory.

Multiple Server Configurations

The multiple component root method has several downsides:

- Modules are shared by all the developers. If a change is made to a module, everybody will see it. This means that API changes are forced out to everyone at once, and a runtime error will affect all the developers. Additionally, you may need to stop and start the server every time a module is changed, interrupting everyone (although you could use Apache::Reload from CPAN to avoid this).

- You can't test different server configurations without all the developers being affected.

- Truly catastrophic errors that bring down the web server affect everyone.

- The logs are shared, so if you like to send messages to the error log for debugging you'd better hope that no one else is doing the same thing or you'll have a mess.

The alternative is to run a separate daemon for each developer, each on its own port. This means maintaining either one fairly complicated configuration file, with a lot of <IfDefine> directives or separate configuration files for each developer.

The latter is probably preferable as it gives each developer total freedom to experiment. The configuration files can be generated from a template (possibly using Mason) or a script. Then each developer's server can listen on a different hostname or port for requests.

You can have each server's component root be the developer's working directory, which should mirror the layout of the real site. This means that there is no need to tweak any paths in the components.

This method's downside is that it will inevitably use up more memory than having a single server. It also requires a greater initial time investment in order to generate the configuration file templates. But the freedom it gives to individual developers is very nice, and the time investment is fixed.

Of course, since each developer has a computer, there is nothing to stop a developer from simply setting up Apache and mod_perl locally. And the automation would be even easier since there's no need to worry about dealing with unique port numbers or shared system resources. Even better (or worse, depending on your point of view), a developer can check out the entire system onto a laptop and work on the code without needing to be on the office network.

Managing DBI Connections

Not infrequently, we see people on the Mason users list asking questions about how to handle caching DBI connections.

Our recipe for this is really simple:

```
use Apache::DBI
```

Rather than reinventing the wheel, use Apache::DBI, which provides the following features:

- It is completely transparent to use. Once you've used it, you simply call DBI-> connect() as always and Apache::DBI gives you an existing handle if one is available.
- It makes sure that the handle is live, so that if your RDBMS goes down and then back up, your connections still work just fine.
- It does not cache handles made before Apache forks, as many DBI drivers do not support using a handle after a fork.

Using Mason Outside of Dynamic Web Sites

So far we've spent a lot of time telling you how to use Mason to generate spiffy web stuff on the fly, whether that be HTML, WML, or even dynamic SVG files.

But Mason can be used in lots of other contexts. For example, you could write a Mason app that recursively descends a directory tree and calls each component in turn to generate a set of static pages.

How about using Mason to generate configuration files from templates? This could be quite useful if you had to configure a lot of machines similarly but with each one slightly different (for example, a web server farm).

Generating a Static Site from Components

Many sites might be best implemented as a set of static files instead of as a set of dynamically created responses to requests. For example, if a site's content changes only once or twice a week, generating each page dynamically upon request is probably overkill. In addition, you can often find much cheaper web hosting if you don't need a mechanism for generating pages dynamically.

But we'd still like some of the advantages a Mason site can give us. We'd like to build the site based on a database of content. We'd also like to have a nice consistent set of headers and footers, as well as automatically generate some bits for each page from the database. And maybe, just maybe, we also want to be able to make look-and-feel changes to the site without resorting to a multi-file find-and-replace. These requirements suggest that Mason is a good choice for site implementation.

For our example in this section, we'll consider a site of film reviews. It is similar to a site that one of the authors actually created for Hong Kong film reviews. Our example site will essentially be a set of pages that show information about films, including the film's title, year of release, director, cast, and of course a review. We'll generate the site from the Mason components on our home GNU/Linux box and then upload the site to the host.

First, we need a directory layout. Assuming that we're starting in the directory */home/dave/review-site*, here's the layout:

```
/home/dave/review-site (top level)
  /htdocs
    - index.html
    /reviews
       - autohandler
       - Anna_Magdalena.html
       - Lost_and_Found.html
       - ... (one file for each review)

  /lib
    - header.mas
    - footer.mas
    - film_header_table.mas
```

The index page will be quite simple. It will look like Example 11-10.

Example 11-10. review-site/htdocs/index.html

```
<& /lib/header.mas, title => 'review list' &>
<h1>Pick a review</h1>
<ul>
% foreach my $title (sort keys %pages) {
 <li><a href="<% $pages{$title} | h %>"><% $title | h %></a>
% }
</li>
<%init>
 my %pages;

 local *DIR;
 my $dir = File::Spec->catfile( File::Spec->curdir, 'reviews' );
 opendir DIR, $dir
     or die "Cannot open $dir dir: $!";

 foreach my $file ( grep { /\.html$/ } readdir DIR ) {
     next if $file =~ /index\.html$/;

     my $comp = $m->fetch_comp("reviews/$file")
       or die "Cannot find reviews/$file component";

     my $title = $comp->attr('film_title');

     $pages{$title} = "reviews/$file";
 }

 closedir DIR
     or die "Cannot close $dir dir: $!";
</%init>
```

This component simply makes a list of the available reviews, based on the files ending in *.html* in the */home/dave/review-site/reviews* subdirectory. We assume that the actual film title is kept as an attribute (via an <%attr> section) of the component, so we load the component and ask it for the film_title attribute. If it doesn't have one Mason will throw an exception, which we think is better than having an empty link. If this were a dynamic web site, we might want to instead simply skip that review and go on to the next one, but here we're assuming that this script is being executed by a human being capable of fixing the error.

We make sure to HTML-escape the filename and the film title in the <a> tag's href attribute. It's not unlikely that the film could contain an ampersand character (&), and we want to generate proper HTML.

Next, let's make our autohandler for the *reviews* subdirectory (Example 11-11), which will take care of all the repeated work that goes into displaying a review.

Example 11-11. review-site/htdocs/reviews/autohandler

```
<& /lib/header.mas, title => $film_title &>
<& /lib/film_header_table.mas, comp => $m->base_comp &>
```

Example 11-11. review-site/htdocs/reviews/autohandler (continued)

```
% $m->call_next;
<& /lib/footer.mas &>

<%init>
 my $film_title = $m->base_comp->attr('film_title');
</%init>
```

Again, a very simple page. We grab the film title so we can pass it to the header component. Then we call the *film_header_table.mas* component, which will use attributes from the component it is passed to generate a table containing the film's title, year of release, cast, and director.

Then we call the review component itself via call_next() and finish up with the footer.

Our header (Example 11-12) is quite straightforward.

Example 11-12. review-site/lib/header.mas

```
<html>
<head>
<title><% $real_title | h %></title>
</head>
<body>

<%args>
 $title
</%args>
<%init>
 my $real_title = "Dave's Reviews - $title";
</%init>
```

This is a nice, simple header that generates the basic HTML pieces every page needs. Its only special feature is that it will make sure to incorporate a unique title, based on what is passed in the $title argument.

The footer (Example 11-13) is the simplest of all.

Example 11-13. review-site/lib/footer.mas

```
<p>
<em>Copyright &copy; David Rolsky, 1996-2002</em>.
</p>

<p>
<em>All rights reserved.  No part of the review may be reproduced or
transmitted in any form or by any means, electronic or mechanical,
including photocopying, recording, or by any information storage and
retrieval system, without permission in writing from the copyright
owner.</em>
</p>
```

Example 11-13. review-site/lib/footer.mas (continued)

```
</body>
</html>
```

There's one last building block piece left before we get to the reviews, the */lib/film_header_table.mas* component (Example 11-14).

Example 11-14. review-site/lib/film_header_table.mas

```
<table width="100%">
 <tr>
  <td colspan="2" align="center"><h1><% $film_title | h %></h1></td>
 </tr>
% foreach my $field ( grep { exists $data{$_} } @optional ) {
 <tr>
  <td><strong><% ucfirst $field %></strong>:</td>
  <td><% $data{$field} | h %></td>
 </tr>
% }
</table>

<%args>
 $comp
</%args>

<%init>
 my %data;
 my $film_title = $comp->attr('film_title');
 my @optional = qw( year director cast );
 foreach my $field (@optional)  {
     my $data = $comp->attr_if_exists($field);
     next unless defined $data;
     $data{$field} = ref $data ? join ', ', @$data : $data;
 }
</%init>
```

This component just builds a table based on the attributes of the component passed to it. The required attribute is the film's title, but we can accommodate the year, director(s), and cast.

There are only two slightly complex lines.

The first is:

```
% foreach my $field ( grep { exists $data{$_} } @optional ) {
```

Here we are iterating through the fields in @optional that have matching keys in %data. We could have simply called keys %data, but we want to display things in a specific order while still skipping nonexistent keys.

The other line that bears some explaining is:

```
$data{$field} = ref $data ? join ', ', @$data : $data;
```

We check whether the value is a reference so that the attribute can contain an array reference, which is useful for something like the cast, which is probably going to have more than one person in it. If it is an array, we join all its elements together into a comma-separated list. Otherwise, we simply use it as-is.

Let's take a look at what one of the review components might look like:

```
<%attr>
 film_title => 'Lost and Found'
 year => 1996
 director => 'Lee Chi-Ngai'
 cast => [ 'Kelly Chan Wai-Lan', 'Takeshi Kaneshiro', 'Michael Wong Man-Tak' ]
</%attr>

<p>
Takeshi Kaneshiro plays a man who runs a business called Lost and
Found, which specializes in searching for lost things and people. In
the subtitles, his name is shown as That Worm, though that seems
like a fairly odd name, cultural barriers notwithstanding. Near the
beginning of the film, he runs into Kelly Chan. During their first
conversation, she says that she has lost something. What she says
she has lost is hope. We soon find out that she has leukemia and
that the hope she seeks seems to be Michael Wong, a sailor who works
for her father's shipping company.
</p>

<p>
blah blah blah...
</p>
```

This makes writing new reviews really easy. All we do is type in the review and a small number of attributes, and the rest of the framework is built automatically.

A more complex version of this site might store some or all of the data, including the reviews, in a database, which would make it easier to reuse the information in another context. But this is certainly good enough for a first pass.

All that's left is the script that will generate the static HTML files. See Example 11-15.

Example 11-15. review-site/generate_html.pl

```perl
#!/usr/bin/perl -w

use strict;  # Always use strict!

use Cwd;
use File::Basename;
use File::Find;
use File::Path;
use File::Spec;
use HTML::Mason;
```

Example 11-15. review-site/generate_html.pl (continued)

```perl
# These are directories.  The canonpath method removes any cruft
# like doubled slashes.
my ($source, $target) = map { File::Spec->canonpath($_) } @ARGV;

die "Need a source and target\n"
    unless defined $source && defined $target;

# Make target absolute because File::Find changes the current working
# directory as it runs.
$target = File::Spec->rel2abs($target);

my $interp =
    HTML::Mason::Interp->new( comp_root => File::Spec->rel2abs(cwd) );

find( \&convert, $source );

sub convert {
    # We don't want to try to convert our autohandler or .mas
    # components.  $_ contains the filename
    return unless /\.html$/;

    my $buffer;
    # This will save the component's output in $buffer
    $interp->out_method(\$buffer);

    # We want to split the path to the file into its components and
    # join them back together with a forward slash in order to make
    # a component path for Mason
    #
    # $File::Find::name has the path to the file we are looking at,
    # relative to the starting directory
    my $comp_path = join '/', File::Spec->splitdir($File::Find::name);

    $interp->exec("/$comp_path");
    # Strip off leading part of path that matches source directory
    my $name = $File::Find::name;
    $name =~ s/^$source//;

    # Generate absolute path to output file
    my $out_file = File::Spec->catfile( $target, $name );
    # In case the directory doesn't exist, we make it
    mkpath(dirname($out_file));

    local *RESULT;
    open RESULT, "> $out_file" or die "Cannot write to $out_file: $!";
    print RESULT $buffer or die "Cannot write to $out_file: $!";
    close RESULT or die "Cannot close $out_file: $!";
}
```

We take advantage of the File::Find module included with Perl, which can recursively descend a directory structure and invoke a callback for each file found. We simply have our callback (the convert() subroutine) call the HTML::Mason::Interp object's exec( ) method for each file ending in *.html*. We then write the results of the component call out to disk in the target directory.

We also use a number of other modules, including Cwd, File::Basename, File::Path, and File::Spec. These modules are distributed as part of the Perl core and provide useful functions for dealing with the filesystem in a cross-platform-compatible manner.

You may have noticed in Example 9-1 that when we invoked the Interpreter's exec( ) method directly, it didn't attempt to handle any of the web-specific elements of the request.

The same method is employed again here in our HTML generation script, and this same methodology could be applied in other situations that have little or nothing to do with the web.

Generating Config Files

Config files are a good candidate for Mason. For example, your production and staging web server config files might differ in only a few areas. Changes to one usually will need to be propagated to another. This is especially true with mod_perl, where web server configuration can basically be part of a web-based application.

And if you adopt the per-developer server solution discussed earlier, a template-driven config file generator becomes even more appealing.

Example 11-16 is a simple script to drive this generation.

Example 11-16. config_maker.pl

```
#!/usr/bin/perl -w

use strict;

use Cwd;
use File::Spec;
use HTML::Mason;
use User::pwent;

my $comp_root =
    File::Spec->rel2abs( File::Spec->catfile( cwd(), 'config' ) );

my $output;
my $interp =
    HTML::Mason::Interp->new( comp_root  => $comp_root,
                              out_method => \$output,
                            );

my $user = getpwuid($<);

$interp->exec( '/httpd.conf.mas', user => $user );
```

Example 11-16. config_maker.pl (continued)

```
my $file = File::Spec->catfile( $user->dir, 'etc', 'httpd.conf' );
open FILE, ">$file" or die "Cannot open $file: $!";
print FILE $output;
close FILE;
```

An *httpd.conf.mas* from the component might look like Example 11-17.

Example 11-17. config/httpd.conf.mas

```
ServerRoot <% $user->dir %>
PidFile <% File::Spec->catfile( $user->dir, 'logs', 'httpd.pid' ) %>
LockFile <% File::Spec->catfile( $user->dir, 'logs', 'httpd.lock' ) %>
Port <% $user->uid + 5000 %>

# loads Apache modules, defines content type handling, etc.
<& standard_apache_config.mas &>

<Perl>
 use lib <% File::Spec->catfile( $user->dir, 'project', 'lib' ) %>;
</Perl>

DocumentRoot <% File::Spec->catfile( $user->dir, 'project', 'htdocs' ) %>

PerlSetVar MasonCompRoot <% File::Spec->catfile( $user->dir, 'project', 'htdocs' ) %>
PerlSetVar MasonDataDir <% File::Spec->catfile( $user->dir, 'mason' ) %>
PerlModule HTML::Mason::ApacheHandler

<FilesMatch "\.html$">
 SetHandler perl-script
 PerlHandler HTML::Mason::ApacheHandler
</FilesMatch>

<%args>
$user
</%args>
```

This points the server's document root to the developer's working directory. Similarly, it adds the *project/lib* directory the Perl's @INC via use lib so that the user's working copy of the project's modules are seen first. The server will listen on a port equal to the user's user id plus 5,000.

Obviously, this is an incomplete example. It doesn't specify where logs, or other necessary config items, will go. It also doesn't handle generating the config file for a server intended to be run by the root user on a standard port.

CHAPTER 12

Custom Mason Subclasses

Something that we have tried very hard to do beginning with the 1.10 release of Mason is to make it easier to customize Mason's behavior. Jon Swartz was already on this track even back with the release of 0.80, which saw the first appearance of the HTML::Mason::Resolver classes, but 1.10 tries to bring this to new levels.

Starting with 1.10 it has become possible to subclass almost every core class that comes with Mason. Some obvious candidates for subclassing include the Lexer, Compiler, and Resolver. This chapter will demonstrate how you might go about implementing subclasses of various Mason objects.

Class::Container as a Superclass

A number of modules in Mason are subclasses of Class::Container. This is a class that was created to encapsulate some common behaviors for Mason objects. Originally, it was called HTML::Mason::Container, but Ken Williams decided to package this class separately and release it to CPAN, as it solves some fundamental problems of a large object-oriented system. Any Mason object that takes parameters to its constructor *must* inherit from this module. Of course, since all of the classes that you might consider subclassing inherit from Class::Container already, you shouldn't need to inherit from it directly. However, you may need to use some of its methods. We will briefly cover a few of them here, but see the Class::Container documentation for more details.

The modules in the Mason core distribution that are Class::Container subclasses are HTML::Mason::ApacheHandler, HTML::Mason::CGIHandler, HTML::Mason::Interp, HTML::Mason::Compiler, HTML::Mason::Lexer, HTML::Mason::Resolver, and HTML::Mason::Request.

The most important methods that Class::Container provides are valid_params() and contained_objects(), both of which are class methods.

The first, valid_params(), is called in order to register the valid parameters for a class's new() constructor. The second method, contained_objects(), is used to register the objects, if any, that a given class contains.

The contained_objects() method is not something you will have to use for all of your subclasses, since most of the time you won't be altering the structure of Mason's framework, you'll just be plugging your own classes into it. This method is called with a hash that contains as its keys parameter names that the class's constructor accepts and as its values the default name of the contained class.

For example, HTML::Mason::Compiler contains the following code:

```
__PACKAGE__->contained_objects( lexer => 'HTML::Mason::Lexer' );
```

This says that the HTML::Mason::Compiler->new() method will accept a lexer parameter and that, if no such parameter is given, then an object of the HTML::Mason::Lexer class will be constructed.

Class::Container also implements a bit of magic here, so that if HTML::Mason::Compiler->new() is called with a lexer_class parameter, it will load the class, instantiate a new object of that class, and use that for the lexer. In fact, it's even smart enough to notice if parameters given to HTML::Mason::Compiler->new() are really intended for this subclass, and it will make sure that they get passed along.

The valid_params() method is a bit more complex. It also takes a list of key/value pairs as arguments. The keys are the names of parameters accepted by the new() method, while the values are hash references defining a validation specification for the parameter. This specification is largely the same as that used by the Params::Validate module, with a few additions (but no subtractions).

One addition is that each parameter, excluding those that represent contained objects, may also define a value for parse. This tells Mason how to parse this parameter if it is defined as part of an Apache configuration file. If no parse parameter is provided, a sensible default will be guessed from the value of the Params::Validate type argument.

The upshot of this is that your subclasses can define their own constructor parameters and Mason will then check for these parameters in an Apache configuration file.

As an example, HTML::Mason::Compiler contains the following:

```
__PACKAGE__->valid_params
    (
     allow_globals =>
     { parse => 'list',   type => ARRAYREF, default => [],
       descr => "An array of names of Perl variables that are" .
                " allowed globally within components" },

     default_escape_flags =>
         { parse => 'string', type => SCALAR,   default => '',
```

```
            descr => "Escape flags that will apply by default to" .
                   " all Mason tag output" },

      lexer =>
        { isa => 'HTML::Mason::Lexer',
          descr => "A Lexer object that will scan component" .
                   " text during compilation" },

      preprocess =>
        { parse => 'code',   type => CODEREF,  optional => 1,
          descr => "A subroutine through which all component text" .
                   " will be sent during compilation" },

      postprocess_perl =>
        { parse => 'code',   type => CODEREF,  optional => 1,
          descr => "A subroutine through which all Perl code" .
                   " will be sent during compilation" },

      postprocess_text =>
        { parse => 'code',   type => CODEREF,  optional => 1,
          descr => "A subroutine through which all plain text will" .
                   " be sent during compilation" },
    );

    __PACKAGE__->contained_objects( lexer => 'HTML::Mason::Lexer' );
```

The type, default, and optional parameters are part of the validation specification used by Params::Validate. The various constants used, ARRAYREF, SCALAR, and so on, are all exported by Params::Validate. The parameters passed to valid_params() correspond to the MasonAllowGlobals, MasonDefaultEscapeFlags, MasonLexerClass, MasonPreprocess, MasonPostprocessPerl, and MasonPostprocessText *httpd.conf* configuration variables. Yes, Class is added automatically to the lexer param because lexer was also given to the contained_objects() method.

The descr parameter is used when we generate the HTML::Mason::Params documentation and is probably not something you'd need to use.

For more details, see both the Class::Container and Params::Validate documentation.

Syntax: Your Very Own Lexer

A request heard every so often on the Mason users list is for some way to create an XML-based markup language that can be used with Mason and that can be compiled to a Mason component object.

Despite the panic the thought of such a thing inspires in us, in the interests of good documentation, we will show the beginnings of such a lexer.

This lexer object will make use of several modules from CPAN, including XML::SAX::ParserFactory and XML::SAX::Base. The former is what it sounds like, a factory for SAX parsers (SAX2 parsers, actually). The latter is what any SAX2 handler should use as a base class. It implements a default no-op method for all the possible SAX2 methods, allowing you to simply implement those that you need. Our lexer will be a SAX2 handler, so we will inherit from XML::SAX::Base.

A quick side note on SAX (Simple API for XML): SAX is an event-based API for parsing XML. As the parser finds XML constructs, such as tags or character data, it calls appropriate methods in a SAX handler, such as start_element() or characters(). The parser is an event producer and the handler, like our Lexer, is an event consumer. In our case, the Lexer will also be generating events for the Compiler, though these will not be SAX events.

For more information on Perl's implementation of SAX2, see the *perl-xml* project on Sourceforge at *http://perl-xml.sourceforge.net/*.

For the purposes of our example, let's assume that any element that is not in the mason XML namespace will be output verbatim, as will any text. For tags, we'll just implement `<mason:args>`, `<mason:init>`, `<mason:perl>`, and `<mason:output>` in this example.* The `<mason:init>` tag will contain XML-escaped Perl code, while the `<mason:args>` tag will contain zero or more `<mason:arg>` tags. Each `<mason:arg>` tag will have the attributes name and default, with name being required.

We will also implement a `<mason:component>` tag in order to provide a single top-level containing tag for the component, which is an XML requirement.

This is only a subset of the Mason syntax set, but it's enough to show you how to customize a fairly important part of the system.

Using these tags, we might have some XML like this:

```
<?xml version="1.0"?>
<mason:component xmlns:mason="http://www.masonbook.com/">
 This is plain text.
 <b>This is text in an HTML tag</b>
 <mason:perl>
  my $x;
  if ($y &gt; 10) {
      $x = 10;
  } else {
      $x = 100;
  }
 </mason:perl>
$x is <mason:output>$x</mason:output>
$y is <mason:output>$y</mason:output>

<mason:args>
 <mason:arg name="$y" />
 <mason:arg name="@z" default="(2,3)" />
</mason:args>
```

---

* The equivalent of `<% %>` in the sane world where people don't use XML for everything!

```
<mason:init>
  $y *= $_ foreach @z;
</mason:init>
</mason:component>
```

OK, that looks just beautiful!

Let's start with the preliminaries.

```
package HTML::Mason::Lexer::XML;
$VERSION = '0.01';

use strict;

use HTML::Mason::Exceptions( abbr => [ qw( param_error syntax_error error ) ] );

use HTML::Mason::Lexer;
use Params::Validate qw(:all);
use XML::SAX::Base;
use XML::SAX::ParserFactory;
use base qw(HTML::Mason::Lexer XML::SAX::Base);  # Lexer comes first
```

As mentioned before, XML::SAX::Base provides default no-op methods for all of the possible SAX2 events, of which there are many. Since we're not interested in most of them, it's nice to have them safely ignored. We inherit from HTML::Mason::Lexer because it provides a few methods that the compiler class needs, such as object_id().

Because we're staunch generalists, we won't insist that the XML namespace of our tags needs to be 'mason'. We'll let the user override this with a parameter if desired:

```
__PACKAGE__->valid_params
  (
   xml_namespace => { parse => 'string', type => SCALAR, default => 'mason',
                      descr => "Prefix of XML tags indicating Mason sections" },
  );
```

We don't need to make a separate new() method in our module, since we can just inherit the one provided by our base Lexer class. The main action will happen in the lex() method:

```
sub lex {
    my ($self, %p) = @_;

    local $self->{name} = $p{name};
    local $self->{compiler} = $p{compiler};
```

We need a convenient place to keep these, so we stick them into $self for the duration of lexing. Perl's local() function makes sure these entries expire at the end of the lex() method:

```
$self->{state} = [];
```

We'll need to keep a stack of what tags we've seen so we can check that tags aren't improperly nested and in order to handle characters() events correctly:

```
my $parser = XML::SAX::ParserFactory->parser( Handler => $self );
```

We could have created the parser object in our new() method, but to store it we would have had to save it in the lexer object's structure, which would have created a circular reference. Doing it this way guarantees that the reference to the parser will go out of scope when we're finished using it.

```
    $parser->parse_string( $p{comp_source} );
}
```

The last bit tells the parser to parse the component text we were given. That will cause the parser to in turn call methods for each SAX event that occurs while parsing the string.

Now we'll take a look at our event-handling methods. The first is start_element(), which will be called whenever an XML tag is first encountered:

```
sub start_element {
    my $self = shift;
    my $elt  = shift;

    if ( ! defined $elt->{Prefix} ||
         $elt->{Prefix} ne $self->{xml_namespace} ) {
        $self->_verbatim_start_element($elt);
        return;
    }
```

If we got something that isn't in our designated namespace we'll just pass it through to the compiler as text to be output:

```
if ( $elt->{LocalName} eq 'component' ) {
    $self->{compiler}->start_component;
}
```

When the component starts, we notify the compiler so it can do any initialization that it needs to do:

```
foreach my $block ( qw( init perl args ) ) {
    if ( $elt->{LocalName} eq $block ) {
        $self->_start_block($block);
      last;
    }
}

if ( $elt->{LocalName} eq 'output' ) {
    $self->_start_output;
}

if ( $elt->{LocalName} eq 'arg' ) {
    $self->_handle_argument($elt);
}
    }
```

The rest of this method is basically a switch statement. Depending on what type of element we receive, we call the appropriate internal method to handle that element.

Let's look at some of the individual methods that are called:

```
sub _verbatim_start_element {
    my $self = shift;
    my $elt  = shift;
    my $xml = '<' . $elt->{Name};

    my @att;
    foreach my $att ( values %{ $elt->{Attributes} } ) {
        push @att, qq|$att->{Name}="$att->{Value}"|;
    }

    if (@att) {
        $xml .= ' ';
        $xml .= join ' ', @att;
    }

    $xml .= '>';

    $self->{compiler}->text( text => $xml );
}
```

Basically, this method goes through some contortions to regenerate the original XML element and then passes it on to the compiler as plain text. It should be noted that this implementation will end up converting tags like <foo/> into tag pairs like <foo></foo>. This is certainly valid XML but it may be a bit confusing to users. Unfortunately, there is no easy way to retrieve the exact text of the source document to determine how a tag was originally written, and with XML you're not supposed to care anyway.

Back to our subclass. The next method to implement is our _start_block( ) method. This will handle the beginning of a number of blocks in a simple generic fashion:

```
sub _start_block {
    my $self  = shift;
    my $block = shift;

    if ( $self->{state}[-1] &&
         $self->{state}[-1] ne 'def' &&
         $self->{state}[-1] ne 'method' ) {
        syntax_error "Cannot nest a $block tag inside a $self->{state}[-1] tag";
    }
```

What we are doing here is making it impossible to do something like nest a <mason: init> tag inside a <mason:perl> block. In fact, the only tags that can contain other tags are method and subcomponent definition tags, which are unimplemented in this example.

We notify the compiler that a new block has started and then push the block name onto our internal stack so we have access to it later:

```
$self->{compiler}->start_block( block_type => $block );

push @{ $self->{state} }, $block;
    }
```

Again, we check for basic logical errors:

```
sub _start_output {
    my $self = shift;

    if ( $self->{state}[-1] &&
         $self->{state}[-1] ne 'def' &&
         $self->{state}[-1] ne 'method' ) {
        syntax_error "Cannot nest an output tag inside a $self->{state}[-1] tag";
    }
```

Again, we push this onto the stack so we know that this was the last tag we saw:

```
push @{ $self->{state} }, 'output';
    }
```

The variable name and default are expressed as attributes of the element. The weird '{}name' syntax is intentional. Read the Perl SAX2 spec mentioned earlier for more details on what this means.

```
sub _handle_argument {
    my $self = shift;
    my $elt  = shift;

    my $var = $elt->{Attributes}{'{}name'}{Value};
    my $default = $elt->{Attributes}{'{}default'}{Value};
```

We want to check that the variable name is a valid Perl variable name:

```
unless ( $var =~ /^[\$\@%][^\W\d]\w*/ ) {
    syntax_error "Invalid variable name: $var";
}
```

Then we tell the compiler that we just found a variable declaration.

```
$self->{compiler}->variable_declaration( block_type => 'args',
                                         type => substr( $var, 0, 1 ),
                                         name => substr( $var, 1 ),
                                         default => $default );

    }
```

That wraps up all the methods that start_element() calls. Now let's move on to handling a characters() SAX event. This happens whenever the SAX parser encounters data outside of an XML tag.

```
sub characters {
    my $self  = shift;
    my $chars = shift;

    if ( ! $self->{state}[-1] ||
         $self->{state}[-1] eq 'def' ||
         $self->{state}[-1] eq 'method' ) {
```

```
        $self->{compiler}->text( text => $chars->{Data} );
        return;
    }
```

If we're in the main body of a component, subcomponent, or method, we simply pass the character data on as text:

```
    if ( $self->{state}[-1] eq 'init' ||
         $self->{state}[-1] eq 'perl' ) {
        $self->{compiler}->raw_block( block_type => $self->{state}[-1],
                                      block => $chars->{Data} );
        return;
    }
```

Character data in a <mason:init> or <mason:perl> section is passed to the compiler as the contents of that block. The compiler knows what type of tag is currently being processed and handles it appropriately.

```
    if ( $self->{state}[-1] eq 'output' ) {
        $self->{compiler}->substitution( substitution => $chars->{Data} );
    }
  }
```

If we are in a substitution tag, we call a different compiler method instead. Otherwise, we'll simply end up discarding the contents.

Since we may be dealing with text where whitespace is significant (as opposed to HTML), we'll want to pass on whitespace as if it were character data:

```
    sub ignorable_whitespace { $_[0]->characters($_[1]->{Data}) }
```

This method may be called if the XML parser finds a chunk of "ignorable whitespace." Frankly, we can never ignore whitespace, because it is just *so* cool, and without it our code would be unreadable. But apparently XML parsers can ignore it.[*]

The last thing we need to handle is an end_element() event:

```
    sub end_element {
        my $self = shift;
        my $elt  = shift;

        if ( ! defined $elt->{Prefix} ||
             $elt->{Prefix} ne $self->{xml_namespace} ) {
            $self->_verbatim_end_element($elt);
            return;
        }
    }
```

Again, XML elements not in our designated namespace are passed on verbatim to the compiler:

```
    if ( $elt->{LocalName} eq 'component' ) {
        $self->{compiler}->end_component;
```

---

[*] See Section 2.10 of the W3C XML 1.0 Recommendation for the definition of "ignorable whitespace."

```
      return;
    }
```

If we have reached the end tag of the component, we inform the compiler that the component is complete and we return:

```
    return if $elt->{LocalName} eq 'arg';
```

We don't need to do anything to end argument declarations. The work needed to handle this element happened when we called _handle_argument() from our start_element() method.

```
    if ( $self->{state}[-1] ne $elt->{LocalName} ) {
      syntax_error "Something very weird happened.  " .
                   "We encountered an ending tag for a $elt->{LocalName} tag " .
                   "before ending our current tag ($self->{state}[-1]).";
    }
```

Actually, this should just never happen: XML does not allow tag overlap and, if the parser finds overlapping tags, it should die rather than passing them to us. But we believe in being paranoid. If there is an error in the logic of this lexer code, this might help us in catching it.

```
    if ( $elt->{LocalName} eq 'output' ) {
        pop @{ $self->{state} };
        return;
    }
```

Any output that needed to be sent has already been dealt with via the characters() method so we simply need to change our state if the end tag was </mason:output>:

```
    $self->{compiler}->end_block( block_type => $elt->{LocalName} );

    pop @{ $self->{state} };
      }
```

The only remaining possibilities at this point are either <mason:perl>, <mason:init>, or <mason:args>. For these we simply tell the compiler that the block is over, change our state, and finish.

The last method we need to write is _verbatim_end_element() to pass through tag endings for non-Mason tags:

```
    sub _verbatim_end_element {
        my $self = shift;
        my $elt  = shift;

        $self->{compiler}->text( text => "</$elt->{Name}>" );
    }
```

This concludes our sample lexer subclass. Note that there are a couple of things missing here. First of all, there is no handling of subcomponents or methods. This wouldn't be too terribly hard as it's mostly an issue of calling the right methods on the compiler.

We also would want to handle line numbers. The default Mason lexer keeps track of line numbers in the source file so that the compiler can output appropriate #line directives in the object file, meaning that errors are reported relative to the source file. This feature isn't required but can be very nice to have.

Some of the unhandled potential tags like <mason:text> would be extremely trivial to implement. The <mason:flags> and <mason:attr> tags could be modeled on the code for handling <mason:args>. And of course, we need to handle component calls too. This is the point in this example where we say, "finishing this is left as an exercise to the reader."

To use this new lexer class, we would either place the following in the *httpd.conf* file:

```
PerlSetVar MasonLexerClass HTML::Mason::Lexer::XML
```

or, when creating the ApacheHandler object, we would simply pass in 'HTML::Mason::Lexer::XML' as the value of the lexer_class parameter.

Output: Compiling to a Different Output

So you've decided that you really hate Mason and you want to use Embperl instead. But you have a number of Mason components you've already written that you'd like to save. Well, you can create your own compiler to generate Embperl code from Mason. In this case, we'll use the lexer as is and rewrite the compiler from scratch. There isn't really a one-to-one match between Mason and Embperl's features so this example will, like the lexer example, be limited in scope. Finding an intelligent way to convert Mason's methods and subcomponents to Embperl is beyond the scope of this book.

In case you are unfamiliar with Embperl, it uses the following syntax: [+ +] tags contain code whose results should be sent to the browser, like Mason's substitution tag (<% %>). The [* *] tags contain Perl code that is not intended to generate output. This is equivalent to Mason's %-lines and <%perl> blocks. Finally, Embperl also has a [! !] tag similar to Mason's <%once> block.

There are other Embperl tags but, once again, this is a simplified example.

Embperl does have a feature similar to Mason's inheritance system called EmbperlObject, but translating between the two is nontrivial.

So let's make our new compiler:

```
package HTML::Mason::Compiler::ToEmbperl;

$VERSION = '0.01';

use strict;

use HTML::Mason::Lexer;
```

```
use HTML::Mason::Exceptions ( abbr => [qw(syntax_error)] );
use HTML::Mason::Compiler;
use base qw(HTML::Mason::Compiler);
```

This pulls in the basic packages we'll need. Even though we really aren't inheriting much from HTML::Mason::Compiler, we still subclass it as anything expecting a compiler will check that what it is given is a subclass of HTML::Mason::Compiler.

Of course, in our case, we won't be using this compiler with the HTML::Mason::Interp class, so the point is moot but important to mention.

```
sub compile {
    my ($self, %p) = @_;

    $self->lexer->lex( comp_source => $p{comp_source},
                       name => 'Embperl',
                       compiler => $self );

    return $self->component_as_embperl;
}
```

The only parameter we expect is comp_source. We tell the lexer the name of the component is 'Embperl' since we don't really care what the name is in this context. Presumably we are being called by some sort of script that is simply going to take the Embperl-ized component and write it to disk somewhere. The name is used for reporting syntax errors when a component is run, but that won't be an issue in this case.

```
sub start_component {
    my $self = shift;

    $self->{once_header} = '';
    $self->{header} = '';
    $self->{body}   = '';
    $self->{footer} = '';

    $self->{current_block} = '';
}
```

This method is called to give the compiler a chance to reset its state, so that's what we do.

We will be storing blocks of code in each of the first four attributes. When we encounter a <%once> block, it will go in the once_header attribute. For <%init> blocks, we can put then in the header attribute. %-lines, <%perl> blocks, <%text> blocks, substitution tags, and text will be placed immediately into the body attribute. Finally, any <%cleanup> blocks will go into the footer attribute.

The current_block() attribute will be used to keep track of what type of block we are in after a call to our start_block() method.

This example will ignore other Mason syntax such as component calls, subcomponents, methods, and <%shared>. Again, this will be left as an exercise for the reader.

```
sub start_block {
    my ($self, %p) = @_;

    syntax_error "Cannot nest a $p{block_type} inside a $self->{in_block} block"
        if $self->{in_block};
```

This is to make sure that the component is following the syntax rules we expect.

```
    $self->{in_block} = $p{block_type};
}
```

Then we record what kind of block we are starting, which will be something like init or perl.

The next method, raw_block(), is called for all of the blocks that we handle except the <%text> block:

```
sub raw_block {
    my ($self, %p) = @_;

    for ($self->{in_block}) {
        /^once$/    and   $self->{once_header} .= $p{block};
        /^init$/    and   $self->{header}      .= $p{block};
        /^perl$/    and   $self->{body}        .= "[* $p{block} *]";
        /^cleanup$/ and   $self->{footer}      .= $p{block};
    }
}
```

This switchlike statement stores the code given to us in the appropriate attribute. If it is a <%perl%> block, we wrap it in the relevant Embperl tag; otherwise, we simply store it as is in the appropriate slot.

```
sub text_block {
    my ($self, %p) = @_;
    $self->{body} .= $p{block};
}

sub text {
    my ($self, %p) = @_;
    $self->{body} .= $p{text};
}
```

The first method is called when the lexer finds a <%text> block. The second is called for regular text. Both of these get placed into the body attribute for later use.

```
sub substitution {
    my ($self, %p) = @_;
    $self->{body} .= "[+ $p{substitution} +]";
}
```

This method handles substitution tags (<% %>) though it ignores the fact that this method can also be given an escape parameter. This could be handled via Embperl's $escmode variable (again, left as an exercise for the reader).

```
sub perl_line {
    my ($self, %p) = @_;
```

```
        $self->{body} .= "[* $p{line} *]";
    }
```

This method is called for %-lines.

Then we need to implement the end_block() method:

```
sub end_block {
    my ($self, %p) = @_;

    syntax_error "end of $p{block_type} encountered while in $self->{in_block} block"
        unless $self->{in_block} eq $p{block_type};
```

Another sanity check is in the start_block() method. It's always a good thing to make sure that the lexer is giving us the kind of input that we would expect.

```
    $self->{in_block} = undef;
    }
```

And we reset our in_block attribute so that the next call to start_block() succeeds.

The last method to implement is the component_as_embperl() method, which simply will return a big block of text, our new Embperl page:

```
sub component_as_embperl {
    my $self = shift;

    my $page = '';

    if ( length $self->{once_header} ) {
        $page .= "[! $self->{once_header} !]\n";
    }

    if ( length $self->{header} ) {
        $page .= "[* $self->{header} *]\n";
    }

    if ( length $self->{body} ) {
        $page .= "$self->{body}\n";
    }

    if ( length $self->{footer} ) {
        $page .= "[* $self->{footer} *]\n";
    }

    return $page;
}
```

And there you have it—a perfectly good Mason component brutally butchered and turned into an Embperl page. I hope you're happy with yourself!

Storage: Replacing the Resolver

Occasionally, people on the Mason users list wonder if they can store their component source in an RDBMS. The way to achieve this is to create your own HTML::Mason::Resolver subclass.

The resolver's job is take a component path and figure out where the corresponding component is.

We will show an example that connects to a MySQL server containing the following table:

```
MasonComponent
----------------------------------------
path           VARCHAR(255)  PRIMARY KEY
component      TEXT          NOT NULL
last_modified  DATETIME      NOT NULL
```

Our code starts as follows:

```
package HTML::Mason::Resolver::MySQL;
$VERSION = '0.01';

use strict;

use DBI;
use Params::Validate qw(:all);

use HTML::Mason::ComponentSource;
use HTML::Mason::Resolver;
use base qw(HTML::Mason::Resolver);

__PACKAGE__->valid_params
    (
     db_name  => { parse => 'string', type => SCALAR },
     user     => { parse => 'string', type => SCALAR, optional => 1 },
     password => { parse => 'string', type => SCALAR, optional => 1 },
    );
```

These parameters will be used to connect to the MySQL server containing our components. Readers familiar with the Perl DBI will realize that there are a number of other parameters that we could take.

Our constructor method, new( ), needs to do a bit of initialization to set up the database connection, so we override our base class's method:

```
sub new {
    my $class = shift;
    my $self = $class->SUPER::new(@_);
```

We invoke the new( ) method provided by our superclass, which validates the parameters in @_ and makes sure they get sent to the right contained objects. The latter concern doesn't seem so important in this case since we don't have any contained objects, but the point is that if somebody subclasses our HTML::Mason::Resolver::MySQL class and adds contained objects, our new( ) method will still do the right thing with its parameters.

Now we connect to the database in preparation for retrieving components later:

```
    $self->{dbh} =
        DBI->connect
            ( "dbi:mysql:$self->{db_name}",
              $self->{user}, $self->{password}, { RaiseError => 1 } );

    return $self;
}
```

A resolver needs to implement two methods left unimplemented in the parent HTML::Mason::Resolver class. These are get_info() and glob_path(). The first is used to retrieve information about the component matching a particular component path. The second takes a glob pattern like /path/* or /path/*/foo/* and returns the component paths of all the components that match that wildcard path.

Additionally, if we want this resolver to be usable with the ApacheHandler module, we need to implement a method called apache_request_to_comp_path( ), which takes an Apache object and translates it into a component path.

Given a path, we want to get the time when this component was last modified, in the form of a Unix timestamp, which is what Mason expects:

```
sub get_info {
    my ($self, $path) = @_;

    my ($last_mod) =
        $self->{dbh}->selectrow_array
            ( 'SELECT UNIX_TIMESTAMP(last_modified)
               FROM MasonComponent WHERE path = ?',
              {}, $path );
    return unless $last_mod;
```

If there was no entry in the database for the given path, we simply return, which lets Mason know that no matching component was found:

```
    return
        HTML::Mason::ComponentSource->new
            ( comp_path => $path,
              friendly_name => $path,
              last_modified => $last_mod,
              comp_id => $path,
              source_callback => sub { $self->_get_source($path) },
            );
}
```

The get_info() method returns its information in the form of a HTML::Mason::ComponentSource object. This is a very simple class that holds information about a component.

Its constructor accepts the following parameters:

comp_path

This is the component path as given to the resolver.

friendly_name

The string given for this parameter will be used to identify the component in error messages. For our resolver, the component path works for this parameter as well because it is the primary key for the MasonComponent table in the database, allowing us to uniquely identify a component.

For other resolvers, this might differ from the component path. For example, the filesystem resolver that comes with Mason uses the component's absolute path on the filesystem.

last_modified

This is the last modification time for the component, as seconds since the epoch.

comp_id

This should be a completely unique identifier for the component. Again, since the component path is our primary key in the database, it works well here.

source_callback

This is a subroutine reference that, when called, returns the source text of the component.

Mason could have had you simply create an HTML::Mason::ComponentSource subclass that implemented a source() method for your resolver, but we thought that rather than requiring you to write such a do-nothing subclass, it would be easier to simply use a callback instead.

Our _get_source() method is trivially simple:

```
sub _get_source {
    my $self = shift;
    my $path = shift;

    return
        $self->{dbh}->selectrow_array
            ( 'SELECT component FROM MasonComponent WHERE path = ?', {}, $path );
}
```

comp_class

This is the component class into which this particular component should be blessed when it is created. This must be a subclass of HTML::Mason::Component. The default is HTML::Mason::Component.

extra

This optional parameter should be a hash reference. It is used to pass information from the resolver to the component class.

This is needed since an HTML::Mason::Resolver subclass and an HTML::Mason::Component subclass can be rather tightly coupled, but they must communicate with each other through the interpreter (this may change in the future). Next is our glob_path() method:

```
sub glob_path {
    my $self = shift;
    my $pattern = shift;

    $pattern =~~ s/*/%/g;
```

The pattern given will be something that could be passed to Perl's glob() function. We simply replace this with the SQL equivalent for a LIKE search:

```
return
    $self->{dbh}->selectcol_array
        ( 'SELECT path FROM MasonComponent WHERE path LIKE ?', {}, $pattern );
}
```

Then we return all the matching paths in the database.

Since we may want to use this resolver with ApacheHandler, we will also implement the apache_request_to_comp_path() method:

```
sub apache_request_to_comp_path {
    my $self = shift;
    my $r = shift;

    my $path = $r->uri;

    return $path
        if $self->{dbh}->selectrow_array
            ( 'SELECT 1 FROM MasonComponent WHERE path = ?', {}, $path );

    return undef unless $r->path_info;

    $path .= $r->path_info;

    return $path
        if $self->{dbh}->selectrow_array
            ( 'SELECT 1 FROM MasonComponent WHERE path = ?', {}, $path );

    return undef;
}
```

We generate a component path by taking the requested URI and looking for that in the database. If it doesn't exist, we will try appending the path info if possible or just give up. Finally, we try the altered path and, if that doesn't exist either, we just give up and return undef, which will cause the ApacheHandler module to return a NOT FOUND status for this request.

That's it, all done. And nothing left as an exercise for the reader this time.

As with the lexer, this can be used either via a *httpd.conf* directive:

```
PerlSetVar  MasonResolverClass  HTML::Mason::Resolver::MySQL
```

or by passing the resolver_class parameter to the new() method for HTML::Mason::Interp.

Request: A Request Object with a Built-in Session

Wouldn't it be cool to have a request object with a built-in session? "Yes, it would," you answer. "Child's play," we say.

When a request is made using this object, it should either find an old session or create a new one. Then in our components we will simply call `$m->session()` to get back a hash reference that will persist between requests.

For simplicity's sake, we won't make this class configurable as to what type of session to use, though it could be done.*

```
package HTML::Mason::Request::WithSession;
$VERSION = '0.01';

use strict;

# Import a subroutine error() which throws an HTML::Mason::Exception
# object
use HTML::Mason::Exceptions ( abbr => [ 'error' ] );

use HTML::Mason::ApacheHandler;
use base qw(HTML::Mason::Request);
```

One problem unique to subclassing to the Request object is that Mason already comes with two of its own Request subclasses. These are `HTML::Mason::Request::ApacheHandler` and `HTML::Mason::Request::CGIHandler`, which are used by the ApacheHandler and CGIHandler, respectively.

In order to cooperate with the ApacheHandler and CGIHandler modules, we want to subclass the appropriate class. However, we can't know which one to subclass when we are loaded, because it is possible that we will be loaded *before* the Apache-Handler or CGIHandler module. We'll take care of this in our `new()` method, which will be discussed momentarily.

Our session will be implemented using cookies and `Cache::FileCache` for storage, just as we saw in Chapter 11:

```
    use Apache::Cookie;
    use Cache::FileCache;
    use Digest::SHA1;
```

We solve our subclassing problem with the following code. There is nothing wrong with changing a class's inheritance dynamically in Perl, so that's what we do. The

---

* This is left as an exercise... Actually, this was left to the one of the authors. Dave Rolsky recently created HTML::Mason::Request::WithApacheSession, which is a highly configurable module that expands on the example shown in this section. This module is available from a CPAN mirror near you.

alter_superclass() method is provided by the HTML::Mason::Request base class, and does the right thing even given multiple inheritance. It also cooperates with Class::Container to make sure that it sees any changes made to the inheritance hierarchy:

```
sub new {
    my $class = shift;

    $class->alter_superclass( $HTML::Mason::ApacheHandler::VERSION ?
                              'HTML::Mason::Request::ApacheHandler' :
                              $HTML::Mason::CGIHandler::VERSION ?
                              'HTML::Mason::Request::CGI' :
                              'HTML::Mason::Request' );

    return $class->SUPER::new(@_);
}
```

We make a session, call exec() in our parent class, taking care to preserve the caller's scalar/list context, and then save the session. If an exception is thrown, we simply rethrow it:

```
sub exec {
    my $self = shift;

    $self->_make_session;

    my @result;
    if (wantarray) {
        @result = eval { $self->SUPER::exec(@_) };
    } elsif (defined wantarray) {
        $result[0] = eval { $self->SUPER::exec(@_) };
    } else {
        eval { $self->SUPER::exec(@_) };
    }

    # copy this in case _save_session overwrites $@
    my $e = $@;

    $self->_save_session;

    die $e if $e;

    return wantarray ? @result : defined wantarray ? $result[0] : undef;
}
```

Making a new session for subrequests is probably incorrect behavior, so we simply reuse our parent's session object if a subrequest is exec()'d:

```
sub _make_session {
    my $self = shift;

    if ( $self->is_subrequest ) {
        $self->{session} = $self->parent_request->session;
        return;
    }
```

This code is pulled almost verbatim from Chapter 11:

```
my %c = Apache::Cookie->fetch;
my $session_id =
    exists $c{masonbook_session} ? $c{masonbook_session}->value : undef;

$self->{session_cache} =
    Cache::FileCache->new( { cache_root => '/tmp',
                             namespace  => 'Mason-Book-Session',
                             default_expires_in  => 60 * 60 * 24, # 1 day
                             auto_purge_interval => 60 * 60 * 24, # 1 day
                             auto_purge_on_set => 1 } );

my $session;
if ($session_id) {
    $session = $self->{session_cache}->get($session_id);
}

unless ($session) {
    $session = { _session_id => Digest::SHA1::sha1_hex( time, rand, $$ ) };
}

Apache::Cookie->new( $self->apache_req,
                     name => 'masonbook_session',
                     value => $session->{_session_id},
                     path => '/',
                     expires => '+1d',
                   )->bake;

$self->{session} = $session;
  }
```

Also just like Chapter 11:

```
sub _save_session {
    my $self = shift;

    $self->{session_cache}->set
        ( $self->{session}{_session_id} => $self->{session} );
}
```

And to finish it off, a simple accessor method:

```
sub session { $_[0]->{session} }
```

Wow, nice and simple. Of course, this would need to be customized for your environment, or you can use the previously mentioned HTML::Mason::Request:: WithApacheSession module available from CPAN.

Once again, you have two options to use this new subclass. If you are configuring Mason via your *httpd.conf* file, do this:

```
PerlSetVar  MasonRequestClass  HTML::Mason::Request::WithSession
```

or in your *handler.pl* you can load the module and then pass a request_class parameter to the HTML::Mason::Interp class's constructor.

Argument Munging: ApacheHandler

One of the main reasons that you might consider creating your own ApacheHandler class is to change the way arguments are processed. For example, we might want to create objects based on certain objects.

Our subclass starts like many others:

```
package HTML::Mason::ApacheHandler::AddObjects;
$VERSION = '0.01';

use strict;

use HTML::Mason::ApacheHandler;
use base qw(HTML::Mason::ApacheHandler);
```

This should look pretty familiar. Now we'll load a few more classes, which we'll be using to create objects:

```
use Date::ICal;  # date object
use MyApp::User; # user object
```

And now we override the argument-processing subroutine, request_args():

```
sub request_args {
    my $self = shift;

    my ($args, $r, $cgi_object) = $self->SUPER::request_args(@_);
```

ApacheHandler's request_args() method returns three items. The first is a hash reference containing the arguments that will be passed to the component. The second is the Apache or Apache::Request object for the current request, and the third is a CGI.pm object. The CGI.pm object is created only when the ApacheHandler's args_method attribute is set to CGI.

```
if ( exists $args->{epoch} ) {
    $args->{date} = Date::ICal->new( epoch => $args->{epoch} );
}

if ( exists $args->{user_id} ) {
    $args->{user} = MyApp::User->new( user_id => $args->{user_id} );
}
```

This bit of code simply creates some useful objects if certain incoming arguments exist. Finally we return the munged $args hash reference, along with the other return values from our superclass's request_args() method:

```
return ($args, $r, $cgi_object);
    }
```

Now, whenever the client submits an argument called epoch, there will be an additional argument, date, a Date::ICal object, available in components. Similarly, a

---

request with a user_id parameter means that there will be an argument user containing a MyApp::User object passed to components.

Using this class is a little different from what we've seen previously. In our *httpd.conf* file, we'd have something like this:

```
<Location /mason>
 SetHandler perl-script
 PerlHandler HTML::Mason::ApacheHandler::AddObjects
</Location>
```

Similarly, in our *handler.pl* file, we'd simply create this object *instead* of an HTML::Mason::ApacheHandler object.

More Reader Exercises

Consider the following possibilities for Mason subclasses:

* A resolver subclass that allows you to have two files per component. One file could be primarily HTML and the other would be code. The resolver subclass would simply concatenate the two together.

* A lexer subclass enabling ASP-style syntax.

* An ApacheHandler subclass that munges incoming strings into Unicode, using the Encode module from CPAN.

* A CGIHandler subclass that performs the same argument-to-object transformation seen in our example ApacheHandler subclass.

The Mason API

To provide a convenient reference to the main elements of the Mason class hierarchy, we've collected the APIs of the Interpreter, Resolver, Compiler, Lexer, Apache-Handler, CGIHandler, Component, and Request classes. The parameters to each class's new( ) method are listed in Appendix B. Many of these parameters also correspond to simple accessor methods for getting/setting their values; those methods are not listed here, so see Appendix B for a complete list.

We have attempted to show the arguments taken by each method. Replaceable text is shown in angle brackets (<>). indicating a value you must specify. An ellipsis (...) indicates a list of values. Optional arguments are indicated by square brackets ([ ]). An optional list of arguments doesn't get both kinds of brackets, because we figure that's just a list with no elements in it. If alternate sets of parameters can be given (such as `comp_source` versus `comp_file` for the Interpreter's `make_component( )` method), we sometimes indicate this by separate listings.

We intend this appendix to be a quick reference; in many cases the official Mason documentation will provide more detail.

Interpreter

The Interpreter is the main entry point for Mason and coordinates the efforts of several other classes. The default Interpreter class is `HTML::Mason::Interp`.

new(<parameters...>)
> Creates a new Mason Interpreter and returns it. See Appendix B for a list of parameters accepted.

Object Properties

compiler()
> Returns the Compiler object associated with this Interpreter.

resolver()

Returns the Resolver object associated with this Interpreter.

static_source()

Returns true or false, depending on whether the static_source parameter is currently set for this Interpreter.

autoflush([<true or false>])

Returns true or false, depending on whether the output buffers will be flushed immediately upon receiving output or not. An optional argument sets the value.

autohandler_name()

Returns the name of the file to be used for Mason's autohandler mechanism (i.e., "autohandler").

dhandler_name([<name>])

Returns the name of the file to be used for Mason's dhandler mechanism (i.e., "dhandler"). An optional argument sets the value.

code_cache_max_size([<size>])

Returns the number of bytes allowed for caching of compiled component code. An optional argument sets the value.

ignore_warnings_expr([<regex>])

Returns a regular expression indicating warnings to ignore when calling or compiling components. An optional argument sets the value.

data_cache_defaults([<hash reference>])

Returns a hash reference of parameters that will be passed to the caching methods by default. An optional hash reference argument sets the value.

max_recurse([<integer>])

Returns an integer indicating the level of nesting allowed in component calls, as a deterrent to infinite component call loops. An optional argument sets the value.

use_object_files()

Returns true or false, depending on whether the Interpreter will cache compiled components to disk as "object files."

preloads()

Returns reference to an array of glob-like patterns specifying components to be loaded when the Interpreter is created.

files_written()

Returns a list of all files created by the Interpreter. This may be useful if you want to enforce certain file permissions or ownership.

Directories

comp_root()
> A pass-through method to the Resolver method of the same name.

object_dir()
> Returns a string containing the name of the directory in which Mason's component objects will be cached.

data_dir()
> Returns the current value of the data_dir parameter.

Runtime Methods

exec(<component>, <args...>)
> Initiates a new Mason request. The first argument should be the component to execute, specified either as an absolute pathname or as a component object. Any additional arguments will be passed to the component.

load(<absolute component path>)
> Returns the component at the path specified by the argument. Throws an exception if no such component exists.

comp_exists(<absolute component path>)
> Returns true or false, depending on whether a component exists at the path specified by the argument.

make_component(comp_file => <path> [, name => <string>])
make_component(comp_source => <string> [, name => <string>])
> Creates a component object and returns it. The text of the component may be specified as a string in the comp_source parameter or as a filename in the comp_file parameter. You may also provide a name parameter to associate with this component. If no name is provided, the name will default to a string like "<anonymous component>".

set_global(<name> => <value>)
> Sets the value of a Perl global variable so that it will be available to components at runtime. The first argument names the variable in a string (i.e., '$user'), including the leading $, @, or % character. The remaining arguments specify the value to assign. The name of the variable should *not* be fully package-qualified with :: characters; the variable will be created in the same package in which components execute.

Request

The Request class represents a chain of components executing in a particular context. A request is begun by invoking the Interpreter's exec( ) method. The current Request object is available by default in components as the variable $m.

new(<parameters...>)

Creates a new Request object. See Appendix B for a list of parameters accepted. Typically a Request is not created directly, but rather by invoking the Interpreter's exec( ) method. The default Request class is HTML::Mason::Request, though it is different when using ApacheHandler or CGIHandler.

instance()

Returns the Request currently running. This can be called as a class method (i.e., HTML::Mason::Interp->instance( )) from code in which $m is unavailable. In a subrequest, the subrequest object, not the main request, will be returned.

Object Properties

interp()

Returns the Interpreter object associated with this Request.

count()

Returns the Interpreter's counter value for this Request.

error_mode([<'fatal' or 'output'>])

Returns the string fatal or output, depending on whether error conditions should trigger an exception (fatal) or display an error message in the regular output channel (output). The mode can be set with an optional argument.

error_format([<format>])

Returns a string indicating how error messages will be formatted. The currently available choices are brief, text, line, and html. An optional argument sets the format.

out_method([<subroutine_reference or scalar_reference>])

Returns the current value of the out_method parameter or optionally sets it if you pass a subroutine reference or a scalar reference as an argument.

cgi_object()

This method is not present in the regular HTML::Mason::Request class, but it is added as a way to access the CGI.pm request object when using HTML::Mason::CGIHandler. It is also added when using HTML::Mason::ApacheHandler with the CGI args_method.

ah()

Only available when using HTML::Mason::ApacheHandler, in which case the Apache Handler object is returned.

apache_req()

Only available when using HTML::Mason::ApacheHandler, in which case the mod_perl request object $r is returned.

Altering the Request Flow

abort([<value>])

Terminates the current Request. You may optionally specify a value to be returned by the Interpreter's exec() method. In a web environment this value will ultimately become the HTTP response code. Accepts an optional exception argument to examine, otherwise $@ will be examined.

aborted()

Returns true if the current request was aborted (and caught by an eval block), or false otherwise. Accepts an exception argument to examine, otherwise $@ will be examined.

aborted_value()

If the current request was aborted, this returns the value passed to the abort method.

decline()

Stops the execution of the current component and passes control to the next applicable dhandler. Any output already generated will be discarded. If no dhandler exists to handle this request, an exception will be thrown.

dhandler_arg()

If the current request is being handled by a dhandler, this method will return the remainder of the request path with the dhandler's directory removed. If no dhandler is executing, this method will return undef.

Caching

See Chapter 4 for more information on the data cache and how to use it.

cache(<arguments...>)

Returns the Cache::Cache object that manages this component's data cache.

cache_self(<arguments...>)

Facilitates automatic caching of the current component's output and return value. The arguments to cache_self() specify how long the cached data should persist, whether it should be associated with a particular key, and the details of how the data should be cached.

Introspection

caller()

Returns the component that invoked the currently executing component or undef if this is the topmost component executing.

callers([<n>])

When called with no arguments, returns a list of all components currently executing. This is known as the "component stack." When called with an integer argument n, returns the component n levels up the execution stack. For instance, $m->callers(1) is equivalent to $m->caller.

caller_args(<n>)

Given an integer argument n, returns an array (if called in list context) or a hash reference (if called in scalar context) of the arguments passed to the component n levels up the execution stack.

depth()

Returns the current depth of the component stack. For instance, with components /autohandler, /dir/autohandler, and /dir/component.html in the default setup, the depth will be 1 when queried in /autohandler, 2 in /dir/autohandler, and 3 in /dir/component.html. If /dir/component.html calls another component, the depth will be 4 inside that component.

Content and Output

print(<strings...>)

A synonym for print(). This method will output the content of any arguments. In recent versions of Mason you may also print to Perl's STDOUT filehandle, as this is tied to Mason's buffers.

clear_buffer()

Discards the contents of Mason's output buffers.

flush_buffer()

Sends the contents of Mason's output buffers to their destination.

content()

Returns the content block passed to the current component or undef if this component was called without a content block. The content block will be evaluated in the lexical context of the calling component. See "Components called with content" in Chapter 2 for more details.

file(<path>)

Given a file path, Mason will look for this file and return its contents as a string.

An absolute path refers to a file on the filesystem. If a relative path is given, Mason will prepend the current component's directory, if it has one. Otherwise Mason will simply make the path absolute by prepending the system's root directory to the path.

Fetching/Running Components

These methods deal with fetching and running components. Some of the methods (in particular comp() and scomp()) let you specify the component by path or by supplying a component object, while other methods (fetch_comp() and comp_exists())

allow only a path. For any of these four methods, if a relative pathname is given, it is considered relative to the dir_path of the current component.

fetch_comp(<path>)

Given a string argument specifying a component path, returns the component at that path or undef if no such component exists.

fetch_next()

Fetches the next component in the content-wrapping chain. This is the same component that will be invoked by the call_next() method.

fetch_next_all()

Fetches all remaining components in the content-wrapping chain and returns them as a list. This is usually called from an autohandler and will return multiple components when multiple autohandlers are in use.

comp(<component>, <arguments...>)

Calls a Mason component. The component is specified by the first argument, which should be either the name of the component to call or a component object. Any remaining arguments to comp() are fed to the called component, either as key/value pairs declared in the component's <%args> section, the special %ARGS variable, or the Perl argument array @_. Any component output will be sent to the current component's output stream, and the component's return value will become the return value of comp().

scomp(<component>, <arguments...>)

Identical to the comp() method, but instead of sending the called component's output to the output stream, is returned as a string. Any return value from the component will be discarded.

comp_exists(<path>)

Given a string argument, returns true if a component exists with that path or false otherwise.

call_next(<arguments...>)

Calls the next component in the component execution stack. Typically this is used by an autohandler to call the component it is wrapping around. Mason will pass any current component arguments (the %ARGS hash) to the next component, as well as any additional arguments passed to the call_next() method.

current_comp()

Returns an object representing the currently executing component.

request_comp()

Returns an object representing the component that was originally requested in the Interpreter's exec() method.

base_comp()

Returns the current base component for methods and attributes. The base component is initially set to the request_comp(). Calling a component method will set the base component to the component used in the method call. Calling a regular (nonmethod) component will set the base component to the called component.

request_args()

Returns the arguments passed to the originally requested component. If called in a list context, the arguments will be returned as a list. If called in a scalar context, the arguments will be returned as a hash reference.

Subrequests

make_subrequest(comp => <path>, args => [...], <parameters...>)

Returns a new Request object with the given parameters. Other parameters will be inherited from the current request.

exec()

Sets the new request in motion with the given arguments passed to the given component. This should be used only when the request was created with the make_subrequest() method, since exec() can happen only once for each request. In particular, it is illegal to call $m->exec(...) inside a component.

subexec(<component>, <arguments...>)

Combines the make_subrequest and exec methods into one step. Any arguments are passed to the given component, and the subrequest created will inherit all inheritable properties from the current request.

Component

This class represents a Mason component. It may be a file-based component on disk, a component created on the fly, or a method or subcomponent. The default Component class is HTML::Mason::Component::FileBased.

new(<parameters...>)

Creates a new component. See Appendix B for a list of parameters that affect the component behavior.

The new() method is not the proper way to create a component from scratch, since components must be associated with an Interpreter. See the make_component() Interpreter method if you wish to create a component from scratch.

Object Properties

title()

Returns a unique string identifying this component.

name()

> Returns a short string identifying this component. There may be more than one component with the same name.

path()

> Returns the path of this component relative to the source root.

dir_path()

> Returns the component's notion of a current directory, relative to the component root.

source_dir()

> Returns the component's enclosing directory if it is a file-based component. Note that Mason does not actually `chdir()` to a component's directory before executing it, so you may need to use `source_dir` to establish context.

object_file()

> Returns the full pathname of the object file associated with this component or `undef` if this component is not associated with any object file.

load_time()

> Returns the time this component object (not its source file) was created, in number of seconds since the epoch.

declared_args()

> Returns a hash reference indicating the variables declared in this component's `<%args>` section. Each key in this hash reference is the name of a Perl variable (including the initial sigil, `$`, `@`, or `%`), and the value is a hash reference containing (at least) a `default` key. Its value, in turn, contains Perl code to be evaluated to get the default value for this component argument.

flag(<name>)

> Given a string argument, returns the value of the Mason flag by that name for this component, as declared in a `<%flags>` section. Throws an exception if the argument is not the name of a valid Mason flag. Currently, there is only one flag allowed in `<%flags>` sections, the `inherit` flag that specifies a parent component.
>
> Note that flag values do not inherit from parent components.

is_subcomp()

> Returns true if the component is a subcomponent or method or false otherwise.

is_file_based()

> Returns true if the component was loaded from a source or object file or false otherwise.

Component Relationships

subcomps()

> Returns a reference to a hash containing all subcomponents declared by this component, with names as keys and component objects as values. If you provide

a string argument, returns only the subcomponent with that name or undef if no such subcomponent exists.

methods()

Returns a reference to a hash containing all methods declared by this component, with names as keys and component objects as values. If you provide a string argument, returns only the method with that name or undef if no such subcomponent exists.

Note that this does not search for methods in any parent components. See the method_exists and call_method entries in the next section if you wish to perform such a search.

parent()

Returns the parent component of this component or undef if this component has no parent.

owner()

If this component is a subcomponent or method, returns the component object in which it was declared.

Inheritance

attr(<name>)

Given a string argument, returns the value of the attribute (declared in an <%attr> block) by that name in this component or its parents. If no such attribute exists, an exception will be thrown.

attr_exists(<name>)

Given a string argument, returns true if an attribute by that name exists in this component or its parents or false otherwise.

attr_if_exists([<name>])

Given a string argument, returns the value of the attribute by that name in this component or its parents. If no such attribute exists, returns undef.

call_method(<name> [, <arguments...>])

Given a string argument, searches for a method by that name in this component or its parents and executes it. If no such method exists, a fatal exception will be thrown.

scall_method(<name> [, <arguments...>])

Just like call_method, but returns the component's output as a string instead of outputting it. Any return value will be discarded.

method_exists(<name>)

Given a string argument, returns true if a method by that name exists in this component or its parents or false otherwise.

Resolver

The Resolver is responsible for handling the interactions between the Interpreter and the storage medium of component source files. The default resolver class is `HTML::Mason::Resolver::File`.

new(<parameters...>)
> Returns a new Resolver object. See Appendix B for a list of parameters accepted by the new( ) method.

get_info(<path>)
> Given a component path, returns an `HTML::Mason::ComponentSource` object that may be queried to get information about the component source.

comp_root([<new_root>])
> Returns the current value of the component root. The value returned may be a string or a reference to an array of arrays, depending on whether you're using one or several component roots. Optionally sets the value of the component root if you provide an argument, whose form is the same.

comp_root_array()
> Like `comp_root( )`, but in a list context always returns a list of arrays, one per component root. If there is only one root and its name is unspecified, it will be given the name `MAIN`. In a scalar context, returns the number of component roots.

glob_path(<pattern>)
> Given a "glob"-style pattern, returns a list of paths of all components that match that pattern in the component root.

apache_request_to_comp_path(<Apache request object>)
> Given an Apache request object, this method is expected to return a component path, or `undef` if the request cannot be translated to a component path.

ApacheHandler

The `HTML::Mason::ApacheHandler` class provides the necessary glue between the Mason Interpreter and the Apache web server's `mod_perl` module. Its main task is to accept an incoming Apache request and invoke the Interpreter with the proper parameters for handling that request.

The ApacheHandler class makes the Apache request object available inside components as the global variable `$r`. This may be an object blessed into the `Apache::Request` class or the `Apache` class, depending on whether the Mason administrator has configured the ApacheHandler to use the `mod_perl` `args_method`.

ApacheHandler also turns `$m`, the Request object, into an `HTML::Mason::Request::ApacheHandler` object by subclassing `HTML::Mason::Request`.

new(<parameters...>)

Creates a new ApacheHandler object. See Appendix B for a listing of the parameters accepted.

interp([<interpreter>])

Returns the current Interpreter associated with this ApacheHandler. An optional argument sets the value to a new Interpreter.

handle_request($r)

Initiates a Mason request, processing any incoming arguments to the web server and calling the appropriate component.

handler($r)

A wrapper around handle_request() suitable for using as a mod_perl "handler." You must enable PERL_METHOD_HANDLERS when compiling mod_perl in order to use this handler.

prepare_request($r)

Returns a new Mason Request object for the given Apache Request or an HTTP status code if an error was encountered.

apache_status_title([<string>])

Returns the title of the Mason status page generated by Apache::Status. An optional argument sets the title.

args_method()

Returns the current args_method setting, which can be either mod_perl or CGI depending on whether you're using Apache::Request or CGI.pm for HTTP argument processing.

decline_dirs([true or false])

Returns true or false, depending on whether requests for directories will be declined or accepted. An optional argument sets the value. If a request for a directory is accepted, it should usually be caught by using a dhandler mechanism, so Mason has a component to execute.

CGIHandler

The HTML::Mason::CGIHandler class is similar to ApacheHandler but runs under the CGI paradigm instead of the mod_perl paradigm. Its task is to accept an incoming CGI request and invoke the Mason Interpreter with the proper parameters for handling that request.

new(<parameters...>)

Creates a new CGIHandler object. See Appendix B for a listing of the parameters accepted.

handle_request()

    Initiates a Mason request, processing any incoming arguments to the web server and calling the appropriate component. The initial component will be the one specified in $ENV{PATH_INFO}.

handle_comp(<component>)

    Like handle_request( ), but explicitly specifies the component as an argument, either as a component path or a component object.

handle_cgi_object(<CGI object>)

    Also like handle_request( ), but takes component path from the given CGI object's path_info method. Additionally, this CGI object is available to the called components.

CGIHandler also turns $r, normally the Apache request object, into an HTML::Mason::FakeApache object. It provides the following methods for compatibility with a mod_perl-based setup:

header_out(<header> => <value>)

    Adds an outgoing header to the HTTP response.

content_type()

    Sets the content type of the response to the argument given. If you don't set the content type, the type will be set to text/html by default.

Compiler

The Compiler is responsible for turning a hierarchical component structure, as fed to it by the Lexer, into a usable form. The default Compiler is HTML::Mason::Compiler::ToObject, which creates a Component object.

new(<parameters...>)

    Creates a new Compiler object and returns it. Called by the Interpreter object. See Appendix B for a list of parameters accepted.

Object Properties

allow_globals([<variables...>])
allow_globals([undef])

    Returns a list of variable names (including the initial $, @, or % type-identifying sigil) that have been declared as allowable globals within components or the number of such variables in a scalar context. The list of allowed globals can optionally be set by passing the variable names (again, including the initial sigils) as arguments. This replaces any previously set globals. To clear the list of allowed globals, pass an argument list containing the single element undef.

```
my @allowed = $compiler->allow_globals;      # Get list of globals
$compiler->allow_globals('$dbh','%session'); # Set list of globals
$compiler->allow_globals(undef);             # Clear list of globals
```

add_allowed_globals(<variables...>)

Adds one or more variable names (including the initial $, @, or % type-identifying sigil) to the list of globals allowed within components. Returns a list of variable names (again, including the initial sigils) in a list context or the number of such variables in a scalar context.

object_id()

Returns a string identifier that uniquely identifies this compiler and its current settings. This identifier is used mainly to make sure that components compiled under a different compiler, or under the same compiler with different settings, are declared stale.

compile(comp_source => <string>, name => <string>)

Compiles a component from source text and returns the compiled component. The source text is passed in a `comp_source` parameter, and a unique identifier for this component is passed in a mandatory `name` parameter. The compiled component may take any of several forms, but the default `HTML::Mason::Compiler::ToObject` class returns a bunch of Perl code in a string.

Compilation Callbacks

These are methods called by the Lexer while processing a component source. You may wish to override some of these methods if you're implementing your own custom Compiler class.

start_component()

Called by the Lexer when it starts processing a component.

end_component()

Called by the Lexer when it finishes processing a component.

start_block(block_type => <string>)

Called by the Lexer when it encounters an opening Mason block tag like `<%perl>` or `<%args>`. Its main purpose is to keep track of the nesting of different kinds of blocks within each other. The type of block (`init`, `once`, etc.) is passed via the `block_type` parameter.

end_block(block_type => <string>)

Called by the Lexer when it encounters a closing Mason block tag like `</%perl>` or `</%args>`. Like `start_block()`, its main purpose is to help maintain syntactic integrity.

_block(block => <string>, [block_type => <string>])

Several compiler methods like `doc_block()`, `text_block()`, and `raw_block()` are called by the Lexer after `start_block()` when it encounters blocks of certain types. These methods actually do the work of putting the body of a block into the compiled data structure.

The methods that follow this pattern are init_block(), perl_block(), doc_block(), text_block(), and raw_block(). The last method is called for all <%once>, <%cleanup>, <%filter>, <%init>, <%perl>, and <%shared> blocks.

text(text => <string>)

Inserts the text contained in a text parameter into the component for verbatim output.

This is called when the Lexer finds plain text in a component.

variable_declaration(type => <string>, name => <string>, default => <string>)

Inserts a variable declaration from the <%args> section into the component.

The type will be either $, @, or %, indicating a scalar, array, or hash. The name is the variable name without the leading sigil. The default is everything found after the first => on an <%args> block line and may include a comment.

key_value_pair(block_type => <string>, key => <string>, value => <string>)

Inserts a key/value pair from a <%flags> or <%attr> section into the component.

The block_type parameter will be either flags or attr.

start_named_block(block_type => <string>, name => <name>)

Analogous to start_block, earlier in this section, but starts a "named" block (<%method> or <%def>).

end_named_block()

Called by the Lexer to end a "named" block.

substitution(substitution => <string>, escape => <string>)

Called by the Lexer when it encounters a substitution tag (<% ... %>).

The value of the escape parameter will be everything found after the pipe (|) in the substitution tag and may be more than one character such as nh.

component_call(call => <string>)

Called by the Lexer when it encounters a component call tag without embedded content (<& ... &>).

The call parameter contains the entire contents of the tag.

component_content_call(call => <string>)

Called by the Lexer when it encounters a component call tag with embedded content (<&| ... &>).

component_content_call_end()

Called by the Lexer when it encounters an end tag for a component call with content (</&>). Note that there is no corresponding component_call_end() method for component calls without content, because these calls don't have end tags.

perl_line(line => <string>)

Called by the Lexer when it encounters a %-line.

Lexer

The Mason Lexer has a very limited API, because it is mostly subservient to (and hidden by) the Compiler. The Compiler calls the Lexer's new( ) and lex( ) methods, then the Lexer calls various Compiler methods to generate the component. The Lexer has more methods than are listed here, but they're internal methods and should not be considered part of its formal API. The default Lexer class is HTML::Mason::Lexer.

new(<parameters...>)
>   Creates a new Lexer object and returns it. In the current version of Mason, the new( ) method doesn't accept any parameters.

lex(name => <string>, compiler => <compiler>, comp_source => string)
>   Begins the process of lexing a component. The name parameter specifies a unique name for this component. For a file-based component, this is its full path relative to the component root. The compiler parameter supplies the compiler object to use when processing this component. The comp_source parameter supplies the source to process.

>   The lex( ) method has no return value. If it encounters an error during processing, it will throw an exception.

line_number()
>   Returns the Lexer's current line number in the component being processed.

name(),
>   Returns the name of the component currently being processed (i.e., the value of the name parameter passed to the lex( ) method).

throw_syntax_error(<error>)
>   Throws an HTML::Mason::Exception::Syntax error with the given error message as well as additional information about the component source.

Object Constructor Parameters

This appendix provides a quick reference to all the constructor parameters of the major pieces of the Mason framework. See Chapter 6 or the official Mason documentation for more detail, including information on how and where to specify them.

It's important to understand the relationships among the various pieces of Mason's framework; Figure B-1 shows how they relate to one another. Keep in mind that you can pass any class's parameters to a class that contains it. For example, you can pass any Compiler parameters to the new( ) method of the Interpreter, ApacheHandler, or CGIHandler. In the figure, the solid arrows indicate a "contains one" relationship, and the dashed arrows indicate a "contains many" relationship.

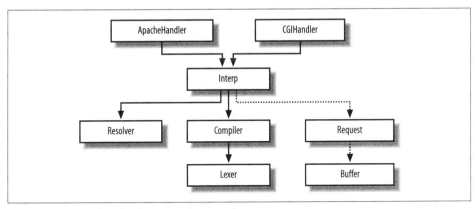

Figure B-1. An outline for the Mason framework

HTML::Mason::Interp

Name	Type	Default	Description
autohandler_name (MasonAutohandlerName)	string	autohandler	The filename to use for Mason's 'autohandler' capability
code_cache_max_size (Mason-CodeCacheMaxSize)	string	10485760	The maximum size of the component code cache
compiler (MasonCompiler)	object	HTML::Mason::Compiler:: ToObject->new	A Compiler object for compiling components
data_dir (MasonDataDir)	string		A directory for storing cache files and other state information
ignore_warnings_expr (Mason-IgnoreWarningsExpr)	regex	qr/Subroutine .* redefined/i	A regular expression describing Perl warning messages to ignore
preloads (MasonPreloads)	list		A list of components to load immediately when creating the Interpreter
resolver (MasonResolver)	object	HTML::Mason::Resolver:: File->new	A Resolver object for fetching components from storage
static_source (MasonStaticSource)	boolean	0	When true, we only compile source files once
use_object_files (MasonUseObjectFiles)	boolean	1	Whether to cache component objects on disk

HTML::Mason::Request

Name	Type	Default	Description
autoflush (MasonAutoflush)	boolean	0	Whether output should be buffered or sent immediately
data_cache_defaults (MasonDataCacheDefaults)	hash		A hash of default parameters for Cache::Cache
dhandler_name (MasonDhandlerName)	string	dhandler	The filename to use for Mason's 'dhandler' capability
error_format (MasonErrorFormat)	string	text	How error conditions are returned to the caller (brief, text, line or html)
error_mode (MasonErrorMode)	string	fatal	How error conditions are manifest (output or fatal)
max_recurse (MasonMaxRecurse)	string	32	The maximum recursion depth for component, inheritance, and request stack
out_method (MasonOutMethod)	code	sub { package HTML:: Mason::Request; print STDOUT grep({defined $_;} @_); }	A subroutine or scalar reference through which all output will pass

HTML::Mason::Resolver::File

Name	Type	Default	Description
comp_root (MasonCompRoot)	list	DocumentRoot in a web setting, current directory in a standalone setting	A string or array of arrays indicating the search path for component calls

HTML::Mason::ApacheHandler

Name	Type	Default	Description
apache_status_title (MasonApacheStatusTitle)	string	HTML::Mason status	The title of the Apache::Status page
args_method (MasonArgsMethod)	string	mod_perl	Whether to use CGI.pm or Apache::Request for parsing the incoming HTTP request
decline_dirs (MasonDeclineDirs)	boolean	1	Whether Mason should decline to handle requests for directories
interp (MasonInterp)	object	HTML::Mason::Interp->new	A Mason interpreter for processing components

HTML::Mason::Compiler

Name	Type	Default	Description
allow_globals (MasonAllowGlobals)	list	[]	An array of names of Perl variables that are allowed globally within components
default_escape_flags (MasonDefaultEscapeFlags)	string		Escape flags that will apply by default to all Mason tag output
lexer (MasonLexer)	object	HTML::Mason::Lexer->new	A Lexer object that will scan component text during compilation
postprocess_perl (MasonPostprocessPerl)	code		A subroutine through which all Perl code will be sent during compilation
postprocess_text (MasonPostprocessText)	code		A subroutine through which all plain text will be sent during compilation
preprocess (MasonPreprocess)	code		A subroutine through which all component text will be sent during compilation

HTML::Mason::Component

None.

HTML::Mason::Buffer

None.

HTML::Mason::CGIHandler

None.

HTML::Mason::Lexer

None.

Text Editors That Understand Mason

In order to write Mason components, you don't need anything fancy. You can do just fine with any old ramshackle text editor—even (horrors!) a word processor that can save as plain text will do.

However, an editor that helps you manage the details of the document you're creating can be a nice mini-luxury. Several different editors can easily be trained to understand the structure of Mason components, with varying degrees of assistance (or interference, depending on how much help you're looking for). In most cases, this is due to the work of Mason developers who created syntax definitions and offered them to the general public. If you find shortcomings, the polite thing to do is to drop a note to the developer, offering a fix if possible.

Emacs

Both authors of this book are enthusiastic users of Emacs and its wonderful cperl-mode for editing plain Perl code, courtesy of Ilya Zakharevich. However, while one can just turn cperl-mode on for an entire Mason component and get some basic syntax highlighting, brace matching, and indentation, the result is necessarily clumsy, since large parts of the component aren't Perl code.

Michael Abraham Shulman, a Mason contributor from way back, developed a much nicer solution. His Multiple-Major-Mode Mode (mmm-mode) is a way to combine cperl-mode and html-mode (or sgml-mode, if you prefer), each in the correct region of the component. Of course, like a true hubristic programmer, Michael addressed the larger problem: mmm-mode is actually a framework for allowing several major modes to coexist in a single buffer. Mason syntax definitions are provided, but there are also definitions for embedding JavaScript in HTML documents, embedding HTML code in Perl here-docs, embedding Perl in HTML using Embperl, and more.

Note that since this is a book on Mason and not a book on Emacs and Lisp, we're just going to give you installation and configuration instructions as if they were magical incantations. If you know alternate ways to achieve the same ends, you'll probably be fine using them.

To use mmm-mode's mason-mode, you'll need to download mmm-mode from *http://mmm-mode.sourceforge.net/* and install the *.el* files as described in the *README* file.* Create a file called *.emacs* in your home directory if it doesn't already exist, and add the statement (require 'mmm-auto) to it. Then you can manually invoke mason-mode while editing a component by first turning on html-mode (type Meta-x† html-mode and press Return) for the outer region, then turning on mason-mode for the Mason sections (type Meta-x mmm-ify-by-class, press Return, type mason, and press Return). mmm-mode will then scan your component to figure out which sections are which, turning on cperl-mode in the sections that contain Perl code.

If you want mason-mode to start up automatically whenever you edit files with a certain suffix, say *.mas*, you can add a few lines to your *.emacs* file after the (require 'mmm-auto) line, as in Example C-1.

Example C-1. mmm-mode configuration for Mason by extension

```
(require 'mmm-auto)
(setq mmm-global-mode 'maybe)
(add-to-list 'auto-mode-alist '("\\.mas\\'" . html-mode))
(mmm-add-mode-ext-class 'html-mode "\\.mas\\'" 'mason)
```

Alternately, if you'd like to enable mmm-mode for all HTML files in a certain directory, you could use the code in Example C-2.

Example C-2. mmm-mode configuration for Mason by directory

```
(require 'mmm-auto)
(setq mmm-global-mode 'maybe)
(add-to-list 'auto-mode-alist '("/usr/local/apache/htdocs" . sgml-mode))
(mmm-add-mode-ext-class 'sgml-mode "/usr/local/apache/htdocs" 'mason)
```

As of this writing, mmm-mode doesn't scan your Mason component continually, so if you type <& &> in your component, the inside of that tag won't be treated as a cperl-mode region until you rescan the file. You can rescan by typing Control-c % Control-b. If you know of a way to automatically keep the regions current while typing, be sure to drop a line to Michael. His email address is in the mmm-mode *README* file.

You can download Emacs from several different places on the Internet, but the original distribution is available at *http://www.gnu.org/software/emacs/*. Precompiled binaries for your system may also be available from other sources, greatly simplifying the installation process if you're not using Unix.

---

* Debian users can find an mmm-mode package in Woody and Sid.

† If you don't know what the Meta key is, you can probably use your keyboard's Escape key instead.

Vim

Not to be outdone in the so-called editor wars, Vim has some pretty slick Mason syntax highlighting of its own. Vim is a widely used variant of the standard Unix editor *vi*. Vim stands for "*vi* improved," and syntax highlighting is one of several major improvements offered by Vim.

The Mason syntax module is part of the standard distribution of Vim, so if you have a fairly modern version of Vim (Version 6.0 or later should be fine), you should already have all the necessary files. To invoke Mason highlighting while you're editing a Mason component, you can enter the command `:set syntax=mason`. This will turn on Perl syntax for the Perl portions of the component and HTML syntax for the other parts.

If you want Mason syntax highlighting to start automatically when you edit Mason components, you have a few options. First, Vim will automatically turn on Mason highlighting when you begin editing a file that starts with the string `<%args>`. This is nice, because it both simplifies configuration and encourages you to standardize the structure of your components.

Another alternative is to configure Vim to invoke Mason highlighting when you begin editing files ending with a certain suffix like *.mas*. To do this, you can add the following directives to your own *.vimrc* file (usually located in your home directory):

```
au syntax mason so /usr/local/share/vim/vim60ax/syntax/mason.vim
au BufNewFile,BufRead *.mas set ft=mason
```

Alternatively, you could edit Vim's *filetype.vim* file (usually located in */usr/local/ vim60/share/vim/vim60/*, though it depends on where Vim is installed on your system) to contain the following line:

```
au BufNewFile,BufRead *.mas setf mason
```

For more information on Vim configuration, consult the thorough Vim documentation. If you add something significant to the Vim Mason support, be sure to contact the maintainer of the Mason syntax file to see whether he'd be interested in integrating your changes into the main distribution.[*]

---

[*] The maintainer is currently Andrew Smith, *andrewdsmith@yahoo.com*.

Content Management with Bricolage

This appendix was kindly written for this book by David Wheeler, Bricolage Maintainer, *david@wheeler.net.*

As your site grows, the amount of content to be managed grows. At some point—particularly if you're part of a large organization with a *lot* of pages on its site—the amount of content that needs to be continually updated becomes unwieldy. Most sites start out with one or two people doing everything manually in a text editor and then FTPing the files to the web server. As the demands on the site grow, savvy site operators discover and deploy flexible templating systems such as Mason to ease the demands of site management.

However, for all its flexibility and power, Mason still requires manual updates to its files. By using Mason, you may reduce the number of files you have to edit every time your marketing department wants to change its message from "adaptively monetizing holistic market-driven systems" to "utilizing proactive meta-services,"* but wouldn't it be nice if the marketing department could make those changes itself, without having to bother you? And wouldn't it be helpful if the interface for making those changes was simple enough for every user in your organization to comprehend and use?

Content management systems (CMSs) endeavor (or at least claim) to respond to such wishes. The CMS market is a packed one, with entries from startups to established industry players. But if you're reading this book, it's safe to assume that you'd be most interested in a Perl-oriented, or perhaps even *Mason*-oriented, CMS.

Bricolage is such a CMS. It is built on Mason, and you can use it to build large Mason-powered sites as well as sites driven by other technologies.

The idea behind a CMS is to centrally manage content in such a way that any user who needs to edit text, graphics, or other media can do so through a structured inter-

---

* Thanks to Tels' `Dev::Bollocks` module for these lovely aphorisms.

face. The presentation of content for editing is independent of the final format of the content or of the distribution of the content to your site. All such content is managed by a version control system, so that its history can be reviewed and the content rolled back to an earlier version if necessary. Furthermore, content moves through a workflow that subjects it to various stages of review and approval before publication and distribution. And when published, the CMS formats the content for output by pushing it through content-independent formatting templates created for that purpose. (See the "Bricolage Terminology" sidebar, later in this chapter, for definitions of some of the terms carelessly littered throughout this paragraph.)

These features form the foundation for Bricolage, a robust, actively developed opensource CMS built to centrally support a distributed organization of content and formatting specialists via an intuitive, browser-based interface. By rigidly separating content from formatting, Bricolage allows nontechnical users to quickly update and publish content relevant to them without having to coordinate with the production folks for formatting in HTML or with IT for getting the content on the site. Rather, a marketing wordsmith or copy editor can search for and check out the "story" (as text-based Bricolage content is called) that needs changing, make the changes, and then check in and possibly publish the story. Bricolage handles formatting the story, writing it to a file, and distributing the file to the production web server—all without the alignment of stars that a traditional, hand-maintained infrastructure requires.

A brief introduction to Bricolage follows, including the basics of installation and configuration, terminology, element administration, content editing, and template development. Although Bricolage offers many more features than those presented here (indeed, comprehensive documentation of Bricolage could fill its *own* book!), the majority of your and your users' time will be spent on these tasks. And don't worry, we'll soon get to the importance of Mason for formatting content. So let's install it and get going!

Installing Bricolage

Bricolage is a complex application with a long list of requirements. Nevertheless, it strives to make installation and configuration as painless as possible. The key to an easy Bricolage installation is to get its requirements satisfied ahead of time. The Bricolage installation process does its best to verify those dependencies and to suggest what you need to complete the installation.

To get started, download Bricolage from its home page, *http://www.bricolage.cc/*, and unpack it. Bricolage uses a standard make process for its installation, so simply execute the following:

```
cd bricolage-1.x.x
make
```

The first thing the make process does is verify that you have all the necessary software requirements satisfied. Thus it's a convenient first step since, based on its printout, you'll know very quickly what it needs installed that's not already on your system.

Fortunately, the list of requirements consists of well-known and widely deployed applications and libraries. Indeed, some of the more popular GNU/Linux distributions, notably Red Hat and Debian, are compatible with Bricolage. Binary RPMs and DEBs can be used to install Perl, Apache, and PostgreSQL on those platforms, and Bricolage supports FreeBSD and the ports-installed versions of Perl, Apache, and PostgreSQL, too. Bricolage even runs well on Mac OS X! Consult the platform-specific *README* files that come with the Bricolage distribution and the *INSTALL* file for detailed installation instructions.

Here's a quick overview of what you'll need to run Bricolage:

Perl

    The first thing you'll need to run Bricolage is Perl 5.6 or later (5.6.1 is *strongly* recommended, since it fixes many bugs in 5.6.0). Although Mason supports earlier versions of Perl, Bricolage's design and many of its key features demand the feature set provided by Perl 5.6. To compile and install Perl yourself, download it from *http://www.perl.com/* and follow its installation instructions.

PostgreSQL

    Bricolage stores the vast majority of its data in a PostgreSQL database. PostgreSQL is a well-respected open source RDBMS with an impressive feature set. Download PostgreSQL 7.1 or later (Version 7.2 or later is *strongly* recommended) from *http://www.postgresql.org/*. If you're installing it manually, be sure to compile it with the `--enable-multibyte=UNICODE` configuration option, as Bricolage stores all text in Unicode character encoding.

Perl modules

    Bricolage provides a comprehensive feature set thanks in large part to the benefits of the CPAN. As a natural result, Bricolage requires quite a lot of CPAN modules to be installed—more than 30 as of this writing. The simplest way to install them all is to let Bricolage's make process use the `CPAN` module to download and install everything for you. If you don't have dedicated Net access while running make, check the *INSTALL* file for a list of the required modules you'll need to acquire and install.

Apache/`mod_perl`

    The Mason-powered Bricolage user interface is browser-based. It therefore requires the Apache web server and `mod_perl`. The process for installing Apache and `mod_perl` to work with Bricolage is no different than your typical install, so if you've already installed Apache and `mod_perl` for Mason, it should also work fine for Bricolage. Note that at the time of this writing, Apache 2.0 and `mod_perl` 2.0 have not been tested with Bricolage; you'll need to install the latest 1.3 Apache and 1.x `mod_perl`. You can also optionally include support for secure sockets (e.g., mod_ssl) in your Apache install. Doing so allows Bricolage to encrypt passwords for logging in and even provides an option to encrypt all requests, so that remote users can protect all content they're editing. Download mod_perl from *http://perl.apache.org/* and Apache from *http://httpd.apache.org/*. For SSL support use either mod_ssl (*http://www.modssl.org*) or Apache-SSL (*http://www.apache-ssl.org*); both require the OpenSSL library (*http://www.openssl.org*).

Once all the preceding pieces are in place and functioning, return to the Bricolage source directory and run make again:

```
cd bricolage-1.x.x
make
```

Once make has verified all of the necessary dependencies, it will prompt you for other important information relevant to the installation, such as the Apache username, the PostgreSQL administrator name and password, the name to be given to the Bricolage PostgreSQL database, and the name and password of the PostgreSQL user for Bricolage itself to use. Consult the *INSTALL* file for more information on the options these prompts set. Once you've successfully answered all of its questions, make will finish its job and you'll be ready to install Bricolage. You must run make install as root:

```
su
make install
```

The installation will take care of everything that needs to be done, including copying the necessary libraries, Mason components, and configuration files to their destinations and creating the Bricolage database.

Now it's time to start Bricolage. Bricolage comes with a startup script, *bric_apachectl*, which reads the necessary configuration files, sets the Apache directives it needs, and fires up Apache. Use this command to start Bricolage:

```
bric_apachectl start
```

Once Bricolage starts, point your browser to the server name you specified during installation and log in. The default user is "admin" and the password is "change me now!" I strongly recommend that you take that advice. In fact, the admin user is a simple default user; you can create a new user in the Global Admin group for yourself, log out, log back in as the new user, and delete the admin user altogether if you like. Better yet, just change the login name of the admin user.

Elements: the Building Blocks of Content

The core of the Bricolage interface is managing different types of assets through a workflow process. When you log in, Bricolage presents you with your own private workspace. Any story, media, or template assets that you have checked out are listed here (see Figure D-1), providing easy access for you to edit them, check them in, view

Bricolage Terminology

As a fairly sophisticated CMS, Bricolage expects you to understand some basic terminology in order to fully take advantage of it. Here are some of the more important terms used in this appendix:

content
> The data an organization needs to manage and publish.

workflow
> An organizational structure that reflects the functional process of content development within an organization. A workflow generally identifies the steps that content goes through from inception to publication and associates certain people with each step. Workflows vary from organization to organization—and even from department to department—so a core Bricolage feature allows organizations to create custom workflows that work for them. The steps in a Bricolage workflow are called "desks," and a typical example that might apply to a media organization would be to have workflow desks called "Editorial," "Copy Edit," "Legal," and "Publish." As you work with content in Bricolage, you can check out content from a desk and, when you're done, check it in to another desk. Then, those responsible for that next step in the content creation process can check it out and do their part. This process continues until all the required steps in the editorial creation process have been followed and the content is ready for publication.

desk
> A logical stop through which content passes as it makes its way through a workflow. Generally corresponds to the duties of a person or group in the organization.

asset
> A meaningful aggregation of data—generally content—that needs to be managed as an atomic entity. These are the conceptual parts that make up the whole of the content managed by a CMS, although they are themselves nearly always made up of collections of smaller pieces of content. In Bricolage, there are three types of assets: stories, media, and templates.

story
> A collection of mostly textual content. Stories are the objects that editors will spend most of their time working with and generally correspond well to the idea of an article, essay, or, well, story to be published as an coherent whole.

media asset
> A collection of content that centers around a media file. The media file may be of any type, including graphics, video, audio, spreadsheets, or even text. (New media types can be defined via an administrative interface.) Textual data may be associated with the media file, either to add metadata (such as file size or play length) or as additional content (such as a title). Media assets are first-class content objects in Bricolage and can be managed just as stories are managed.

—continued—

template
> A formatting asset that takes the content in a story and formats it for output. In Bricolage, templates can be written in Mason or in HTML::Template, and other templating architectures will be added in the future. Like stories and media, templates can be managed through workflows appropriate to their development.

elements
> The collection of independent parts that make up the whole of a story or media asset. A story-type element or media-type element defines the structure of a whole story or media asset, respectively. All other elements reflect various things that one thinks of as being a part of a story. Typical examples include "Feature Story," "Illustration," "Page," and "Sidebar."

subelement
> An element contained in another Bricolage element. Any elements that are not story type elements or media type elements can be used as subelements.

category
> The hierarchical organization of content. Categories can be nested and arbitrarily deep. They are generally used to create part of the URI for a story.

burner
> The Bricolage object that applies templates to story content and writes the resulting files to disk. Naturally enough, this process is called "burning."

output channel
> A collection of templates specific to a particular type of output. Using multiple output channels, the same story can be output in multiple ways. This approach is useful for creating new channels for your content, such as HTML for the web, WSDL for mobile phones, and even PDF or PostScript for high-quality rendering.

publishing
> The process of burning content to files in one or more output channels and then distributing those files to destination servers where they can be made available to an audience. Typically, the distribution is to a public web server.

their event logs, or delete them. You can also preview a story or media asset—see how it will look when it gets published—by clicking its title. You can sort the assets by many of their properties, including title, category, cover date, and priority. The navigation menu on the left side of the screen presents a hierarchical view of the workflows and administrative tools available for your use.

Descending through the ADMIN → PUBLISHING → Elements menus presents the Bricolage Element Manager (Figure D-2). The Element Manager, like all of the Bricolage managers, provides an interface to search for existing elements for editing or deletion as well as a link to create new elements. Selecting to edit an element, such as the default-installed "Book Review" element, brings up the Element Profile (Figure D-3).

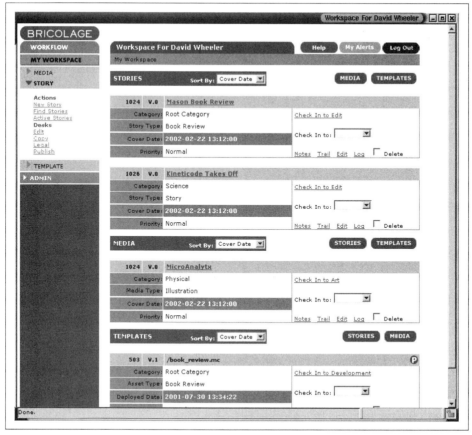

Figure D-1. My Workspace

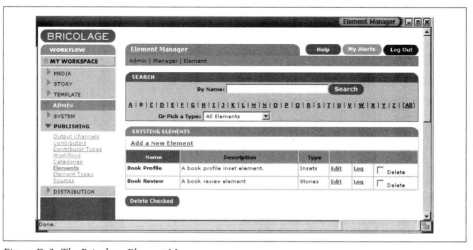

Figure D-2. The Bricolage Element Manager

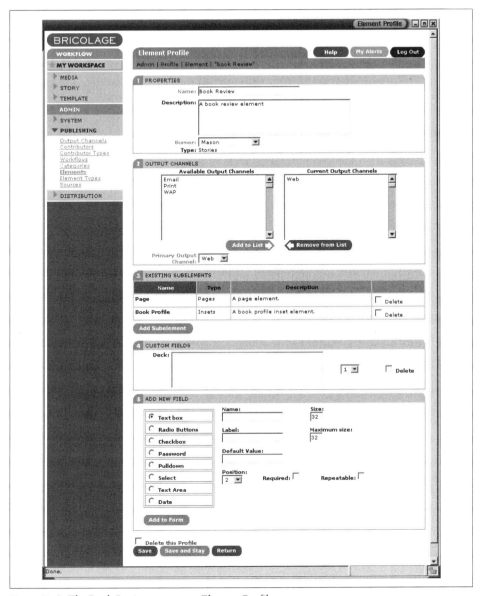

Figure D-3. The Book Review story type Element Profile

There are essentially three types of elements in Bricolage: those that define stories, those that define media assets, and subelements of either stories or media assets. The "Book Review" element shown in Figure D-3 is an example of an element that defines the structure of a story, hereafter called a "story type element."

Figure D-3 reveals a multitude of relevant data points that describe stories based on this element. In the first section of the profile, the "Burner" select list determines what kind of template will be used to "burn" the content of "Book Review" stories into files. The options supported as of this writing are Mason and HTML::Template. This means that the templates that format the content of "Book Review" stories are actually Mason components! Other templating architectures may also be added by the time you read this, but isn't it fortuitous that Bricolage already supports our favorite?

All story type and media type elements are set to publish to particular output channels. An output channel is a named collection of templates used to output the content of a story in a particular way. For example, in Figure D-3, notice that the "Book Review" story type element publishes to the "Web" output channel. Other output channels available to this element are "Email," "Print," and "WAP." Should any of these be added to the "Book Review" element, upon publication a story built from the "Book Review" element will be formatted by templates specific to each output channel. In this way, it's possible to publish the same content in multiple ways and to multiple destinations—a useful feature for maximizing the reach of your content. For example, adding the "WAP" output channel and publishing a story based on the "Book Review" element would format and distribute the content of the story for both the Web and for WAP phones. Bricolage allows you to create as many output channels as necessary to get your content where it needs to go. You'll then just have to create the templates for them (see "Templates" later in this chapter).

Examining sections 3, 4, and 5 of the Element Profile, you'll notice that Bricolage provides for a great deal of element customization. Section 3, "EXISTING SUBELE-MENTS," lists subelements of the "Book Review" element. This list derives from all of the non-media type and non-story type elements in Bricolage. Furthermore, subelements can themselves contain subelements. In this way, one can create a structured hierarchy of elements, and this hierarchy can be as arbitrarily deep as necessary. In this example, "Page" and "Book Profile" have been added as subelements of the "Book Review" story type element. Thus, a content editor building a story based on the "Book Review" element will have a choice of adding page and book profile subelements. This componentized architecture closely mirrors Mason's idea of assembling a page from a library of components—in fact, if you use the Mason burner, every element has a one-to-one relationship to a Mason component.

Sections 4 and 5 of the "Book Review" story type element profile illustrate Bricolage's support for custom fields. As an element administrator, you determine what fields need to be in an element, the default order in which they appear, and whether they're required or repeatable. Note that one field—Deck—has already been added. By using the form in section 5, you can add more fields and make them any of several familiar types: text box, radio button, checkbox, select list, and so on.

The key to element administration in Bricolage is to think of it in terms of logical data modeling. Think about how meaningful aggregations of content (e.g., stories or pages) on your site are structured, and then create the necessary elements and subelements to model those structures. Then, when content editors create the content, they'll be presented with only the choices of elements and fields that adhere to the models you create for them. In this way, not only do you provide an intuitive interface for your content editors to work with, but you also assure the integrity of the resulting structure's content.

Content Editing

Once you have designed your element hierarchy to meet the needs of your content editors, those editors can start to create content. Figure D-4 illustrates a typical story profile, this one for a story based on the "Book Review" element we examined in the last section. Note that the value for "Story Type" is "Book Review." In the content editing space, the elements that define stories and media assets are called "story types" or "media types," respectively, while all other elements are simply called "elements." This distinction prevents confusing your editors about the difference between elements that are subelements and elements that define stories or media.

The first section of the Bricolage story profile, "INFORMATION," lists properties of the story common to every story in the system. In addition to the aforementioned "Story Type" property, notice the "URI" property. Bricolage constructs this property from the primary category of the story, the story's cover date, and its slug. The cover date is an arbitrary date with which to associate the story, while the slug is a kind of one-word description. Categories, discussed later, make up the directory structure of your site. Notice that the slug and cover date can be edited; whenever you change any of these values, Bricolage will automatically update the URI. Previews are an important function of the URI in the story profile; click the URI to see how the story will look once it has been formatted by its templates and published.

Other properties managed in this section include the story's source (where the content comes from) its title, a description, and the expire date. The expire date is particularly useful, as Bricolage's distribution architecture will automatically delete the story from your site on this date—a critical feature for time-sensitive content.

The second section of the story profile, "CONTENT," provides the interface for building the meat of your content. The element hierarchy mapped out in the "Book Review" story type element profile defines the structure of this section. The "Add Element" button and the select list next to it offer the elements that one can add to this story. Note that in the interest of simplicity, the "Add Element" select list offers both subelements and custom fields as options—the two concepts are not distinguished in this interface. The reason for this simplification is that editors don't really care whether something they're adding to the story is a subelement or a field; they just know they need to add something—a deck, a page, a book profile, and so forth. So all they have to do is pick something from this list and then click "Add

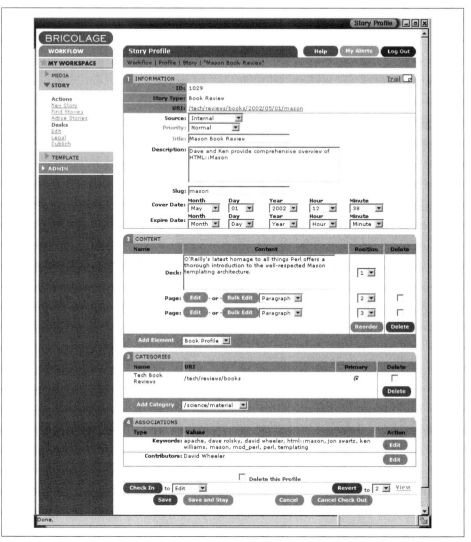

Figure D-4. A story profile for a 'book review' story

Element"—no need to stop and think about whether the thing they want to add is a field or a subelement, because everything is in one place.

A "Deck" and two "Page" elements have been added to the sample story in Figure D-4. Custom fields such as "Deck" display the values that the editor has put in, while subelements such as "Page" provide buttons to edit those elements. The "Position" select lists allow the editor to easily reorder the elements she has added to the story, while the "Delete" checkboxes allow her to remove nonrequired elements she no longer wants.

Sharp readers will have noticed that there are in fact *two* edit buttons associated with each "Page" element, "Edit" and "Bulk Edit." The "Edit" button presents the editor with an element profile. The element profile essentially mimics the "CONTENT" section of stories, listing the subelements and fields that have been added to the element. Figure D-5 illustrates the element profile for the first "Page" element in the story profile displayed in Figure D-4. The usual "Position" and "Delete" options are once again available, as is the ability to add more elements. Note that three paragraphs have been added to this element. While it makes sense to add *some* elements one at a time—particularly those that can be added only once, such as the "Deck" field in the story profile—adding a *repeating* field over and over disrupts the editing process. No editor wants to interrupt his editing every time he has to start a new paragraph by stopping to select "Paragraph" from the select list, click "Add Element," wait for the page to reload, scroll down to find the new field, and then continue with his writing.

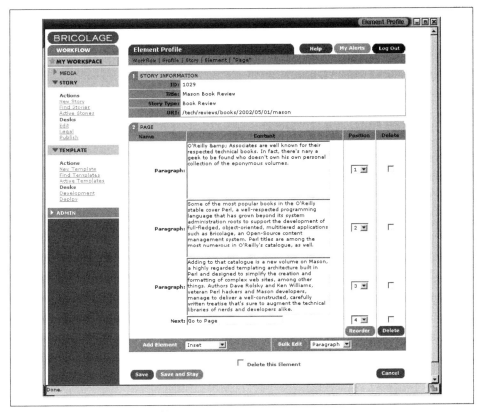

Figure D-5. A page element profile

The "Bulk Edit" button addresses this issue. The select list next to the "Bulk Edit" button lists fields that can be added multiple times to a story—in this example,

"Paragraph." Notice that each repeatable element listed in the story profile illustrated in Figure D-4 has a "Bulk Edit" button. The element profile duplicates this interface, so that an editor can jump straight from a list of elements to the bulk edit page for one of the repeatable fields in one of the elements or can edit the element itself in its profile and bulk edit its repeatable fields from there.

Figure D-6 illustrates the result of selecting "Paragraph" and clicking the "Bulk Edit" button. This interface allows an editor to edit contiguous fields, well, contiguously—without having to interrupt her train of thought to deal with managing the architecture of the story. She may choose to use whatever field separators she likes (the default is a blank line) and gains the added benefit of word and character counts. In fact, the bulk edit interface is smart enough to properly wrap broken and mangled lines pasted from another application, such as an email client or word processor.

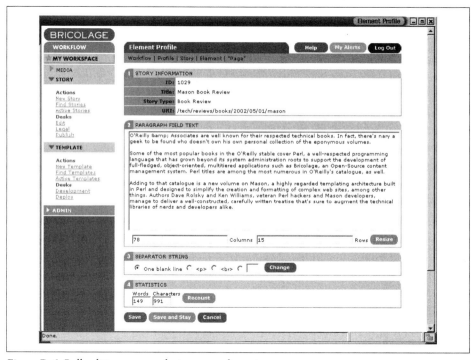

Figure D-6. Bulk editing paragraphs in a page element

Let's return to the story profile in Figure D-4. The third section, "CATEGORIES," manages the categories in which the story will be published. Each category defines a directory on the filesystem, and because categories may contain subcategories, you can easily construct a meaningful hierarchy for the content on your site. In Figure D-4, the category */tech/reviews/books* has been selected, and you can tell from the URI path that it is a subcategory of */tech/reviews*, which is itself a subcategory of */tech*, which in turn is a subcategory of the permanent / root category. Upon publication, the story will be written to files in this category, as reflected in the full URI of the story listed in the "INFORMATION" section of the story profile. You can add a story to multiple categories, and it will be written to all of those categories when published. This feature is useful for stories that cut across categories and when the categories are formatted differently by their templates. Multiple categories can even be useful for designating different sites. In that sense, selecting multiple categories forces the story to be published to multiple sites. One category is always designated as the primary category and will be used as the default for previews and for searching for an existing story in Bricolage.

The last section of the story profile defines associations between the story and other objects in Bricolage—namely keywords and contributors. Keywords are exactly what you think they are: keywords associated with the story. Most often these will be used for creating a keywords metatag in your story HTML files, but it can also be used for archiving, indexing, search engine populating, and so on. Contributors are the people who contributed content to a story. Bricolage offers comprehensive features for managing contributors, including the ability to create types of contributors, to define custom fields for those types (e.g., "Bio"), and to create variations (called "roles") on a given contributor within a type, so that the same contributor can be used for different stories with different information in his custom fields.

The button bar at the bottom of the story profile provides numerous options for managing the story. Click "Save" to save the story and return to your workspace. Click "Save and Stay" to save the story and continue editing it. Select the "Delete" checkbox and click "Save" to delete the story. Select a desk from the select list next to the "Check In" button, click that button, and the story will be saved and checked into that desk, incrementing the version number in the process. You can revert to a previous version of the story by selecting a version number from the select list on the right end of the button bar, and clicking "Revert." Click "View" if you just want to see what a previous version looked like. Click "Cancel" to return to your workspace without saving your changes, and "Cancel Checkout" to remove all the changes you made since you checked out (or created) the story and remove the story from your workspace.

Templates

Because this is a Mason book, I'm sure you're now saying to yourself, "Self, where's the Mason? I want to see some code!" This is the section you've been waiting for. You should have at least skimmed the other sections, though, because in Bricolage templates are closely tied to elements.

As mentioned earlier, non-media type elements in Bricolage are associated with a "burner." A burner is merely a templating architecture available for formatting your content. At the time of this writing, the list includes HTML::Mason and HTML::Template.

In the element we examined earlier, the "Book Review" story type element, the Mason burner was selected. Subelements of the "Book Review" element were "Page" and "Book Profile," both of which also use the Mason burner. Ultimately, this means that the templates that format the content for these elements are Mason components.

Figure D-7 illustrates a template profile, *book_review.mc*, which formats stories created from the "Book Review" story type element. In Bricolage, templates, like story and media assets, are managed through workflow. You check them out, make your changes, and check them in. When you're ready to put them to work formatting your content, you deploy them from a workflow desk designated for that task. Managing templates through workflow allows an organization to manage an approval process when necessary, as well as create various stops that may be necessary to create templates—e.g., from production (when somebody creates a raw HTML template) to development (when a Masonite adds the code to do the formatting) to deployment.

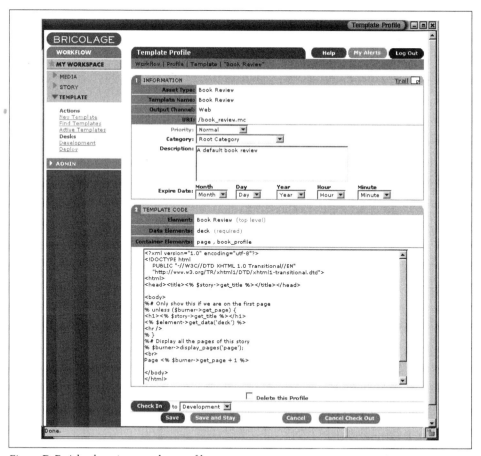

Figure D-7. A book review template profile

In Figure D-7, you'll notice that the template looks pretty much like any Mason component. The difference, however, is that the Bricolage burner system makes a number of global objects available to the component. These objects are a $story object, which represents the story itself; an $element object, which represents the element that the template is formatting; and a $burner object, which represents the Bricolage burner executing the Mason template. These objects provide all the methods you need to get and format story content. The $story object, for example, allows you to access the primary properties of the story being burned, such as (in this example), the title: $story->get_title. Here is the complete *book_review.mc* template code:

```
<?xml version="1.0" encoding="utf-8"?>
<!DOCTYPE html
    PUBLIC "-//W3C//DTD XHTML 1.0 Transitional//EN"
    "http://www.w3.org/TR/xhtml1/DTD/xhtml1-transitional.dtd">
<html>
<head><title><% $story->get_title %></title></head>

<body>
% # Only show this if we are on the first page.
% unless ($burner->get_page) {
<h1><% $story->get_title %></h1>
<h3><% $element->get_data('deck') %></h3>
<hr />
% }

% # Display all the pages of this story.
% $burner->display_pages('page');
<h4>Page <% $burner->get_page + 1 %></h4>

</body>
</html>
```

The $element object allows you to retrieve the custom data attached to the element that's currently being formatted (remember, elements are hierarchically created, so you can have many elements for a given story). The example retrieves the contents of the "Deck" field from the story element: $element->get_data('deck'). The $element object also offers properties to retrieve the subelements added to the story. Note that, in Figure D-7, the fields listed above the Mason code provide a cheat sheet listing what "Data Elements" (fields) and "Container Elements" (subelements) are available.

The $burner object provides special methods that allow you to affect the burn process itself. In this example, $burner->display_pages('page') causes the burner to execute the relevant template for the "Page" element for each page element in the story. Pages in Bricolage are elements of a specific type that have been marked as pages in the UI (see Figure D-8). The "Page" element happens to be an element of an element type that's marked "Page" (makes sense, don't it?), so we can use the display_pages() method to burn "Page" elements. The burner is smart enough to find the proper template and use it to format each page.

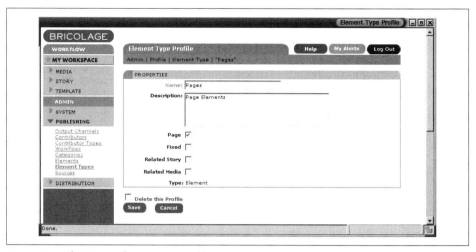

Figure D-8. The 'Pages' element type profile

The display_pages() method formats each page in the context of the template that calls it. Thus, all of the Mason code on either side of the call to $burner->display_pages('page') is executed for every page in the story. This is similar to the Mason $m->call_next method in that the context of the surrounding code always remains intact for each page; but unlike $m->call_next, $burner->display_pages writes each page of the story to a separate file. This functionality allows the burner to determine how many pages a story has and how many to burn to the filesystem without you as the template developer needing to worry about it. All you need to do in that context is to determine the page number, when necessary, to display contextual information that varies depending on the page.

The *book_profile.mc* template, listed earlier, does just that: because Bricolage elements are ordered as a Perl array, the first page element is 0, the second page is 1, and so on. Thus it's a straightforward matter to determine what page is currently being burned and therefore what contextual data to display. Here, the title and deck go on only the first page ($burner->get_page returns 0, or false), and page number labels get displayed by simply adding 1 to every call to get_page().

The *page.mc* template uses the same approach to add links to the different pages in a story. Here is a sample *page.mc* template:

```
<!-- Start "Page" -->
<%perl>;
# Display all elements except 'prev' and 'next'.
foreach my $e ($element->get_elements) {
    next if $e->has_name('prev') || $e->has_name('next');
    if ($e->has_name('paragraph')) {
        $m->print('<p>'. $e->get_data . "</p>\n");
    } else {
        $burner->display_element($e);
```

```
        }
    }

    $m->print("\n<hr />\n\n");

    # Get file name info from the output channel.
    my $oc = $burner->get_oc;
    my $filename = $oc->get_filename;
    my $file_ext = $oc->get_file_ext;

    # $burner numbers pages from '0' not '1'.
    my $pnum = $burner->get_page + 1;

    # Show 'previous' link
    if (my $prev = $element->get_data('previous')) {
        my $pageindex = $pnum-2 != 0 ? $pnum-2 : '';
        my $prev_pnum = $pnum - 1;
        $m->print(qq{<p><a href="$filename$pageindex.$file_ext">}
                . qq{&lt;-- $prev $prev_pnum</a></p>});
    }

    # Show 'next' link
    if (my $next = $element->get_data('next')) {
        $m->print(qq{<p><a href="$filename$pnum.$file_ext">}
                . qq{$next --></a></p>});
    }
</%perl>
<!-- End "Page" -->
```

The first thing you'll notice is a new method call, $element->get_elements. This method returns a list of all the subelements and field elements of the current element in the order specified by the editor in the story profile. Note that in this template the $element object represents the "Page" element currently getting burned, rather than the story type element; the global $element object *always* represents the current element relevant to the template. Since the elements returned by $element->get_elements can be either subelements or fields, we use has_name() to check each one so that, based on our knowledge of the story structure, we can decide what to do with each element.

In this example, we choose to skip the 'next' and 'previous' elements because they'll be handled later. The 'paragraph' elements, on the other hand, are formatted as one would expect, while any other elements are merely passed to $burner-> display_element. This method, like the display_pages() method, finds the relevant template for the element, formats the element, and adds it to the output of the template. It differs from the display_pages() method in that it doesn't output a separate page for each element. In this respect, it somewhat resembles Mason's $m->comp method, although it takes no other arguments.

The rest of the *page.mc* element is given over to creating links to the previous and next pages of the story. Bricolage outputs all pages according to a strict set of rules:

a) all pages for a single story are in the same directory; b) each file is named according to the filenaming properties of the current output channel; and c) pages 2 and up get a number attached to the base name of the file. So if the current output channel has its 'filename' property set to 'index' and its 'file_ext' property set to 'html', the filenames of a story will be *index.html*, *index1.html*, *index2.html*, and so on. The previous *page.mc* template draws on this knowledge to create links to the previous and next pages in the story—if, that is, the story editor filled in values for the 'next' or 'previous' fields.

Figure D-9 illustrates the result of previewing the story shown in Figure D-4.

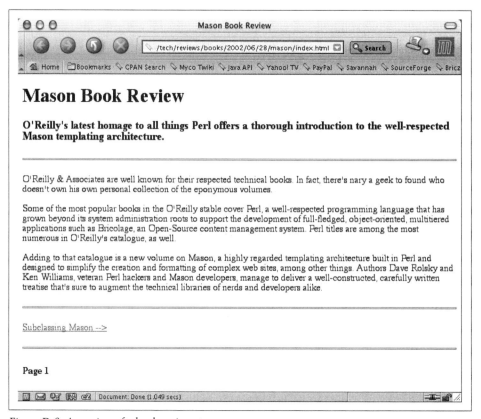

Figure D-9. A preview of a book review story

Where to Learn More

Although the componentized architecture for building and formatting content constitutes the core functionality of Bricolage, this brief introduction has but scratched the surface of what's possible in this flexible application. Element design and implementation is an art of its own, and the templates, of course, feature all of the flexibility and power of Perl. But there's more. Bricolage offers a vast array of features commonly found in commercial CMSs. Here's a partial list of some of the features not mentioned earlier:

- Autohandler-type templates
- Scheduled publishing
- Content files distributed to production web servers
- Event-based alerting
- Filtering actions applied to content files
- Complete user and group administration
- A fine-grained permission architecture
- A SOAP server for:
  - Importing and exporting assets
  - Automatically publishing content
  - Mass publishing content
  - Loads of other things no one has even thought of yet

To learn more about Bricolage, visit its home page, *http://www.bricolage.cc/*. There you'll find user documentation to help get you started, the complete API documentation, more screen shots, and links to downloads of the latest version. There are also active discussion lists (and their archives) for Bricolage users and developers. Feel free to join the fun!

Glossary

argument

In this book, generally used to refer to the arguments passed to a component, declared in an <%args> block.

attribute

A named property of a component that can be inherited via the inheritance hierarchy. Attributes are set using the <%attr> tag and queried using the $component->attr() method.

autohandler

A component that "wraps" other components and serves as a default parent. See also *inheritance hierarchy* and *wrapping chain*.

base component

The bottommost child of the current component as invoked in a component call. This may be the current component itself. Analogous to the "self" in object-oriented programming. The base component changes several times throughout a request as components call one another.

child component

The opposite of a "parent" component. Each component may have zero or more children. Children are not specified explicitly; rather, a component becomes a child by virtue of having a parent.

Compiler

A class responsible for turning a body of Mason source code into Perl code suitable for execution by the Interpreter. Available in Mason components as $m->interp->compiler.

component

The basic building block of a Mason site. A component is usually defined in a source file inside the component tree, though one file may define several components. Components can also be created on the fly by feeding component source text to the Interpreter's make_component() method.

component root

Depending on context, may refer to a named, ordered list of directories in which Mason will search for components or to a single element of this list. This linguistic ambiguity arises because Mason uses the parameter comp_root to refer to the entire list, but many people also use the phrase "multiple component roots" to refer to a component root with more than one element. See also *component tree*.

component stack

The runtime chain of components that have invoked one another. Analogous to the runtime stack of subroutines in a typical programming language. Components call one another via $m->comp(), $m->scomp(), $m->call_next(), $component->call_method(), or <& &> tags. The current component is always at the bottom of the component stack, and the top-level autohandler is usually at the top.

component tree

An ordered list of directories in which Mason will search for components. See also *component root*.

current component

The component currently executing at any given point in a Mason request.

data directory

A directory in which Mason will store temporary files, including object files and cached data.

dhandler

Stands for "default handler." A component invoked when no component matching the requested component path exists.

flag

A named property of a component that controls how Mason treats it. Attributes are set using the <%flags> tag and queried using the $component->flag() method. Flags do not inherit via the inheritance hierarchy.

inheritance hierarchy

A tree of parent/child relationships among components. Each component may inherit by default from an autohandler, or it may specify its parent (or declare that it has no parent) by setting its "inherit" flag.

Interpreter

A class responsible for supervising a pool of components and creating Mason Request objects. Available in Mason components as $m->interp.

Lexer

A class responsible for turning a body of Mason source code into meaningful chunks for the Compiler.

method

A special kind of subcomponent that can be inherited via the inheritance hierarchy and called externally. Methods are defined using the <%method> tag and invoked via $component->call_method() or with the colon-containing component:method syntax in $m->comp() calls and the like.

object file

A filesystem-cached version of the Compiler's output for a single component source file.

parameter

In this book, generally used to refer to a settable property of any of the pieces of the Mason framework. Parameters for several classes can be passed to a single class's constructor method, and the Class::Container module will make certain that parameters get routed to their intended destination.

parent component

A single component that another component inherits from. Each component may have zero or one parent. See also *inheritance hierarchy*.

request

Depending on context, may mean the Mason Request object $m, the Apache request object $r, or the HTTP request initiated by the end user in a web context. The three usually exist simultaneously in a one-to-one correspondence, so the term "request" may sometimes even refer to all three of these.

requested component

The component originally specified in the exec() Interpreter method, or if no such component exists, the first dhandler that accepts responsibility for the request. In a web-deployed Mason application, the requested component usually matches the URL seen in a web browser. The value of the requested component remains constant throughout a request.

Resolver

A class responsible for all interaction between the Interpreter and the underlying storage mechanism for component source files.

site

In this book, used to refer to any deployed Mason application. This is most commonly a web site but may be any collection of Mason components together with an Interpreter to render them.

source file

A file containing the Mason source code for a component. A single source file may contain several component definitions if it contains subcomponents or methods. See also *object file*.

subcomponent

A privately scoped component defined in another component. Subcomponents are defined using the `<%def>` tag and invoked via the normal component-calling techniques.

wrapping chain

A list of components constructed at the beginning of the request by finding the parent, grandparent, and so on of the requested component. The requested component is always at the bottom of the wrapping chain, and the top-level auto-handler is usually at the top.

Index

Symbols

<& &> (call tag), 3, 24–25
<% %> (substitution tag), 2, 21, 184, 226
[! !] tag (Embperl), 224
[* *] tag (Embperl), 224
[+ +] tag (Embperl), 224
& (ampersand), 22
: (colon), 67
" (double quote), 22
/ (forward slash), 20, 67
> (greater-than sign), 22
< (less-than sign), 22
% (percent sign), 2
. (period), 22
| (pipe), 21, 81
_ (underscore), 22
$_ variable (Perl), 84

A

<a href> tags, 80
<a> tag, 125, 207
abort( ) method, 53, 112, 241
aborted( ) method, 53, 241
aborted_value( ) method, 54, 241
access controls, 199–200
access levels, 199
add_allowed_globals( ) method, 250
add_session_id( ) subroutine, 191
/admin/autohandler component, 200
/admin directory, 116, 200
admin flag, 115
/admin/add_category.html component, 165
/admin/alter_category.html component, 165
/admin/autohandler component, 164
/admin/delete_category.html
    component, 165
/admin/edit_categories.html
    component, 165
/admin/edit_user.html component, 165
/admin/user_list.html component, 164
advanced inheritance, 84–88
ah( ) method, 63
aliases, 204
allow_globals( ) method, 97, 249
allow_globals parameter, 45, 92–93, 255
/all_projects.mas component, 135–136
Alzabo (database-to-object mapper), 113,
    165
ampersand (&), 22
Apache web servers, 6, 169
    configuration files, 16, 41–42, 116–117
    dhandlers in, 41–42
    ExecCGI mechanism in, 168
Apache::ASP modules, 9–10
Apache::AuthCookie module, 194–197
Apache::Cookie module, 187
Apache::DBI module, 205
ApacheHandler class, 235–236, 247–248
ApacheHandler object, 110, 248
Apache::Reload module, 204
apache_req( ) method, 63
apache_request_to_comp_path( )
    method, 229, 231, 247
Apache::Session module, 185–186
Apache::Session::Generate::MD5
    module, 189
Apache::Status module, 112

We'd like to hear your suggestions for improving our indexes. Send email to *index@oreilly.com*.

apache_status_title( ) method, 248
apache_status_title parameter, 110, 255
Apache::Template module, 12
APIs (Application Programming
        Interfaces), 237
    ApacheHandler class, 247–248
    CGIHandler class, 248–249
    Compiler class, 249–251
    Component class, 244–246
    component object, 64–67
    Interpreter class, 237–239
    Lexer class, 252
    Request class, 50–51, 239–244
    request object, 50–51
    Resolver class, 247
    techniques, 184
/apprentice.css component, 122–124
<%args> blocks, 27, 32
%ARGS hash, 32–33, 145
args_method( ) method, 248
args_method parameter, 110, 255
arguments, 32, 34–35
    accessing arguments with @_, 33
    %ARGS hash, 32–33
    via component calls, 35
    definition of, 281
    via HTTP requests, 35–36
    munging, 235
array reference, 34
ARRAYREF constant, 216
as_line( ) method, 51
ASP (Active Server Pages), 9
assets (Bricolage CMS), 264
as_text( ) method, 51
<%attr> blocks, 29
attr( ) method, 56, 64, 246
<%attr> blocks, 79
attr_exists( ) method, 65, 246
attributes, 78–79
    access controls with, 199–200
    definition of, 281
attr_if_exists( ) method, 65, 246
authentication, 194
    using Apache::AuthCookie, 194–197
    without cookies, 197–199
authorization, 194
    using Apache::AuthCookie, 194–197
    using attributes in access
        controls, 199–200
    without cookies, 197–199
autoflush( ) method, 58, 238
autoflush parameter, 51, 100, 254

autoflushing, 111, 193–194
/autohandler component, 120–122, 199–200
autohandler_name( ) method, 238
autohandler_name parameter, 43, 98, 254
autohandlers, 4, 42–44
    content wrapping in, 79
    definition of, 281
    as filters, 46–47
    implementing access check in, 199–200
    inheritance, 89
    for initialization, 44–46
    setting up sessions in, 188
    using with dhandlers, 49
auto_send_headers parameter, 110
$available_status object, 145

B

<b> tag, 80, 125
base components, 47
    calling, 56
    definition of, 281
base_comp( ) method, 56, 243
Big5 character set, 22
binary data, generating, 111
blocks, 26
    <%args>, 27, 32
    <%attr>, 29
    <%cleanup>, 28
    content, 25–26, 80–84
    <%def>, 30
    <%doc>, 29
    <%filter>, 27–28
    <%flags>, 29
    <%init>, 26, 71
    <%method>, 30
    <%once>, 28, 72–73
    <%perl>, 23
    <%shared>, 30, 72–73
    <%text>, 28
body attribute, 226
<body> tag, 5, 74
bottom-up inheritance, 79
Bricolage (content management
        system), 260–261
    content editing in, 269–273
    elements in, 263–269
    features, 279
    installing, 261–263
    interface, 263–269
    templates, 273–278
    terminology, 264–265
    web site, 279

/browse.html component, 140
browsing, 114
buffers, 58
    clearing, 59
    flushing, 58
    methods, 63–64, 68
buffer_stack( ) method, 64
burners (Bricolage CMS), 265

C

cache( ) method, 51, 59–61, 241
Cache::Cache module, 59, 188–191
Cache::FileCache module, 59, 232
Cache::MemoryCache subclass, 59
cache_self( ) method, 61–62, 241
caching, 5–6
    arguments to, 241
    methods for, 59–62, 241
call tag (<& &>), 3, 24–25
caller( ) function (Perl), 56
caller( ) method, 57, 241
caller_args( ) method, 57, 242
callers( ) method, 56, 241
call_method( ) method, 65, 246
call_next( ) method, 54, 208, 243
CATCH tag, 12
categories (Bricolage CMS), 265
CGI (Common Gateway Interface)
    advantages of, 167–169
    creating sites in Mason, 170–171
    disadvantages of, 169–170
    script, 172
    vs mod_perl, 174–175
    using Mason templates in, 171–174
/cgi-bin directory, 170
CGIHandler class, 248–249
cgi_object( ) method, 63, 240
Chamas, Joshua, 9
character sets, 22
characters( ) method, 223
child components, 56, 281
Class::Container class, 214–216
classes
    ApacheHandler, 247–248
    CGUHandler, 248–249
    Class::Container, 214–216
    Compiler, 249–251
    Component, 244–246
    HTML::Mason::ApacheHandler, 255
    HTML::Mason::CGIHandler, 170–171
    HTML::Mason::Compiler, 92, 255

HTML::Mason::Compiler::ToObject, 92
HTML::Mason::Interp, 254
HTML::Mason::Lexer, 92
HTML::Mason::Request, 254
HTML::Mason::Resolve, 228
Interpreter, 98, 237–239
Lexer, 252
passing parameters to, 91–92
Request, 239–244
Resolver, 247
superclass, 214–216
<%cleanup> blocks, 28, 225
cleanup code, 96
clear( ) method, 68
clear_buffer( ) method, 59, 112, 242
CMS (content management
            system), 260–261
$cnt variable (Embperl), 8
cobrand_colors( ) subroutine, 202
code reference, 52
code_cache_max_size( ) method, 238
code_cache_max_size parameter, 99, 254
$col variable (Embperl), 8
colon (:), 67
color schemes, 200
    with codes, 202
    with stylesheets, 200–202
comp( ) method, 52, 243
comp_class( ) method, 97
comp_class parameter, 94, 230
comp_exists( ) method, 55, 239, 243
comp_id( ) method, 65
comp_id parameter, 230
compile( ) method, 250
Compiler, 90, 249
    compilation callbacks in, 250–251
    definition of, 281
    methods, 97
    object properties, 249–250
    overview, 18
compiler( ) method, 237
compiler methods, 97, 250–251
compiler parameter, 100, 254
compiler_class parameter, 100
component calls, 35
Component class, 244
    component relationships in, 245–246
    inheritance in, 246
    object properties, 244–245
component objects, 64
component path, 19

component roots, 19
  and advanced inheritance, 84–86
  definition of, 281
  vs. document root, 107–108
  multiple, 84–86, 203–204
  two-level, 166
component stacks, 281
component tree, 281
component_as_embperl( ) method, 227
component_call( ) method, 251
component_content_call( ) method, 251
component_content_call_end( )
    method, 251
components, 2–4, 19
  with access controls, 152
  advantages for data processing, 180–182
  altering contents of, 95–97
  arguments, 32
  base, 47, 56, 281
  basic syntax, 20
  calling, 24–25
    using other components, 52–53
    with content blocks, 25–26, 80–84
  child, 56, 281
  creating, 70–71
  current, 47, 282
  definition of, 281
  directories of, 19
  editing, 257–259
  fetching, 242–244
  file extensions, 116, 184
  file-based, 67
  generating static web sites form, 206–212
  as independent units, 182
  inheritance, 4–5
  layout of, 183
  vs. modules, 176–180
  parent, 43, 282
  parsing, 20
  path, 230
  requested, 47, 282
  return codes, 108–109
  return values, 36
  running, 242–244
  sharing data among, 71–73
  subcomponents, 283
  writing, 257–259
  of web sites, 117–118
comp_path parameter, 230
comp_root( ) method, 98, 239, 247
comp_root parameter, 98, 255
comp_root_array( ) method, 247

comp_source parameter, 225
configuration files, 212–213
  adding configuration directives to, 105
  and dhandlers, 41–42
constructors, 51–52
contained_objects( ) method, 215–216
content( ) method, 53, 242
content blocks, 25–26, 80–84
content (Bricolage CMS), 264
content management system
    (CMS), 260–261
content wrapping, 44, 79
content_type( ) method, 175, 249
Content-Type header, 175
convert( ) subroutine, 211
cookies, 10
  storing sessions with, 185–187
  user ID, 119
count( ) method, 55, 240
CPAN, 13, 59, 181
CSS (Cascading Style Sheets), 201
current components, 47, 282
current_block attribute, 225
current_comp( ) method, 57, 243

D

dash (-), 22
data directory, 282
data processing, 180–182
database-to-object mapper, 113
data_cache_defaults( ) method, 238
data_cache_defaults parameter, 51, 100, 254
data_dir( ) method, 239
data_dir parameter, 99, 254
data-driven web sites, 6
dates, 129
dates, formatting, 129, 130
$dbh global variable, 46, 92
$dbh variable, 92
DBI connections, 205
declared_args( ) method, 65, 245
decline( ) method, 54, 241
DECLINED status code, 110
decline_dirs( ) method, 248
decline_dirs parameter, 110, 255
<%def> block, 30, 69–71
default parameter, 216
default.css files, 201
default_escape_flags( ) method, 97
default_escape_flags parameter, 93, 255
delimiters, 12
depth( ) method, 242

descr parameter, 216
desks (Bricolage CMS), 264
DESTROY methods, 97
developer environments, 202
   handling DBI connections in, 205
   multiple component roots, 203–204
   multiple server configurations, 204–205
dhandler parameter, 100
dhandler_arg( ) method, 55, 241
dhandler_name( ) method, 238
dhandler_name parameter, 51, 254
dhandlers, 39–40
   and Apace configuration, 41–42
   customizing, 40–41
   definition of, 282
   methods, 54
   names for, 51
   using with autohandlers, 49
die( ) function (Perl), 19
Digest::SHA1 module, 116, 119
directories, 116
   component roots as, 19
   data, 282
   Interpreter class, 239
   layout of, 184
   methods for, 239
dir_path( ) method, 66, 245
<%doc> blocks, 29
doc_block( ) method, 250
document root, 19, 107–108
Dominus, Mark-Jason, 11
double quote ("), 22
dynamic contents, 76–78
dynamic web programming, 172

E

Element Manager (Bricolage CMS), 265–266
Element Profile (Bricolage CMS), 265, 267
elements (Bricolage CMS), 265
Emacs (text editor), 257–258
email addresses, 114
embedding tag (<% %>), 10
Embperl, 7–9, 224–227
EmbperlObjects, 9, 224
end_block( ) method, 250
end_component( ) method, 250
end_element( ) event, 222
end_named_block( ) method, 251
error_format( ) method, 240
error_format parameter, 51, 100, 254
error_mode( ) method, 240
error_mode parameter, 51–52, 100, 254

errors, 51
escape flags, 21
   global default for, 93
escape parameter, 226
escaping, 21
   newline, 31
   substitutions, 21–23
$escmode variable(Embperl), 226
eval {} block (Perl), 71
event handlers, 10
   examples of, 34–35
exceptions, 51
exec( ) method, 172, 239, 244
ExecCGI mechanism (Apache), 168
execution trace, 96
extra parameter, 230

F

FastCGI execution model, 169
/featured_project.mas component, 133–135
fetch_comp( ) method, 243
fetch_next( ) method, 54, 243
fetch_next_all( ) method, 54, 243
file( ), 242
file( ) method, 55
file extensions, 116, 184
file naming, 184
file uploads, 169
file-based components, 67
<FilesMatch> pattern, 170
FilesMatch section, 103
files_written( ) method, 238
 blocks, 58
<%filter> blocks, 27–28, 80–81
FILTER tag, 12
filters, 46–47, 125
flag( ) method, 66, 245
<%flags> block, 29
flags, 282
flush( ) method, 68
flush_buffer( ) method, 58
tag, 220
footer attribute, 225
FOREACH tag, 12
forward slash (/), 20, 67
friendly_name parameter, 230

G

GET request, 34
get_info( ) method, 229, 247
get_keys( ) method, 60

GIF images, 1
glob function (Perl), 231
global variables, 37
glob_path( ) method, 229, 247
GNU/Linux box, 206
greater-than sign (>), 22

H

h escape flag, 21
<h1> tags, 3
hacking, 115
handle_cgi_object( ) method, 249
handle_comp( ) method, 173, 249
handler( ) method, 248
handle_request( ) method, 106, 108,
    248, 249
handler.pl files, 104–107
handler.pl script, 188
<head> tag, 74
header( ) method, 175
header attribute, 225
header.mas component, 3–4
header_out( ) method, 175, 249
headers, 75–76, 175
hostnames, 204
HTML editors, 8, 95
<html> </html> tags, 74
HTML (Hypertext Markup Language), 7, 11
    error format, 51
    escape flags, 21
    standards, 118
HTML tables, 8
HTML::Embperl, 7
HTML::Entities module, 22
HTML::Mason::ApacheHandler class, 167
    constructor parameters, 255
    vs. HTML::Mason::CGIHandler
        class, 174–175
    methods, 63
    objects, 105
HTML::Mason::Buffer subclass, 58, 256
HTML::Mason::CGIHandler class, 256
    creating CGI-based sites with, 170–171
    vs. HTML::Mason::ApacheHandler
        class, 174–175
    methods, 63, 248
HTML::Mason::Commands package, 94
HTML::Mason::Compiler class, 92, 215,
    225, 255
HTML::Mason::Compiler::ToObject
    class, 92

HTML::Mason::Component class, 64,
    94, 256
HTML::Mason::Component object, 20
HTML::Mason::Component::FileBased
    class, 64
HTML::Mason::ComponentSource
    object, 229
HTML::Mason::Component::Subcomponent
    objects, 64
HTML::Mason::Exception::Syntax
    error, 252
HTML::Mason::Interp class, 237, 254
HTML::Mason::Interp object, 105
HTML::Mason::Lexer class, 92, 218, 256
HTML::Mason::Request class, 240, 254
HTML::Mason::Resolver class, 228
HTML::Mason::Resolver::File class, 97,
    247, 255
HTML::Template module, 10–11
HTTP headers, 110
HTTP requests, 35–36
httpd.conf configuration variables, 216
httpd.conf files, 51, 102–104, 185–188

I

IF tag, 12
<IfDefine> directive, 204
if-elsif clauses (CGI), 182
ignore_warnings_expr( ) method, 238
ignore_warnings_expr parameter, 99, 254
index files, 204
index pages, 114
/index.html component, 121, 131
inherit flag, 43
inheritance, 4–5, 78–79, 165
    advanced, 84–88
    and multiple component roots, 84–86
    autohandler, 89
    in Component class, 246
    methods, 246
    top-down vs. bottom-up, 79
inheritance hierarchy, 282
<%init> blocks, 26, 71, 225
init_block( ) method, 251
in_package( ) method, 97
in_package parameter, 94
instance( ) method, 51, 240
internal caching, 5
interp( ) method, 55, 240, 248
Interp object, 55
interp parameter, 255

Interpreter, 90, 237
  definition of, 282
  directories, 239
  exec( ) method, 172
  object properties, 237–238
  overview, 18
  parameters, 98–100
  Request parameters passed to, 100
  runtime methods, 239
introspection methods, 55–57, 241
IPC::Shareable module, 73
is_admin flag, 153
is_file_based( ) method, 66, 245
ISO-8859-1 character set, 22
is_subcomp( ) method, 66, 245
is_subrequest( ) method, 62

J

Java Server Page, 82
JPEG files, 39
JScript, 9

K

key/value pairs, 57
key_value_pair( ) method, 251
keyword search, 136

L

last_modified parameter, 230
/latest_projects.mas component, 120, 129–130
/left_side_menu.mas component, 120, 124–128
less-than sign (<), 22
lex( ) method, 252
Lexer, 90, 92, 282
  methods, 252
lexer( ) method, 97
lexer parameter, 95, 255
lexer_class parameter, 95
/lib directory, 116
/lib/check_access_level.mas component, 152–153
/lib/format_date.mas component, 130–131
/lib/paging_controls.mas component, 137–140
/lib/redirect.mas component, 148
/lib/set_login_cookie.mas component, 150
/lib/url.mas component, 128–129
$limit arguments, 135

line_number( ) method, 252
load( ) method, 239
load_time( ) method, 65, 245
local( ) method, 186
Location header, 175
/logged_in directory, 116
/logged_in/add_project_member.html component, 164
/logged_in/autohandler component, 152
/logged_in/check_access_to_project.mas component, 159
/logged_in/edit_project_submit.html component, 159–161
/logged_in/delete_project.html coponent, 164
/logged_in/editable_project_list.html component, 159
/logged_in/edit_members.html component, 161–164
/logged_in/edit_project.html component, 159
/logged_in/edit_self.html component, 153
/logged_in/edit_user_submit.html component, 153–154
/logged_in/new_project.html component, 154
/logged_in/new_project_submit.html component, 159
/logged_in/project_form.mas component, 154–158
/logged_in/remove_project_member.html component, 164
/login_form.html component, 144
loop control syntax (Embperl), 9
LRU (least recently used) cache, 18
lush_buffer( ) method, 242

M

$m global variable, 37
MAC (Message Authentication Code), 119
MACRO tag, 12
macros, 12
mailing list archives, 40
mainpage.mas component, 4
make_component( ) method, 70–71, 173, 239, 244
make_subrequest) method, 88–89
make_subrequest( ) method, 50, 62, 244
markup language, 20

Mason, 1
 advantages for data processing, 180–182
 alternatives to, 6–13
 and Apache::Status module, 112
 basic concepts, 19–20
 CGI (Common Gateway Inteface) vs.
   mod_perl, 174–175
 compiling in, 224–227
 configuring under mod_perl, 102
   via custom code, 104–107
   via httpd.conf, 102–104
 converting components into Embperl
   pages, 224–227
 creating CGI (Common Gateway
   Interface)-based sites in, 170–171
 generating config files with, 212–213
 generating non-HTML files
   with, 111–112
 generating static web sites with, 206–212
 installing
   mod_perl, 15–16
   standalone, 14–15
 integration with Apache, 6
 integration with mod_perl, 6
 lexer, 216–224
 main features of, 2–6
 markup language, 20
 modules vs. components, 176–180
 objects in, 90
 online resources, 17
 overview, 1
 passing parameters to classes in, 91–92
 processing requests in, 18–19
 sample codes, 2
 setting up under CGI (Common Gateway
   Interface), 167–169
 storing components
   in RDBMS, 228–231
 syntax, 216–224
 test program for, 16–17
 text editors for, 257–259
 using templates inside CGI
   scripts, 171–174
mason_handler.cgi script, 170–171
max_recurse( ) method, 238
max_recurse parameter, 52, 254
$m->call_next( ) method, 190
$m->comp( ) method, 36, 148
media assets (Bricolage CMS), 264
<META> tags, 75
metadata, 165
<%method> block, 30
<%method title> block, 76–77

method_exists( ) method, 65, 246
methods, 73–74
 ApacheHandler class, 247–248
 for buffers, 58, 63–64, 68
 for caching, 59–62, 241
 CGIHandler class, 248–249
 compiler, 97
 Compiler class, 249–251
 Component class, 244–246
 definition of, 282
 for dhandlers, 54
 for directories, 239
 for file-based components, 67
 for headers, 75–76
 HTML::Mason::CGIHandler class, 63
 for inheritance, 246
 Interpreter class, 237–239
 introspection, 55–57, 241
 Lexer, 252
 for Request class, 239–240
 Request class, 239–244
 Resolver class, 247
 runtime, 239
 for subrequests, 62, 244
 for titles, 75–76
 TML::Mason::ApacheHandler class, 63
 with dynamic content, 76–78
methods( ) method, 67, 246
mod_perl, 6
 vs. CGI (Common Gateway
   Interface), 174–175
 configuring Mason
   via custom code, 104–107
   via httpd.conf, 102–104
 configuring Mason in, 102
 installing, 15–16
 publications on, 101–102
 web site, 101
modules, 1
 Apache::ASP, 9–10
 Apache::AuthCookie, 194–197
 Apache::Cookie, 187
 Apache::DBI, 205
 Apache::Reload, 204
 Apache::Session, 185–186
 Apache::Status, 112
 Cache::Cache, 59, 188–191
 vs. components, 176–180
 HTML::Entities, 22
 HTML::Template, 10–11
 loading, 186
 Text::Template, 11–12
$m->redirect( ) method, 175

$m->request_args( ) method., 138
multiple component roots, 84–86, 203–204
multiple server configurations, 204–205
my( ) function (Perl), 3
MySQL server, 228–231

N

n escape flag, 21
name( ) method, 66, 67, 245, 252
namespace, 189
navigation menu, 114
new( ) method, 50, 95, 98
   ApacheHandler class, 248
   CGIHandler class, 248
   Compiler, 249
   Component class, 244
   HTML::Mason::Compiler, 215
   Interpreter class, 98
   Lexer class, 252
   Request class, 240
   Revolver class, 247
newline, 31
/news.mas component, 133
$new_user object, 145

O

object files, 238, 282
object_dir( ) method, 239
object_file( ) method, 67, 245
object_id( ) method, 250
object-oriented programming, 43
objects
   buffer, 58
   Compiler, 249–250
   Component, 244–245
   component, 64
   constructor parameters, 253–255
   Interpreter, 237–238
   Request, 240
   schema, 119
<%once> block, 72–73, 225, 28
once_header attribute, 225
optional parameter, 216
out_method( ) method, 240
out_method parameter, 52, 100, 254
output( ) method, 68
output channels (Bricolage CMS), 265
owner( ) method, 66, 246

P

param( ) method (CGI), 173
parameters, 282
   allow_globals, 92–93, 255
   apache_status_title, 110, 255
   args_method, 110, 255
   autoflush, 51, 100, 254
   autohandler_name, 43, 98, 254
   auto_send_headers, 110
   code_cache_max_size, 99, 254
   comp_class, 94, 230
   comp_id, 230
   compiler, 100, 254
   compiler_class, 100
   comp_path, 230
   comp_root, 98, 255
   comp_source, 225
   data_cache_defaults, 51, 100, 254
   data_dir, 99, 254
   decline_dirs, 110, 255
   default, 216
   default_escape_flags, 93, 255
   descr, 216
   dhandler, 100
   dhandler_name, 51, 254
   error_format, 51, 100, 254
   error_mode, 51–52, 100, 254
   escape, 226
   extra, 230
   friendly_name, 230
   HTML::Mason::ApacheHandler
      class, 255
   HTML::Mason::Compiler class, 255
   HTML::Mason::Interp class, 254
   HTML::Mason::Request class, 254
   ignore_warnings_expr, 99, 254
   in_package, 94
   interp, 255
   last_modified, 230
   lexer, 95, 255
   lexer_class, 95
   max_recurse, 52, 254
   optional, 216
   out_method, 52, 100, 254
   passing to classes, 91–92
   postamble, 96
   postprocess_perl, 96, 255
   postprocess_text, 96, 255
   preamble, 96
   preloads, 99, 254
   preprocess, 96, 255
   resolver, 100, 254

parameters (*continued*)
    resolver_class, 100
    source_callback, 230
    static_source, 99, 254
    type, 216
    use_object_files, 254
    use_strict, 93–94
Params::Validate, 15, 181, 215, 216
parent( ) method, 66, 246
parent components, 43, 282
parent_request( ) method, 62
parsers, 216
parsing, 20
passwords, 114
path( ) method, 66, 245
PATH_INFO environment variable
    (CGI), 40
PATH_INFO mechanism (Apache), 40
PDF files, 39
percent sign (%), 2
period (.), 22, 184
Perl, 262
    embedding syntax, 10
    installing, 14
    loop control, 9
<%perl> blocks, 23, 225–226
Perl code, 2
    editing, 257
    embedding into text, 23
Perl interpreter, 169
Perl lines, 23, 184
Perl modules, 262
perl_block( ) method, 251
PerlContentHandler directive, 102
PerlHandler directive, 105
perl_line( ) method, 251
PerlModule directive, 186
PerlSetVar directive, 103
PHP (PHP: Hypertext Preprocessor), 13
pipe (|), 21, 81
PNG files, 40
pop_buffer_stack( ) method, 64
POST request, 34
postamble( ) method, 97
postamble parameter, 96
PostgreSQL, 262
postprocess_perl( ) method, 97
postprocess_perl parameter, 96, 255
postprocess_text( ) method, 97
postprocess_text parameter, 96, 255
preamble( ) method, 97

preamble parameter, 96
preloads parameter, 99, 254
prepare_images( ) function (JavaScript), 74
prepare_request( ) method, 248
preprocess parameter, 96, 255
preprocess_perl( ) method, 97
print( ) function (Perl), 21
print( ) method (Mason), 55, 242
project browsing, 114
/project directory, 116
/project/dhandler component, 141–143
projects, 115
pseudocodes, 113
publishing (Bricolage CMS), 265
push_buffer_stack( ) method, 64

Q

query_form( ) method, 128
quest_args( ) method, 78

R

$r global variable, 37, 109, 247, 37
raw_block( ) method, 226, 250
$r->content_type( ) method, 175
RDBMS (Relational Database Management
    System), 228–231
receive( ) method, 68
redirect( ) method, 63, 148
Request class
    altering request flows in, 241
    caching in, 241
    content and output methods, 242
    fetching and running components
        in, 242–244
    introspection methods, 241
    methods, 239–240
    object properties, 240
    subrequests in, 244
request class, 50–51
request object, 18
    creating, 51–52
    dhandler-related methods, 54
    general-use methods, 55
    introspection methods, 55–57
    methods, 50–51
    passing to handler subroutines, 106
    subrequests, 62, 88–89
    with built-in sessions, 232–234
request_args( ) method, 56, 244
request_comp( ) method, 57, 243

request_depth( ) method, 57
requested components, 47, 282
requests, 18–19, 282
Resolver, 90
    component root, 97–98
    definition of, 282
    methods, 247
    overview, 18
    replacing, 228–231
resolver( ) method, 238
resolver parameter, 100, 254
resolver_class parameter, 100
results paging system, 135
return( ) function (Perl), 36
return codes, 108–109
$return_to value, 146
$r->header_out( ) method, 175
Richter, Gerald, 7
$row variable (Embperl), 8
row_by_plc( ) method, 119
$r->register_cleanup( ) method, 151
runtime methods, 239

S

Safe.pm module, 12
SAX parsers, 216
SAX (Simple API for XML), 217
SCALAR constant, 216
scalar reference, 52
scall_method( ) method, 65, 246
schemas, 119
scomp( ) method, 53, 148, 243
search options, 136
/search_results.mas component, 136–137
security, 115
server-side include (SSI) mechanism, 3
session ID, 191–192
%session variable, 188
sessions, 185
    session ID, 191–192
    storing, 185–187
    using Cache::Cache for, 188–191
set_global( ) method, 94, 239
SetHandler directive, 102
SHA1 algorithm, 119, 189
<%shared> block, 30, 72–73, 77–78
/show_category.html component, 140–141
Shulman, Michael Abraham, 257
site administration, 115
site redundancy, 73
sites, 282
source files, 282

source_callback parameter, 230
source_dir( ) method, 67, 245
source_file( ) method, 67
SQL query, 82
stack index, 57
$start argument, 135
start_block( ) method, 225, 250
start_component( ) method, 250
start_element( ) method, 219, 221
start_named_block( ) method, 251
startup costs, 169
static web sites, 206–212
static_source( ) method, 238
static_source parameter, 99, 254
stories (Bricolage CMS), 264
strict pragma, 93–94
stylesheets, 116, 200–202
subcomponents, 69–70
    definition of, 283
    vs. methods, 73
    naming, 184
subcomps( ) method, 67, 245
subelements (Bricolage CMS), 265
subexec( ) method, 62, 244
$submit_to variable, 146
subrequests, 88–89
    vs. component calls, 62
    method for, 62
    methods for, 244
subroutine reference, 52
subroutines, 3
substitution( ) method, 251
substitution escaping, 21–23
substitution tag (<% %>), 2, 21, 184, 226
superclass, 214–216
SVG files, 205
SWITCH tag, 12
/syshandler component, 118–120

T

taglibs, 82
Template Toolkit, 12–13
templates (Bricolage CMS), 265
templating system, 2, 12
text
    editing, 257–259
    embedding Perl code into, 23
    generating, 111
text( ) method, 251
<%text> blocks, 28, 225–226
text editors, 257–259
text messages, 40

text_block( ) method, 250
Text::Template module, 11–12
throw_syntax_error( ) method, 252
tie( ) method, 186
tied hashes, 191
Time::Piece module, 116
title( ) method, 67, 244
titles, 75–76
top_buffer( ) method, 64
top-down inheritance, 79
top_menu method, 80
Tregar, Sam, 10
TRY tag, 12
two-level component root, 166
type parameter, 216

U

u escape flag, 21
%udat variable (Embperl), 9
undef( ) function (Perl), 168
underscore (_), 22
uploads, 169
URLs (Uniform Resource Locators), 7
    building with /lib/url.mas
        component, 124
    and dhandlers, 40
    path, 203
    storing session IDs in, 191–192
use_object_files( ) method, 238
use_object_files parameter, 254
user accounts, 114–115
user authentication and authorization, 194
/user directory, 116
user information, 114
$User object, 119
/user.html component, 141
usernames, 114
/users/forgot_password.html
        component, 151
/users/forgot_password_submit.html
        component, 151
/users/login_submit.html component, 149
/users/logout.html component, 150
/users/new_user.html component, 144
/users/new_user_submit.html
        component, 147–148
/users/user_form.mas component, 145–147
use_strict( ) method, 97
use_strict parameter, 93–94

V

valid_params( ) method, 215–216, 228
variable_declaration( ) method, 251
Vars( ) method (CGI), 173
VBScript, 9
Vim (text editor), 259
virtual hosting, 106

W

Wardley, Andy, 12
web servers, 6
    config files, 212–213
    document root, 19
web sites, 194
    access levels, 199
    Apache configuration of, 116–117
    co-branding color schemes, 200
        with codes, 202
        with stylesheets, 200–202
    components, 117–118
        /all_projects.mas, 135–136
        /apprentice.css, 122–124
        /autohandler, 120–122
        /browse.html, 140
        /featured_project.mas, 133–135
        /index.html, 121, 131
        /latest_projects.mas, 120, 129–130
        /left_side_menu.mas, 120, 124–128
        /lib/format_date.mas, 130–131
        /lib/paging_controls.mas, 137–140
        /lib/redirect.mas, 148
        /lib/set_login_cookie.mas, 150
        /lib/url.mas, 128–129
        /login_form.html, 144
        /news.mas, 133
        /project/dhandler, 141–143
        /search_resultts.mas, 136–137
        /show_category.html, 140–141
        /syshandler, 118–120
        /user.html, 141
        /users/forgot_password.html, 151
        /users/forgot_password_
            submit.html, 151
        /users/login_submit, 149
        /users/logout.html, 150
        /users/new_user.html, 144
        /users/new_user_
            submit.html, 147–148
        /users/user_form.mas, 145–147
        /welcome.mas, 131–133

web sites (*continued*)
    directory layout, 116
    file extensions in, 116
    functionality of, 114–115
    index page, 114
    navigation menu, 114
    redundancy in, 73
    security of, 115
    site administration, 115
    static, 206–212
    unrestricted areas of, 118
/welcome.mas component, 131–133
whitespace, 184
    ignoring, 222
    in substititation tags, 21
WML files, 205
workflow (Bricolage CMS), 264
wrapping chain, 47–48
    definition of, 283
    methods, 54

X

XML component syntax, 217–224
XML (Extensible Markup
        Language), 217–223
XML::SAX::Base module (CSPAN), 216, 218
XML::SAX::ParserFactory module
        (CSPAN), 216
XSLT (Extensible Style Language
        Transformations), 10

Z

Zakharevich, Ilya, 257

About the Authors

Dave Rolsky has worked as a paperboy, supermarket bagger, temporary secretary, ear-training and music theory-teaching assistant and, every so often, as a computer programmer specializing in Perl. He is an animal rights activist, obsessive reader of the works of Gene Wolfe, Hong Kong film afficionado, and the owner of many black t-shirts.

Dave has been a member of the Mason core team since the summer of 2000, a position he attained primarily by constantly nagging Jon Swartz, Mason's creator. He has written numerous CPAN modules, including Alzabo, Exception::Class, Log::Dispatch, and others. He was never convicted.

Ken Williams enjoys sitting by the park and taking long walks in the fireplace. He has a hard time staying interested in any one thing for very long; he has recently worked as a math teacher, choral conductor, Perl consultant, and liturgical bongoist. He is currently a researcher in Document Categorization at the University of Sydney in Australia.

He has written CPAN modules of varying utility while masquerading under the seedy, secretive pseudonym of "Ken Williams."

Ken joined the Mason core team in the fall of 2000 and has managed to convince the other core members that his flashy looks and his appeal with Mason's ultra-hep Gen-Z users outweighs his tendency to forget what planet he's on.

Colophon

Our look is the result of reader comments, our own experimentation, and feedback from distribution channels. Distinctive covers complement our distinctive approach to technical topics, breathing personality and life into potentially dry subjects.

The animal on the cover of *Embedding Perl in HTML with Mason* is a Hamadryas (Arabian) baboon. This species inhabits the dry plains and rocky hills of northern Africa and the Arabian Peninsula. Though their primary diet consists of roots, seeds, and fruit, Hamadryas baboons also eat insects and small animals, including other monkeys. They travel and forage in bands of 50 to 100 during the day and gather in troops as large as 750 to sleep on steep-sided cliffs during the night. All adults have long, dense, silky fur that is gray in males and brownish in females. Mature males weigh an average of 45 pounds and have a silver cape or mane over the head, neck, and shoulders. Females are considerably smaller and have no mane.

Arabian baboons live in a highly developed social order based on harem groups—a single adult male is accompanied by up to four females and their offspring. Males control their family by brute force, often biting females on the nape of the neck. Their powerful canines are also bared to threaten predators, which include leopards, jackals, hyenas, cheetahs, and lions. When facing an attack, they may yawn, slap their hands and feet, scream, and alert other baboons with a dog-like bark. They are fierce combatants, often winning fights against animals larger than themselves.

Ancient Egyptian artwork frequently pictures Hamadryas baboons as attendants of Thoth, scribe of the gods, and himself the god of wisdom, learning, and magic. The Egyptians recognized the intelligence of "sacred" baboons and reportedly trained them to wait on tables, pluck weeds from garden plots, and assume positions of prayer when in a temple. They also helped make wine; tomb paintings depict them harvesting grapes and using their own body weight to increase the tension of wine presses. Today these baboons are listed as a threatened species, and they no longer inhabit Egypt. Cultivation and development have destroyed much of their natural habitat and forced some bands to rely on crops and garbage dumps for food.

Philip Dangler was the production editor for *Embedding Perl in HTML with Mason*. Norma Emory was the copyeditor. TIPS Technical Publishing, Inc. provided production services and wrote the index. Emily Quill and Mary Anne Weeks Mayo provided quality control.

Ellie Volckhausen designed the cover of this book, based on a series design by Edie Freedman. The cover image is a 19th-century engraving from *Animal Creation*. Emma Colby produced the cover layout with QuarkXPress 4.1 using Adobe's ITC Garamond font.

David Futato designed the interior layout. This book was converted to FrameMaker 5.5.6 with a format conversion tool created by Erik Ray, Jason McIntosh, Neil Walls, and Mike Sierra that uses Perl and XML technologies. The text font is Linotype Birka; the heading font is Adobe Myriad Condensed; and the code font is LucasFont's TheSans Mono Condensed. The illustrations that appear in the book were produced by Robert Romano and Jessamyn Read using Macromedia FreeHand 9 and Adobe Photoshop 6. This colophon was written by Philip Dangler.

Other Titles Available from O'Reilly

Perl

Programming Perl, 3rd Edition

*Larry Wall, Tom Christiansen &
Jon Orwant*
3rd Edition July 2000
1104 pages, ISBN 0-596-00027-8

Programming Perl is not just a book
about Perl; it is also a unique introduction to the language and its culture,
as one might expect only from its authors. This third
edition has been expanded to cover Version 5.6 of Perl.
New topics include threading, the compiler, Unicode,
and other features that have been added or improved
since the previous edition.

The Perl CD Bookshelf, Version 3.0

By O'Reilly & Associates, Inc.
Version 3.0 September 2002 (est.)
768 pages, Features CD-ROM
ISBN 0-596-00164-9

Version 3.0 of O'Reilly's *The Perl CD
Bookshelf* gives programmers convenient online access to their favorite
Perl books, all from their CD-ROM
drive. We've updated this best-selling product with electronic versions of 7 popular books. Included are the second edition of *Perl in a Nutshell*, the third editions of
Learning Perl and *Programming Perl*, the *Perl Cookbook*,
and 3 new titles: *Perl & XML*, *Perl & LWP*, and *Master-
ing Perl/Tk*. A paperback version of *Perl in a Nutshell*
rounds out this incredible package.

Perl & XML

By Erik T. Ray & Jason McIntosh
1st Edition April 2002
216 pages, ISBN 0-596-00205-X

Perl & XML is aimed at Perl programmers who need to work with XML
documents and data. This book gives
a complete, comprehensive tour of the
landscape of Perl and XML, making sense of the myriad
of modules, terminology, and techniques. The last two
chapters of Perl and XML give complete examples of
XML applications, pulling together all the tools at your
disposal.

CGI Programming with Perl, 2nd Edition

By Shishir Gundavaram
2nd Edition July 2000
470 pages, ISBN 1-56592-419-3

Completely rewritten, this comprehensive explanation of CGI for those who
want to provide their own Web servers
features Perl 5 techniques and shows
how to use two popular Perl modules, CGI.pm and
CGI_lite. It also covers speed-up techniques, such as
FastCGI and mod_perl, and new material on searching
and indexing, security, generating graphics through
ImageMagick, database access through DBI, Apache configuration, and combining CGI with JavaScript.

Advanced Perl Programming

By Sriram Srinivasan
1st Edition August 1997
434 pages, ISBN 1-56592-220-4

This book covers complex techniques
for managing production-ready Perl
programs and explains methods for
manipulating data and objects that
may have looked like magic before. It gives you necessary
background for dealing with networks, databases, and
GUIs, and includes a discussion of internals to help you
program more efficiently and embed Perl within C or C
within Perl.

Perl Pocket Reference, 4th Edition

By Johan Vromans
4th Edition July 2002
96 pages, ISBN 0-596-00374-9

The fourth edition of our popular *Perl
Pocket Reference* now covers the latest
release—Perl 5.8—with a summary of
Perl syntax rules, a complete list of
operators, built-in functions, and standard library modules. All with brief,
easy-to-find descriptions. You'll find the newest Perl features, such as enhanced regular expressions, multithread-
ing, the Perl compiler, and Unicode support. *Perl Pocket
Reference* provides a complete overview of Perl, packed
into a convenient pocket-sized guide that's easy to take
anywhere.

How to stay in touch with O'Reilly

1. Visit our award-winning web site

http://www.oreilly.com/

★ "Top 100 Sites on the Web"—PC Magazine
★ CIO Magazine's Web Business 50 Awards

Our web site contains a library of comprehensive product information (including book excerpts and tables of contents), downloadable software, background articles, interviews with technology leaders, links to relevant sites, book cover art, and more. File us in your bookmarks or favorites!

2. Join our email mailing lists

Sign up to get email announcements of new books and conferences, special offers, and O'Reilly Network technology newsletters at:

http://www.elists.oreilly.com

It's easy to customize your free elists subscription so you'll get exactly the O'Reilly news you want.

3. Get examples from our books

To find example files for a book, go to:

http://www.oreilly.com/catalog

select the book, and follow the "Examples" link.

4. Work with us

Check out our web site for current employment opportunities:

http://jobs.oreilly.com/

5. Register your book

Register your book at:

http://register.oreilly.com

6. Contact us

O'Reilly & Associates, Inc.
1005 Gravenstein Hwy North
Sebastopol, CA 95472 USA
TEL: 707-827-7000 or 800-998-9938
     (6am to 5pm PST)
FAX: 707-829-0104

order@oreilly.com
For answers to problems regarding your order or our products. To place a book order online visit:

http://www.oreilly.com/order_new/

catalog@oreilly.com
To request a copy of our latest catalog.

booktech@oreilly.com
For book content technical questions or corrections.

corporate@oreilly.com
For educational, library, and corporate sales.

proposals@oreilly.com
To submit new book proposals to our editors and product managers.

international@oreilly.com
For information about our international distributors or translation queries. For a list of our distributors outside of North America check out:

http://international.oreilly.com/distributors.html

O'REILLY®

To order: *800-998-9938* • *order@oreilly.com* • *www.oreilly.com*
Online editions of most O'Reilly titles are available by subscription at *safari.oreilly.com*
Also available at most retail and online bookstores.